THE
Sensual
TOUCH

A GUIDE TO
MORE EXOTIC LOVEMAKING

THE
Sensual
TOUCH

CONSULTANT
DR GLENN WILSON

Macdonald Orbis

A *Macdonald Orbis* BOOK

House Editor Dorothea Hall
Editor Richard Dawes
Art Editor Gordon Robertson

Macdonald & Co (Publishers) Ltd
66-73 Shoe Lane, London EC4P 4AB

First published in Great Britain in 1989 by
Macdonald & Co (Publishers) Ltd
London & Sydney

A member of Maxwell Pergamon Publishing Corporation plc

Original Text Copyright
© Marshall Cavendish Limited 1989
This edition copyright
© Macdonald & Co (Publishers) Ltd 1989

British Library Cataloguing in Publication Data
The sensual touch,
 1. Sex relations
 T. Wilson, Glenn, *1942–*
 306.7

 ISBN 0-356-17859-5

Phototypeset by Quadraset Limited

Printed and bound by Dai Nippon, Hong Kong

CONTENTS

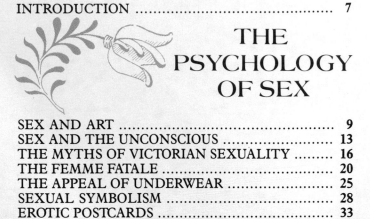

THE
EASTERN
WAY

EXOTIC SEX
AROUND
THE WORLD

SEX
AND
HEALTH

INTRODUCTION

The highly subjective nature of sexual experience makes everyone his or her own expert. Yet its universality means that there is far more to learn than any of us can hope to grasp in a lifetime. This is not to say, though, that we should resign ourselves to a narrow vision of this potentially boundless means of expressing both our individuality and our togetherness.

Sexual practice and morality have followed many complex paths throughout human history and for most of us there is a whole world still to discover. Many books trace those paths, usually spicing the narrative with titillatory tales but offering no practical guidance to the sexually inexperienced or bewildered. Others concentrate solely on improving sexual performance, often at the expense of sensitivity to the complex feelings that flow between partners.

This book bridges the gap, marrying solid advice on achieving a better sex life with an overview of the role sex has played in different ages and in different parts of the world. What characterizes it throughout is the quest for greater understanding of our sexuality, for although sex occupies a significant portion of our waking and dreaming states for most of our life, it does not yield up its secrets lightly.

The wide range of features that follow provide an invaluable key to making the physical dimension of sex more fulfilling. But at the same time they do not sidestep the psychological issues that can make sex heaven or hell. They examine in depth the desires and fears that condition our sexual self-expression, whether they be the simple longing for closeness, the lust for power over another, the pursuit of the ideal, or the worship of the fetish object.

With the wealth of accumulated wisdom from around the world offered by this book, there can be no excuse for not beginning at once the pleasurable quest for lasting sexual fulfilment for you and your partner.

THE PSYCHOLOGY OF SEX

Sex as a mere physical act is only a part of the real contact that is possible between two minds and bodies. Yet when we look below the surface of the feelings that precede, accompany, and follow sex, we enter an emotional minefield. In fact Sigmund Freud went so far as to claim that emotions of a sexual origin are at the root of all neurotic difficulties. For sex to be truly satisfying we certainly need to understand how our bodies work. But we cannot afford to discount the often puzzling workings of our feelings if we are to enjoy closeness with our partner or even to feel at ease with our own impulses towards others in daily life and in our dreams.

This chapter looks at the processes, both conscious and unconscious, that shape our sex life, at how we often transform our sex drive into creativity and other symbolic acts, and at how we depict the humour in sex. It ends with a brief survey of the changes brought about in our attitudes to sex by the great revolutionaries in the field.

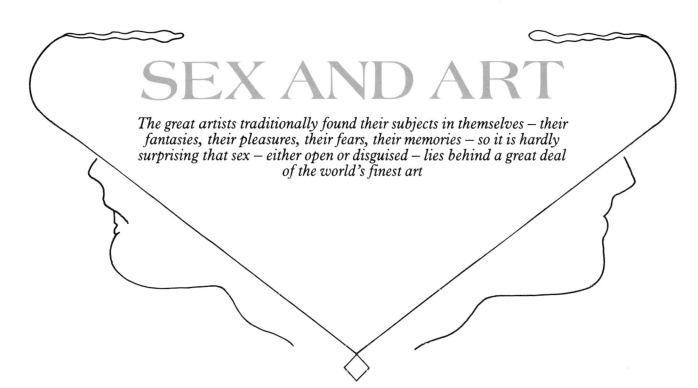

SEX AND ART

The great artists traditionally found their subjects in themselves – their fantasies, their pleasures, their fears, their memories – so it is hardly surprising that sex – either open or disguised – lies behind a great deal of the world's finest art

Primitive societies have always concentrated on sexual themes in their tribal and religious art, and still do today. In the East, sex and religion have frequently been linked, and scenes of intercourse are as common on Indian temples as they are in books of sexual instruction such as the *Kama Sutra*.

In Japan some of the country's greatest art is to be found in the 'pillow-books', so named because they were kept in pillows by courtesans and geisha-girls as sources of inspiration for their customers. The pillow books were scrolls depicting scenes of copulation and were essentially ancient sex manuals.

SEX AND RELIGION

In the great civilizations of Greece and Rome, sex played a central role in art, literature and religion. Temples often contained sexual images. At Ephesus, a statue of Diana showed the goddess with 15 breasts, and visitors to Delos today see giant marble phalluses which represent the god Dionysus.

When Pompeii was excavated 1700 years after its burial by the eruption of Mount Vesuvius, frescoes were found in the brothel showing various positions of intercourse practised by the inmates, and many paintings and sculptures were discovered in other parts of the city which demonstrated the importance of sex in Roman daily life and worship.

In the Christian world, a sense of guilt and shame has become associated with anything to do with sex, and numerous rules and laws have made it very difficult for artists to create erotic art. Much of the excitement of erotic images in our western world comes from our knowledge that there is something 'naughty' about them.

Many of the world's greatest artists have had their works destroyed as obscene. The list includes such masters as Michelangelo, Leonardo da Vinci, Titian, Watteau, Boucher, Turner, and Toulouse-Lautrec. Other great creators of erotic art are Raphael, Rembrandt, Rubens, Goya, Rowlandson, Courbet, Degas and Gauguin.

SEXUAL REPRESSION

The 19th century was the great age of prudery and sexual repression, when a writer like Lewis Carroll could feel so afraid and ashamed of his sexuality that he chose the company of little girls rather than mature women. The result was not only stories like *Alice in Wonderland* but also numerous rather revealing photographs of a series of scantily-clad girls.

THE BIBLE

The Bible provided one favourite subject of erotic art — the reformed adulteress Mary Magdalene. In the 16th century, Titian painted her gazing rapturously up to heaven as she clutched her long silky tresses to her body, leaving her full breasts provocatively exposed.

In the 17th century, Rubens portrayed her in a state of obvious ecstasy, half naked and kneeling before the almost nude figure of Christ. In the 19th century, both Felicien Rops and Van Maele showed her masturbating in front of a crucifix, and in 1894, Rodin created a marble sculpture of her in the nude embracing the naked body of Christ on the cross.

Klimt's Danae *is based on the myth of Acrisius who imprisoned his daughter for fear that she would bear a son who would kill him. Jupiter then descended in a shower of gold and the prophecy came true.*

The great French sculptor, Rodin, flouted convention by having passionate affairs with his beautiful models, resulting in powerful images in marble of couples in sexual embraces. Scandal resulted from his nude Mary Magdalene embracing the naked figure of Christ on the cross, and also from his nude portrayal of the famous dancer Nijinsky, with whom he was said to be having a homosexual relationship.

THE SEVERED HEAD

In both Paris and London, respectable collectors of erotica could happily buy academic nudes representing Greek goddesses or visitors to Roman bath-houses while condemning as obscene the work of Aubrey Beardsley, the most controversial artist of Victorian England.

Beardsley depicted the new, liberated woman of the end of the century as a vampire using her sexuality to trap men. Two of his illustrations for Oscar Wilde's play *Salome* were censored. In a third, the heroine, after dancing provocatively in front of King Herod and having received as a reward the head of John the Baptist, passionately kisses the severed head still dripping blood from the blow of the executioner's axe.

Beardsley's most heavily condemned works were his

Although they caused enormous public outrage at the time, Beardsley commented of his drawings for Aristophanes' Lysistrata, *'They are in a way the best things I have done'.*

BROTHELS

For centuries, brothels have fascinated artists, including Rembrandt, Van Gogh, Gauguin, Degas and Picasso. In 1892, Toulouse-Lautrec spent a year in Parisian brothels, where he was fascinated by the rich Baroque and Oriental architecture and the rooms with swaying beds for those who liked the feeling of movement.

He painted at least fifty pictures of prostitutes, either with their clients, or parading for a medical inspection, enjoying lesbian relationships, or masturbating.

illustrations to *Lysistrata* by Aristophanes. To show their frustration when their wives deny them sex because they insist on going to war, the heroes are given enormous and lovingly drawn erect penises. As re-

Michelangelo's *David*

THE PENIS

Greek and Roman artists considered the male nude to be the prime example of human perfection, but succeeding generations found the nudity of male classical sculptures embarrassing. Before being exhibited to the public, they would be fitted with a fig leaf or suffer the indignity of having the penis knocked off with a special little hammer. Even today most classical male nudes are exhibited in this way.

Famous artists saw their work treated equally unkindly. Michelangelo's *David* was given a fig leaf, to the artist's dis-

gust, before being shown in Florence in 1504. The fig leaf was only removed as late as 1912.

Leonor Fini's The Train Journey *captures the erotic possibilities of a railway carriage. Secluded from the outside world, almost any fantasy could be realized.*

cently as 1966, London's Victoria and Albert Museum was not allowed to show these drawings.

RICH EROTICISM

Also fascinated by the Salome story was the turn-of-the-century Austrian artist Gustav Klimt. Twice, he painted her posing provocatively as she clutched the severed head by its hair. He also sketched many drawings of copulating couples and masturbating women, but his most erotic work is *Danae*, a richly coloured painting of a nude woman with long red hair, her body curled in a foetal position, her eyes closed and her lips parted. One hand grips her breast while the other guides golden coins between her legs.

TERRORS OF SEXUALITY

The most famous artist of the 20th century is Pablo Picasso, and during his long career he produced many erotic pictures. Shortly before his death, he was asked about the difference between art and eroticism, and he replied, 'There is no difference.'

He returned in his work again and again to the excitements and terrors of sexuality, from women masturbating to lesbian couplings, and from scenes of violent rape to tender moments of his own sexual relationships with his many wives and mistresses.

Among his last works, created in his eighties, were a series of masterly engravings showing himself as an old man watching wistfully as the young artist Raphael copulates with his model in his studio.

THE CREATIVE URGE

One of the greatest influences on the 20th century has been Sigmund Freud, the pioneer psychoanalyst who believed that sex lies at the root of artistic creativity, and that our dreams can tell us much about our sexual fears and fantasies.

His ideas were important to artists, and especially to a group called the Surrealists, whose works often explored their sexual dreams. Thus, they could transform the human body into an erotic arena for exciting experiences as in René Magritte's *Rape* – an erect penis which is also a woman's face whose features are replaced by her sexual parts – and Salvador Dali's *Young Virgin Autosodomized by her Own Chastity* – where the girl's naked body is composed of male sexual shapes.

ART AS WISH-FULFILMENT

England's most famous erotic artist of this century is probably Sir Stanley Spencer. Like his eastern forebears, he saw a direct connection between sex and religion. He once said, 'In all my sex experience, I notice the same degree of emotion as in religious experience.'

In the 1930s, he planned to build a Temple of Love,

EDOUARD MANET

The great 19th century French painter, Edouard Manet, was twice branded a pornographer. In 1863 he exhibited *The Picnic* which showed two clothed men relaxing with a naked woman by a stream, and in 1865 his painting entitled *Olympia* provoked a sensation with its nude prostitute receiving an admirer's bouquet from her black servant. A barrier had to be erected to keep the crowds away from the picture, and the Empress is said to have struck it with her riding whip in disgust.

The response epitomized the double standards of the day because while she was expressing her outrage, her husband Emperor Napoleon III purchased *The Birth of Venus*, a very provocative classical nude painted by a 'respectable' academic artist, at the very same Parisian exhibition.

The Picnic (*Le Déjeuner sur l'Herbe*)

Caravaggio was the most notorious Italian artist of the early 1600s. Many of his religious commissions were deemed unacceptable because he was thought to interpret his subjects too literally.

to unite sex and worship, and although it was never built, he did create a series of eight altar pieces which he called *Beatitudes of Love*. He believed that 'each of the pictures shows the entwined and unified soul of two persons' – the male in each case was the artist.

HOMOSEXUAL AND FETISHISTIC IMAGERY

More recently, artists in England have continued to explore personal worlds of erotic excitement. David Hockney concentrates on homosexual imagery. He has often drawn nude boys alone or making love together, and his painting, *The Room, Tarzana*, shows a young man wearing a tee-shirt and white socks posing provocatively on his stomach.

The paintings and sculptures of Allen Jones are more fetishistic, exalting the female form in leather or rubber with long legs and high heels.

Allen Jones has always denied that his images exploit the female as a sexual object, but nevertheless some women have found them objectionable. In April 1986, his sculpture of a chair formed by the body of a woman in black stockings was attacked with acid while in London's Tate Gallery.

FEMALE ARTISTS

Women artists have recently been challenging the tradition of erotic artworks produced solely by men for men. Betty Dodson creates meticulous drawings of nude women engaged in sexual duets or masturbation. Sylvia Sleigh paints her male friends in the nude to capture a virility that she has not found in previous pictures of male nudes. And Nancy Grossman produces sado-masochist nightmares in her sculptures of men imprisoned in leather masks, buckles and zips.

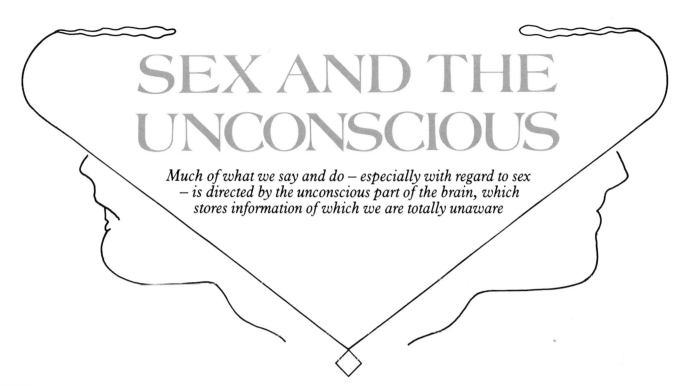

SEX AND THE UNCONSCIOUS

Much of what we say and do – especially with regard to sex – is directed by the unconscious part of the brain, which stores information of which we are totally unaware

People have been interested in the unconscious part of the mind for thousands of years, but it was not until the 19th century that the subject came in for close, scientific scrutiny.

Sigmund Freud paved the way for this interest, but was by no means the first person to grapple with the concept of a part of the mind that controls our thoughts and actions in some mysterious way.

SPONGE EFFECT

The unconscious mind is like a sponge. It soaks up messages – at times without us being aware of it – and often these messages come directly from the unconscious mind of someone else. In this way messages about sensitive issues such as sex are passed on from parents to children, for example, without either side consciously knowing that it is happening.

THE MEMORY BANK

All experiences, both good and bad, are filed away in the unconscious. They can be taken from this store in various ways. The way that most of us are familiar with is in dreams. When we sleep, our internal censor sleeps and so lets the unconscious have a free rein.

This is why dream analysis is so valuable to therapists when trying to assess the unconscious mind of their patients. Sexual fantasies can also give clues as to what is in the unconscious.

But of most interest to therapists, and to anyone who is interested in the subject of the unconscious, is the fact that the mind seems to be especially good at storing away negative feelings. Painful ideas and memories from childhood and other times of life can be eradicated so that they no longer live in the conscious mind to trouble it.

Such thoughts and memories are 'forgotten' by the conscious mind and the individual cannot, however hard he tries, remember them.

For example, very few people can remember the details of their birth, yet by using hypnotherapy or a technique called 'rebirthing' many people can do so, often quite vividly. No memory is ever lost – it is just filed away out of reach.

HIDING YOUR EMOTIONS

All our basic instincts such as sex drive come from and live in the unconscious and most of its contents come from past experience.

Many emotions and ideas, both painful and pleasurable, are filed away in the unconscious out of reach of the conscious mind. But things to do with sex appear to be so more than most. This is partly because the subject generally causes embarrassment, and because western culture tends to play down the importance of sex rather than being relaxed and uninhibited about it.

The processes of the unconscious mind are by no means straightforward. It does not think logically as does the conscious mind. It easily becomes confused as it tries to fulfil its wishes.

Even during dreams our minds play tricks on us and the brain can even dream in symbols to disguise the real objects of the dream. This seems to be especially true of dreams about sex.

DEFENCE MECHANISMS

There are many mechanisms which are active in our unconscious minds all the time, altering the way we behave and think, especially about subjects such as sex. **Repression** is one of the many defences that the unconscious brings into play to protect the conscious mind from material that it finds difficult to cope with.

A good example of this is what we have been told

about sex by our parents. Almost all mothers of teenage girls, for example, say that they have told their daughters about menstruation before they start, yet many girls claim never to have been told anything at all. Neither person is lying. The mother has undoubtedly told the girl but she, because she is shy about discussing such matters with her mother, represses it so that it comes to rest in the unconscious. She then consciously denies all knowledge of the matter.

Denial is the next most common defence. Up to 40 per cent of widowed people experience the illusion that their loved one is actually present with them and 14 per cent say that they have seen them or heard them. This is an example of the unconscious lying to deny the loss.

Projection is a way that we attribute to others those feelings and qualities that we most dislike in ourselves. So, if we are sexually inhibited, we can all too easily claim that our partner is the inhibited one, when in fact he or she is not.

Reaction formation is at the opposite extreme. We obscure unacceptable feelings. For example, if we are untidy by nature we may, quite unconsciously, over-compensate by becoming obsessional about tidiness.

Displacement is another common defence. In this we are afraid, for whatever reason, to express our feelings directly to the person to whom they should be expressed. Unconsciously, we express them to someone else. So, a man can have a row with his boss yet because

Dreams unleash, and tell us much about, the unconscious mind. Freud interpreted water as a sexual symbol and nakedness as wanting to be free.

THE COLLECTIVE UNCONSCIOUS

Carl Jung, the pioneering Swiss psychologist, extended this concept of the unconscious mind to include the idea of the collective unconscious. He asserted that we, as a race, have many notions in our unconscious minds that we have not directly experienced ourselves.

He cited, for example, the almost universal fear of the dark and of snakes in most cultures and claimed that humans, over millions of years, have inherited such fears and passed them on from generation to generation.

---

of the danger of being sacked, he is unable to vent his wrath on him. He then goes home and becomes 'unaccountably' angry with his wife for no reason at all. She is naturally baffled and usually has no way of knowing what the outburst is all about.

Regression is a process in which we return to a former stage of psychological development, often in childhood. We all do this when enjoying things in a childlike way or when we are overwhelmed by threatening experiences, such as going into hospital for an important operation.

In certain sexual circumstances an individual can regress to being a child. This can be pleasant during lovemaking and indeed can be a major part of some couples' sex lives. One or other of the partners 'babies' the other. However, regression of this kind can also act to our disadvantage at times.

During arguments, many couples regress to childhood and act out old patterns of behaviour. What may have started as an adult conversation can deteriorate into the squabbling more common among young children.

Sublimation is yet another common psychological process that we engage in, quite unconsciously, when it comes to sex. We all have a sex drive, but for any one of a number of reasons we might not feel able, or the drive might not be suitable, to find expression in the sexual act at a particular time.

The drive, however, seeks some form of expression and the way in which this is done is called sublimation. Men tend to sublimate their sex drive into work and activities away from home. Women, generally, devote their time to child care, and the care of others – activities which are based in, or close to, the home.

UNCONSCIOUS MESSAGES

Teenagers or adults in any one culture will tend to give much the same answers when asked about basic views of sex. This seems to suggest that we pick up messages about the subject even though we may never have received a formal sex education.

Messages of this kind have usually soaked into us over a period of many years and will have often passed

directly, without our being aware of what is happening, from the unconscious mind of our parents and other figures of authority to our own.

Some common messages in our western culture are:
☐ A woman who does not do what her lover wants sexually does not love him
☐ Men are the sexual aggressors and should make the first move
☐ Sex is dirty, sinful and shameful
☐ Nice girls do not masturbate

These are just a tiny fraction of the more common unconscious messages that plague many relationships and marriages – no matter whether they are based on fact or not.

Such messages may have entered our subconscious at an early stage and been stored away ready to affect us later in life. This puts considerable responsibility on parents to gain access to their own unconscious so that they can do away with negative messages and not pass them on to their children.

This awareness can often be gained in discussion with your partner, or even with a very close friend.

Although the unconscious is a highly complex subject, any steps towards an understanding of it can help clarify the way we behave when there are no obvious explanations to hand.

A warm and trusting relationship can help to release sexual desires hitherto repressed by the unconscious.

APPEALING TO THE UNCONSCIOUS

The effects of sexual messages on the unconscious do not just colour our interpersonal relationships, they also affect us as consumers and individuals.

Much of what goes into advertising images and slogans makes use of people's unconscious aspirations, fears and guilts, among other emotions. We are also encouraged to aspire to certain stereotypes which, in turn, require the purchase of a particular product or service.

Much of this persuasion is extraordinarily subtle, yet it pushes just the right buttons in our unconscious to make us buy whatever is being advertised.

THE MYTHS OF VICTORIAN SEXUALITY

*Prim, proper and prudish is the Victorian image.
But behind the scenes, young actresses
and child prostitutes entertained
'respectable' gentlemen*

The Victorians' attitude towards sex varied enormously between the classes. The lower and the upper classes had much in common – their shared principle being 'Do what you like when you like and damn the consequences'. What is commonly understood as the Victorian attitude to sex, however, is that of the middle classes. They were the most powerful section of society, and, being so, it is their viewpoint that has been handed down.

Ignoring his mother's self-imposed celibacy and its effect on the middle classes, Edward, Prince of Wales, took his pleasures at every opportunity.

THE INFLUENCE OF THE QUEEN

Although Queen Victoria became the embodiment of Victorian sexual thought, until she was 40 she retained all the zest and capacity for sexual enjoyment of her Hanoverian forebears.

After the Prince Consort's death in 1861, the British nation began to take on itself the heavy mantle of Victoria's melancholy, and it was with the Queen's tacit approval that the forces of repression began to tighten their grip over the country. The middle classes identified with her, as they did throughout her reign, and felt guilt when contrasting their own sexual behaviour with the enforced celibacy of their sovereign.

THE VICTORIANS AND HOMOSEXUALITY

As might be expected, the Victorians took a hard line on homosexuality and until 1861 men found guilty of this 'crime' could be sentenced to death. At this time the sentence was reduced, however, but it could still mean anything from life imprisonment downwards.

The degree of homosexuality in Britain during the Victorian era is difficult to discover as most homosexuals, very wisely, kept a low profile. Some idea can be gained, however, from a quote made at the time of the Oscar Wilde trial by William Stead, a famous journalist of the time who was later to go down on the Titanic: 'Should everyone found guilty of Oscar Wilde's crime be imprisoned, there would be a very surprising emigration from Eton, Harrow, Rugby and Winchester to the jails of Pentonville and Holloway. Until then, boys are free to pick up tendencies and habits in public schools for which they may be sentenced to hard labour later on.'

HYPOCRISY

This guilt led naturally to hypocrisy. The middle classes felt impelled to pretend that they were behaving in a manner that would have the approval not only of the Queen but of the Church. Religious thought, both in the Church of England and the non-conformist sects, placed great importance on the family, but it also emphasized that sex, although necessary for the creation of children, was an unfortunate necessity and not something to be enjoyed.

Victoria's self-pitying seclusion angered and then alienated the upper classes, who consequently turned to her son, Edward, the Prince of Wales, the future Edward VII, for a lead. But she was the mother figure incarnate for the middle classes and the 'improved' working classes striving for middle class status.

The Queen hated birth control, which she described as 'that horrid thing', so, ostensibly, did the middle classes, although they secretly practised it. Childbirth was considered by Victoria to be the 'shadow-side of marriage', shaming and degrading, and automatically

THE VIRGIN PROSTITUTES

The Victorians' terror of venereal disease led to a growing demand for virgin prostitutes — indeed a popular myth at that time was that a cure for this dreaded disease could be effected by deflowering such a girl.

This led to virgin prostitutes being highly prized and at one time customers had to pay up to one hundred pounds for the service. Commercialism soon took over, however, and the price dropped to as low as five pounds. This reflected not a slackening in demand but an increase in supply, and one could be forgiven for thinking that not every virgin fitted the description of *virgo intacta*.

Some brothels, mindful of this lucrative trade, employed their own doctors who not only supplied certificates of virginity to customers but also supplemented their earnings from the proceeds of virginity restoration.

this became the attitude of the middle classes. Like sex, it was a dark thing done in secret, and many women, determined to retain their dignity throughout the procedure, wore their corsets right through labour despite intense pain.

MYTHS AND THE MEDICAL PROFESSION

To many women, sex was something to be endured and, to dissuade men from their conjugal rights, a number of myths were determinedly circulated by a body of men crucial in disseminating guilt and fear – the medical profession. Too much intercourse, they suggested, would reduce a man's lifespan or turn him into a gibbering idiot. Doctors also maintained that it was a likely cause of cancer. As for women who claimed to enjoy sex, they were completely beyond the pale, and would certainly die young. Laborious statistics were compiled in prisons and lunatic asylums, 'proving' that such places were the logical destinations of those who indulged themselves too freely.

The most plausible theory as to why doctors should have persisted in perpetuating these myths is that they

---

THE VICTORIANS AND ORAL SEX

Sexual techniques such as fellatio and cunnilingus, now known under the broad heading of oral sex, were discussed only in the context of medical case histories or portrayed in pornographic magazines. Yet there is no question that oral sex was as common in the nineteenth century as it is today, and unquestionably the wide use of prostitutes arose partly from the inability of husbands to ask this of their wives.

This was hinted at by the observer of Victorian London's poor Henry Mayhew, when he spoke of the 'disgusting practices' indulged in by prostitutes in Hyde Park. By 1904, Dr C S Fere had put the matter into perspective. In his book, *The Sexual Instinct*, he maintained that oral sex, like masturbation, was too universal to be regarded as a total aberration.

---

saw themselves as the leaders of middle-class morality, and had a vested interest in damping down promiscuity.

UPPER CLASS MORALITY

The upper classes viewed middle-class morality cynically – among what was known as the 'Top Ten Thousand', free-love ran riot. In great country houses of the nineteenth century, bedrooms were arranged for the convenience of whoever was sleeping with whom. The aristocracy's only stipulation was that such matters were to be kept within their own set and woe betide anyone who disobeyed the code.

The aristocracy took their lead, not from the imposed morality of the middle class, but from their ribald ancestors of the eighteenth century, and from the

example of the Prince of Wales. The Prince did not attempt to hide from the world his amours and his propensity for pretty women, preferably those who were available, such as actresses and professional beauties. Middle-class men secretly envied him. While professing to be respectable members of society, they had the same yearnings.

THE TRUE SITUATION

So, Victorian morality was a front. London, for example, had an immense army of prostitutes, conservatively estimated at 80,000, a large number of whom worked in brothels in the Haymarket and Leicester Square in the centre of the city.

There were, too, the women of the 'demi-monde' – the mistresses of rich and influential men, who lived in considerable comfort on the outer edge of society and were often the unacknowledged leaders of fashion.

CHILD PROSTITUTION

Nor could the passer-by miss the cult of the child prostitutes, the young girls who used match-selling as their cover around Trafalgar Square and Piccadilly Circus. Respectable matrons travelling about central London averted their eyes from the homosexuals who circulated in Charing Cross, in the streets of Tottenham Court Road, and in the areas surrounding barracks.

CURBING EXCESSES

It was considered that the best way to curb sexual excesses was to frighten or imprison. Adolescents, aware of their growing sexuality, were terrified by grave books written by 'A Medical Man'. Masturbation, it was said, meant an early grave, and homosexual behaviour eternal damnation. Young men at Oxford and Cambridge found difficulty in reconciling the teaching of Plato – that the highest form of love was that between men – with the puritan views and supposed moral ethics of their own time.

Few parents informed their children of the facts of life, and it is not surprising that any information obtained was inaccurate and squalid. Small wonder that neuroses multiplied, and that attitudes were engendered that are still present today.

THE MISINFORMED GENERATION

The lack of communication between the generations sometimes had tragic results. After learning the effects of masturbation, many young men castrated themselves, and died as a result.

Venereal disease was regarded with so much loathing and contempt that people found it easier to suffer pain and anxiety than to ask for medical advice, and consequently, many cases went untreated.

The belief that one act of sexual intercourse automatically meant a baby encouraged girls to commit

La marchande de plaisir

London had about 80,000 prostitutes. Fear of disease led many men to seek virgins only and a thriving trade in supplying such girls built up.

Although servant girls were considered fair game for sex by the upper classes, gentlemen also had directories telling them where to pick up prostitutes.

suicide. Masturbation by young women was the sin no one talked about.

Accurate information was hard for the young to come by. The rich were more fortunate, for it was a tradition that their sources were the servants. It was also a tradition that female servants should offer themselves to the 'young master' for sexual experiment.

SEX FOR PROCREATION

It is not surprising that many Victorian men and women were filled with guilt and shame. There were very few men who could claim that they conformed to the code of sexual behaviour demanded of them, which was, briefly, to copulate only to breed children, and then not to enjoy it too much. A woman who was participating in sexual intercourse was brought abruptly back to earth by her husband saying to her sternly 'A lady does not move'. The marital double bed was therefore not only a promise but an ever-present reminder of original sin, and this ambiguity pervaded sexual thought and persisted into everyday life.

A LACK OF BIRTH CONTROL

Unquestionably sexual experiment was a good deal less adventurous than it is today. Birth-control methods were not by any means reliable, which meant that women never had the freedom to have sex free from the thought of pregnancy. And a girl of good family could be ruined if she had an illegitimate child.

A MAN'S WORLD

As regards purity, men were allowed a good deal of discretion. The upper and middle classes were plentifully supplied with nubile servants; and books widely circulated, such as *Hints to Men About Town*, were actually directories of prostitutes, with addresses, descriptions, prices, and specialities. The proportion of men who go chaste to their marriage bed does not alter much over the years – it is a factor depending on disposition rather than social conditions.

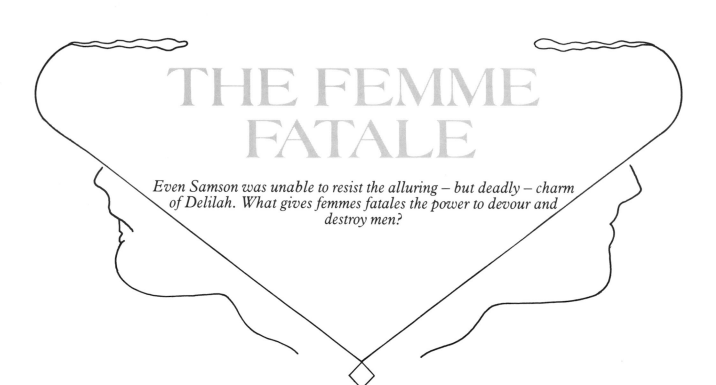

THE FEMME FATALE

Even Samson was unable to resist the alluring – but deadly – charm of Delilah. What gives femmes fatales the power to devour and destroy men?

Some men are attracted to women who are bad. Others are attracted by women whose very goodness and innocence provoke disaster.

Rich men are attracted to vamps who take a pride in squandering their fortunes. Politicians fall for prostitutes who ruin their careers. Old men fall for young girls and end up in jail. Young men fall for older women and kill themselves when spurned.

All of these men are victims of femmes fatales.

WHAT IS A FEMME FATALE?

A femme fatale is a woman who is so attractive that she leads a man to disaster. The archetype draws men to her like moths to a flame. She is so irresistible that they will give up anything for her, and then she destroys them.

She may be motivated by greed and take everything that her looks, her charm and her allure can give her. She may want the power and influence she can only attain by having powerful men as her lovers. She may want another kind of power over men – the kind that comes by having them fall in love with her by the score and never giving her heart to any of them.

Her motivation may not be evil at all. The classic femme fatale became a high-class courtesan after being tragically spurned by a lover. She can never give her heart to any other, and devotes her life to exacting her revenge on all the men she encounters.

THE BEAUTY THAT DESTROYS

A femme fatale may be even more innocent than that, though. She may be the victim of her own beauty. This may drive men to obsessive love, causing tragedy for them and for her.

Delilah, whose name is still synonymous with female perfidy, in the film portrayal.

DO THEY REALLY EXIST?

It is true that the femme fatale inhabits mythology and literature more than real life. Eve, perhaps, was the first femme fatale. She brought tragedy not just on Adam, she brought evil to all men.

The beauty of Helen – she was supposed to have been the daughter of the Greek god Zeus – was said to have caused the Trojan Wars. She married Menelaus,

Agamemnon's younger brother. According to one version of the story, during the absence of her husband, she fled to Troy with Paris, son of the Trojan king Priam. When Paris was killed, she married his brother Delphobus whom she betrayed to Menelaus when Troy fell. Although there is plenty of archaeological evidence that the Trojan Wars actually took place, Helen's part in them is, at best, contentious.

The best documented classical femme fatale is Cleopatra. During a bitter civil war, she used her 19-year-old charms to secure the help of Julius Caesar. He defeated her brother, Ptolemy, and gave her the crown of Egypt.

She joined Caesar in Rome, returning home to Egypt after his murder. When Mark Antony became Caesar's heir apparent, she went to Asia Minor to

Cleopatra, here portrayed by Elizabeth Taylor, seduced Mark Antony in her quest for power. He was so infatuated that he risked his reputation, lost his fortune, and finally killed himself.

seduce him. The couple returned to Egypt together.

But their marriage destroyed Mark Antony's popularity in Rome. The Roman Senate declared war on them, defeating them at sea in the Battle of Actium in 31 BC. And as the Roman army encroached on land, they both committed suicide.

There can be little doubt of Cleopatra's allure, or that their love of her turned the Roman people against both Caesar and Antony. But much of what we know of her belongs to literature – especially Shakespeare – rather than to historical fact.

BIBLICAL SIRENS

The Bible is littered with femmes fatales.

Delilah was a Philistine who was bribed to ensnare Samson, the Jewish champion. After seducing him, she coaxed him into revealing that the source of his strength was his hair. While he was asleep she cut it, betraying him to his enemies who put out his eyes.

Jezebel is practically synonymous with wickedness in a woman. Her sins were purely religious though. She was the wife of King Ahab of Israel and tried to persuade him to worship Baal instead of the Jewish god Yahweh. This annoyed the prophet Elijah who prophesied her death. She did die, ten years later, and her body was torn apart by dogs as he had foretold.

Judith fulfils the femme fatale role better, although the Jews see her as a selfless heroine. A Jewish widow, she gave herself to the Assyrian general Holofernes, then cut his head off after they had made love. Her compatriots then fell on the invaders and defeated them in a great slaughter.

LESS BIBLICAL SIRENS

Another classical character who specialized in demanding men's deaths was Messalina. She was the third wife of the Emperor Claudius and was notorious for her licentious behaviour and love of instigating murderous court intrigues.

In AD 42, she persuaded Claudius to sentence a senator, Appius Silanus, to death because he had rejected her advances. This began a reign of terror during which many senators were executed after being denounced by Messalina. When she caused the death of one of Claudius's secretaries, the rest turned against her. One of them, Narcissus, managed to have her put to death by convincing Claudius that Messalina and her lover, Gaius Silius, had secretly married and were plotting to kill her husband and seize power for themselves.

In the 18th century Catherine the Great of Russia connived in the assassination of her estranged husband, Tsar Peter III. She was also renowned for her sexual appetite. It is said that towards the end of her life she found that no man could satisfy her, so she decided to try having sex with a horse.

Disaster struck when the crane used to lower it broke and the horse fell, crushing her to death.

The exploits of all these women, though, are as much a topic of fable and legend as of history.

MYTHOLOGY

In Greek mythology, Pandora unleashed all the evils of the world by opening her box. But a more accurate mythological representation of the femme fatale are the Sirens. These creatures were half-woman half-bird and their singing was so seductive that it lured ships on to the rocks. Three of them were supposed to inhabit the west coast of Italy near Naples.

When Odysseus passed that way he defeated them by putting wax in his ears and lashing himself to the mast so that he could not change course. Jason and his Argonauts did not hear them because of the sweet singing of their shipmate Orpheus. And after several other failures the Sirens committed suicide.

There has long been a tradition of depicting the femme fatale as half woman and half animal – even the Sphinx with her deadly riddle can be considered

SALOME

Salome (played by Rita Hayworth, *left*, in the 1953 film) has something of a reputation as a femme fatale. She performed her famous dance in front of Herod Antipas who had recently imprisoned John the Baptist for having condemned Herod's marriage to his brother's widow, a violation of Mosaic law.

In appreciation of her dance, Herod promised Salome anything she should wish for. At the prompting of her father, Herodias, she ingratiated herself with Herod by asking for – and receiving – John the Baptist's head on a platter.

a femme fatale. And death by drowning is a common end for the victims of femmes fatales.

MERMAIDS

The mermaid fulfils the requirements of the femme fatale. They were half-woman and half-fish and reputedly lured sailors on to rocks. One of the most well known is the siren of the Rhine who sat on the Lorelei rock, enticing passing sailors with her singing. And a glimpse of the delectable Norwegian Havfrue, sitting on the surface of the water when the mist hangs over the sea, combing her long golden hair, portends imminent disaster to local fishermen.

In Brittany, the mermaids are called morgens and seem to be related to the evil enchantress of the Arthurian legend, Morgan Le Fay. She was King Arthur's half sister who used her evil powers to seduce him. The fruit of their union, Mordred, killed Arthur. The child of unholy incest, he was the only one who could defeat the power of Excalibur.

There is, of course, another femme fatale in the Arthurian legend, Guinevere. Her liaison with Lancelot destroyed the Round Table and led to the war in which Arthur was killed.

THE FEMME FATALE IN ART

The second half of the 19th century saw a great revival of interest in the femme fatale. Suddenly it became fashionable for men to fret over dangerous women. The femme fatale is a product of the art of that age.

There were many reasons for this. One of them was that many prominent artists – among them Delacroix, Corot, Courbet, Degas, Moreau and Munch – avoided marriage in the belief that a woman would sap their creative energy.

Another reason was that in an era when there was no effective cure for syphilis, women were quite often literally the carriers of hideous disease and death. Prostitution was widespread – it has been estimated that in the mid-19th century more than a sixteenth of the entire female population of London was engaged in prostitution.

CARMEN

Bizet's Carmen (shown right in the 1983 film version) was based on the novel by Prosper Mérimée, published in 1852. In it, a young corporal, José, has plans to marry a peasant girl, Micaëla. However, he becomes infatuated with a gypsy girl, Carmen, who works in a local cigarette factory.

When she is involved in a fight with another cigarette girl, José is sent to arrest her. However, using the power of her attraction over him, Carmen gets José to engineer her escape. For this he receives two months' imprisonment.

When he comes out she encourages him to become a smuggler. He refuses. But when he becomes involved in a fight with his superior officer, who is also in love with her, he has no choice but to desert with her. Meanwhile she has become involved with a bullfighter.

In the mountains with the smugglers, Carmen reads her cards. No matter how many times she deals them, they always say that she is about to die, and José's death will follow shortly after.

José is involved in a fight with the bullfighter, but Carmen stops him from killing the toreador. Later, at the bull fight, Carmen admits that she loves the toreador and rather than live without her, José stabs her to death.

It was also the era of 'la vie de bohème' among artists. The belief was that the creative soul should not be bound by the conventions of the bourgeois marriage, which meant that artists and writers were particularly susceptible to the dangers of infection. Baudelaire, Maupassant, Manet and Gauguin all died of syphilis.

THE RUINATION OF MEN

Real femmes fatales abounded too. From mid-century until the First World War, fabled courtesans like Cora Pearl, La Paiva, Lillie Langtry and Otero mixed openly in high society. It was almost fashionable for a young man to be ruined by one of these women. In fact, their reputations rested entirely on the number of vast fortunes they had squandered.

So open was their profession that these women were known as 'les grandes horizontales' after the position in which they earned money.

SARAH BERNHARDT

The other great femme fatale of the 19th century who straddled the gap between life and art was the actress Sarah Bernhardt. She played the femme fatale role both on and off the stage. She had numerous, ruinous love affairs, surrounded herself with Byzantine opulence and a menagerie of wild animals and went so far to cultivate the idea that she slept in a satin-lined coffin.

She was fascinated by executions and attended a hanging in London, a garrotting in Madrid and two beheadings in Paris. Her necklace was said to have been made out of eyes that had turned to stone.

Victorien Sardou, who wrote plays designed to exploit her femme fatale image, said of her, 'If there's anything more remarkable than watching Sarah act, it's watching her live.'

FEMMES FATALES TODAY

There are still plenty of attractive women whom men will do anything to possess. Marilyn Monroe was one. She slept with both John F. Kennedy and his brother Bobby. If that had come out at the time, it would have spelt disaster for both their political careers.

Their younger brother, Edward, narrowly escaped a watery death in 1969 when his car plunged off a narrow bridge at Chappaquiddick. In the car with him was one of the 'boiler room girls' from Bobby Kennedy's 1969 campaign, Mary Jo Kopechne. She drowned.

LOLITA

The 20th century's most famous literary femme fatale is undoubtedly Lolita. The novel, written in English by Russian emigré Vladimir Nabokov, was first published in Paris in 1955. In it, 37-year-old Humbert Humbert writes his life story while awaiting trial for murder in the psychopathic ward of a prison.

Having come to the US from Europe, he meets and marries the widow Charlotte Haze in order to be near her 12-year-old daughter Lolita. Later on, to further

his sexual ambitions, Humbert considers murdering Charlotte, but when she is killed by accident he takes Lolita on a trip across the country with the object of seducing her — only to be seduced by her.

Contrary to his expectations, she is no innocent virgin. Lolita escapes from his jealous protection and he does not learn of her again until she is 17, married and pregnant. She then tells him that during her days with him she had made love to famous

playwright, Clare Quilty. Although their affair is long over, insane jealousy drives Humbert to murder Quilty, but he dies of a heart attack

before coming to trial. The pouting, precocious, promiscuous Lolita had truly driven the long-suffering Humbert Humbert to his untimely end.

What their relationship was and whether she was a femme fatale is still a matter for speculation. But after failing to report the accident for nine hours, he pleaded guilty to a misdemeanour, received a two month suspended sentence and lost his driver's licence for a year. The incident possibly ruined his chances of ever getting to the White House.

In Britain, Edward VIII could be considered the victim of a femme fatale when he gave up the crown in 1936 to marry American divorcee Mrs Simpson. And it could be said that former cabinet minister Cecil Parkinson's political career was, albeit temporarily, seriously threatened by his attraction for and affair with his former secretary Sara Keays.

It could also be argued that John Lennon's overwhelming attraction to Yoko Ono tore the Beatles apart. But the nearest thing that the latter half of the 20th century can get to a femme fatale is Nancy Spungen.

After attempting to seduce the Sex Pistols' lead singer Johnny Rotten, she became attracted to bass guitarist Sid Vicious and encouraged him in his heroin habit.

She was, in part, responsible for tensions within the group which caused their break up at the beginning of their 1978 US tour.

Spungen was later found dead in her room in the Chelsea Hotel in New York and Vicious was charged with her murder. While on bail awaiting trial, he overdosed on heroin supplied by his mother. He was barely 21.

Not even the Greeks could come up with a tragedy more appropriate for our age.

The short, violent affair between Nancy Spungen and Sid Vicious of the Sex Pistols ended in murder and suicide — all in the name of love.

THE APPEAL OF UNDERWEAR

Saucy and sexy, bone-crushing or barely there, underwear has run the gamut of trends. But today, freed from the constraints of exaggerated fashion, it can be both fun and exciting to wear

One of the most exciting moments at the start of a new love affair is when the other person takes off their outer clothes to reveal a new identity – in what they wear underneath. As well as reinforcing masculinity or femininity, underclothes can tell us about a person's erotic personality. With fashion becoming more unisex and masculine for women, perhaps they have turned to underclothes to reveal their sexuality and sensuality. And, just as fashion has evolved and trends have come and gone for top clothes, underwear has also been subject to radical changes and alterations.

THE ROLE OF UNDERWEAR

Throughout history the main motivation for these changes has been a constant wish on the part of women to achieve, or approximate to, the body shape considered to be sexually desirable at the time.

The first significant fashion trend in the West was the narrowed waist, and the item of underwear designed to achieve this was the corset.

Originally made out of stiffened linen, the corset, or 'stays', has undergone many changes.

In Elizabethan days, when it was fashionable to have stiff, elongated bodices, corsets were made of iron. Any woman wearing such a dress would have to fit her naturally curved torso into a stiffened tube-like bodice which encased her body from above the bust down to her hips.

Punctured lungs, weakened thoraxes and broken ribs were among the results of wearing too tight corsets for too long. Some women even went so far as to have their lower ribs removed – all for the sake of fashion.

A fashionable lady of the 1830s could start her day in comfort – but help would soon be on hand to coerce her into a bone-crushingly tight corset.

BLOOMERS

A certain Mrs Amelia Bloomer was the person to launch the fashion of women wearing trousers when, in the mid-19th century, she advocated the wearing of Turkish-style loose pantaloons under dresses. This

EXTREMES OF FASHION

In the mid-16th century, fashion, both for men and women, went to such wild extremes as to make both sexes look twice as large as they ever were created to look. The farthingale, a whalebone contraption, was the cause of the enormously wide skirts which came into vogue. Some were so grotesque that it was almost impossible for a woman to walk comfortably.

After the farthingale, the hooped petticoat seemed relatively tame. But fashion, notorious for taking things to the furthest extreme poss-ible, came up with an amazingly complex array of hoops, some for the sides of the dress and some for surrounding the legs so that by the 18th century, women were once more immobilized.

In the 19th century, the descendant of the hooped petticoat and the farthingale was, in its heyday, made of closely spaced metal hoops, with the intention of creating a bell-like shape for the skirt. Unlike the farthingale and the hooped petticoat, it was not only worn in high society, but by all, even by factory workers.

really caught on when women began riding bicycles and modesty had to be preserved.

In later years, bloomers became known as knickers, a diminutive of knickerbockers, and they began to be seen in a new light.

People suddenly realized, at the beginning of the 20th century, that underwear could be fun to wear, and they entered the realm of treating underwear as luxury rather than merely functional items. Knickers became prettier and more slimline, and have carried on in the same way to the present day.

BREASTS AND BRAS

Women, it would appear, have never been entirely happy with the shape of their breasts. They have been strapped to make them flat, supported to make them more prominent, padded to make a woman seem more well-endowed and just left to 'do their own thing'.

In the 1920s, when the 'boyish' figure was in fashion, women took to flattening their upper half with the aid of 'flatter' bras.

By the 1940s, the 'sweater girl' look was pushed in films and popular magazines and fashion dictated that breasts should be uplifted and accentuated.

By the 1960s, liberated women decided to let it all hang out and burned their bras in a gesture of rebellion against male-dominated society. Bras were seen as symbolizing the repression of women, both physically and generally.

In the 1980s, many women have opted to allow the bust to keep its natural shape. Bras are no more a must, but there are hundreds of different shapes and styles to suit every taste and type of figure.

SUSPENDERS AND STOCKINGS

Ironically what started off as a device to hold stockings up has now become one of the best-selling frivolous, luxury underwear items. The suspender belt has strong links with erotica and sex appeal.

Men were the first to wear suspenders as women kept their legs hidden under voluminous robes, and used simple garters to hold stockings up. The original suspender belt for women was a complicated contraption, consisting of a harness which reached over the shoulders. Then it moved down to be attached to the corset and finally became a simple belt.

In the late 1960s, tights took over in popularity, having become a necessity with the birth of the mini skirt.

But once eliminated for the sake of practicality, the stocking and suspender returned to feature as an impractical, purely erotic underwear duo.

MODERN FASHIONS IN UNDERWEAR

Colour has become important. No longer do people only opt for the more neutral plain colours such as

Once a luxury affordable only by the rich, soft and silky lingerie such as cami-knickers and camisoles are now available at reasonable prices in most chain stores and are a valuable and treasured part of many women's wardrobes.

Frilly and frothy underwear was very much à la mode in post-war France – a cheeky fashion cashed in on by the makers of soap suds.

white, black and beige (although white still remains the firm favourite). Bright splashes of every colour under the sun are now available for both sexes. Coordinating sets are also available – now, you can get T-shirts, bras, briefs, shorts and even socks in the same pattern material.

TURNING YOURSELF ON

The overdrive marketing trend to promote coordinated underwear sets has created a desire, for women especially, not only to dress to please their partners but also to dress to please themselves. After all, feeling confident and comfortable involves all aspects of the way you dress, not only the outer layers.

There has also been an explosion in the demand and supply of romantic, frothy 'nothings'. Lace is back in fashion – and so are satin and silk luxury lingerie sets, which range from skimpy vests, bras and briefs to tights, French knickers and the briefest of briefs.

NAUGHTY BUT NICE

The market for highly erotic underwear is still strong. Well-known sex shops have their own mail order catalogues – and naughty underwear parties can be arranged. Titillating wisps of nylon and lace beckon the consumer and are 'guaranteed' to send your lover wild. Items for sale range from lacy, slinky, 'evening dresses' to the more daring peephole bras and crotchless briefs. Exotic underwear is also to be found on sale in the classified ads of many newspapers.

The common denominator in all these garments is that they must reveal as much as possible – but not everything. And the more slinky or lacy with as many strips, bows and frills, the better. Favourite colours are the obvious reds and blacks with white still the top favourite. But leopard spot designs are sought out by those with more extravagant tastes.

Erotic men's underwear is much more limited, but still available – ranging from G-strings with leopard skin patterned pouches to black see-through nylon briefs. Wet-look underwear also seems popular.

OUTER AND INNER SELVES

What we want our clothes to convey to others about our status, occupation, opinions and sexuality may clash with what we are really like inside. So the outer layer comes to represent the image we wish to present to the outside world, while inner wear reveals the private self.

A woman may try to hide genteel femininity and present an aggressive go-getting attitude in the workplace by wearing a plain unadorned suit. But if she is wearing red and black lacy knickers, suspenders and stockings underneath, there is obviously some difference, most often contrived, between her outer and inner image.

MEN AND UNDERWEAR

At the same time as women have 'come out of the closet' about their underwear, and underwear departments in stores reflect the increased demand for 'extrovert' lingerie, men seem to have progressed much more slowly in their attitudes.

From long shorts earlier in the 20th century, men's underwear has become ever shorter in the leg until the development of Y-fronts.

While the underwear market is much more successful nowadays in the women's sector, many men do not even choose their own underwear. Often it is bought as a gift for them by their partner or relatives.

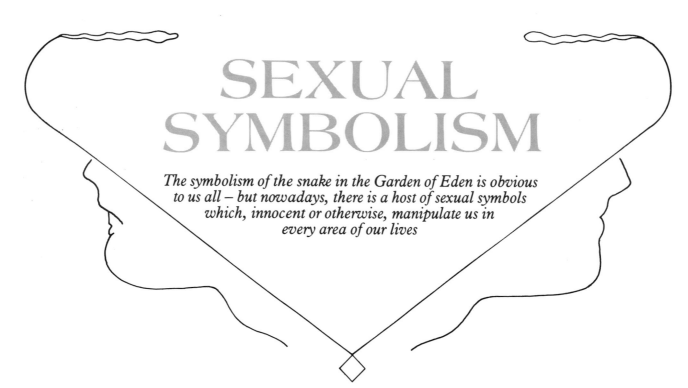

SEXUAL SYMBOLISM

The symbolism of the snake in the Garden of Eden is obvious to us all – but nowadays, there is a host of sexual symbols which, innocent or otherwise, manipulate us in every area of our lives

When a firm of publishers successfully launched a magazine called *Taste* – it was aimed mainly at the cookery and entertaining market – they were pleased but surprised to find that some 35 per cent of the purchasers were men. But, if one school of sex-psychologists is right, the male interest is easily explained. '*Taste*, for example,' wrote the authors of a recent study of 'Subliminal Seduction', 'is read by the unconscious mind as "testes", a sexual word guaranteed to stimulate interest in the product.' In their opinion the unconscious motivation was at least as strong as the conscious feelings about it.

TWO MINDS

The theory is not new. In our head, we have two minds. One, calm and rational, will decide to buy a brand of toothpaste because it will clean our teeth. The other, unconscious and primitive, will urge us to another brand – the one, maybe, that bursts from the TV screen or stands proud and erect between suggestive rocks and waterfalls that evoke sexual exhilaration.

SIMPLE, BUT DANGEROUS

When advertisers win over our unconscious mind by speaking its language directly, no great harm may result. We may find ourself with a lipstick that erects itself smoothly from its tube. At the cinema we may devour more hot dogs – the ones with the longest sausages and squidgy mustard – than we intended. And the car that takes us shopping may have been chosen by our unconscious mind in the hope it would come with the girl on the bonnet.

But matters become more serious if town planners choose the building development that has the highest rise towers or generals are choosing rockets if they are bright red.

THE MYSTERY OF SYMBOLS

The power of symbols – especially where sex is concerned – is mysterious. Just as we have two minds in our heads, we also seem to have two languages. One comes in the shape of words. The other, more ancient by far, is speechless but more or less universal. For example, the grossest insult in one language can sound like an invitation to tea in another. Most people, at some time, have enjoyed teaching foreigners rude words. But an upthrust finger, anywhere in the world, will make its sexual point.

A COMMON LANGUAGE

A few years back, when US explorers met up with a South American Indian tribe that had never encountered anyone else before, a photographer was on hand to record the meeting between naked natives and their visitors. With no common language, both parties swiftly found common symbols.

It is almost as if we were born with that language already in our head, and can speak it as instinctively as a fledgling bird flies. What is currently fascinating some scientists is the idea that the language of symbols really is a universal language that is 'spoken' not just by humans but by everything else that lives. It is an idea that, once grasped, has some odd, even spooky, implications. (It has, in serious American science magazines, been approached in the theory of The Cosmic Joker.)

A JUICY PAIR

Take, for example, the kind of sexual badinage you can hear in any fruit and vegetable street market in the world. It is simple minded stuff – 'Don't squeeze me till I'm yours' – and plentiful reference to big juicy ones, pairs of coconuts and the rest of it. Take a banana,

The Fall. *One of the earliest and most potent examples of sexual symbolism, with the penis as serpent playing a central role.*

cucumber or a big leek and you have the ingredients of a thousand music-hall jokes. Is all this just the exercise of a dirty mind that sees sexy symbols in every shape?

PHALLIC/VULVIC SYMBOLS

Take, as another example, that deadly toadstool *Phallus impudicus*. The name means 'shameless penis' and that is precisely its shape, and coincidentally, is a big one. Curiously imitative, too, is that counterpart of female

human private parts, the sea coconut, whose shape exactly echoes rounded thighs. Man has always been quick to 'see' such symbols and weave them into faith and culture. But arguably, at least, it is no coincidence that the same shapes and colours and scents say 'sex' right across the world and far beyond mere human language. It could, just, mean that symbols are the first language of the universe.

SEX AND MONEY

Certainly, you don't have to be a dyed in the wool Freudian to admit that, even unconsciously, we use

Right A picture of a tyre on its own is purely innocent, but when used to prop up a beautiful, pouting nude, there is a significant about-turn in its symbolic attraction.

Centre This fascinating image holds a wealth of suggestion. The banana is obviously phallic, and the sexual current is enhanced by a black hand reaching from behind and touching a white buttock.

Far right A common sexual image used by advertising firms to promote sales is the close-up of a mouth descending on, in this case, an ice-cream cone. The links with the phallus and oral sex are obvious.

symbolic frames of reference more often than not. For some reason, money – although it has powerful associations with sex – has even more identity with excrement. In any language, everyday expressions make the point plain.

The rich are said to be 'rolling in it' or 'stinking rich'. If they are unwilling to part with their money, they are 'tight-assed'. The first animal that comes to mind as an insult is the pig, where the rich are concerned. Associating pigs with filth is unfair on pigs, but filth and filthy lucre go together in the human mind as inevitably as going to the lavatory means 'spending a penny' and as making a fortune is called 'making a pile'.

BIRDS OF A FEATHER

Nor are humans the only living creatures to use symbols instinctively. If you were an Australian bower bird in search of a successfully active sex life, your triumphs would depend on your ability to collect and display blue objects. Posed casually around your nest, like the avian equivalent of a new Porsche in the drive, will be a quite extraordinary display of objects – buttons, biro pens, even cigarette lighters – stolen from nearby human camp sites, and feathers stolen from someone else's back. Male bower birds will spend as much time stealing such items from each other as in collecting their own. And, as some scientists confirm, the bird with the bluest display of items is always the one that gets the females.

A QUIVER OF ARROWS

After a few million years of using blue as a sex symbol, bower birds took blue biros and cigarette lighters on board with admirable speed. They may yet take to collecting credit cards. Certainly the human race, in its headlong technical inventiveness, is creating and confusing the symbols that denote sex and power – every day new symbols of what is most desirable are added to the heap. And in this, some believe, lies a serious danger.

When a brewer of a popular alcoholic drink uses arrows, thudding into their target, as his key symbol in a TV campaign, he is inviting us to score (to use the word symbolically) in every sense. The arrow has been a

phallic symbol since ancient Greece and Rome – just as the bow and quiver have been female sex symbols. And arrows have been used as brand symbols ever since kings put a fleur-de-lys on their shields.

STIRRING ANCIENT MEMORIES

But when we use powerful and ancient sexual symbols with all the skill of modern advertisers, there is an opportunity for abuse. The target client, propped against the bar, has never seen or handled a bow and arrow. But, deep down, the advertisement raises ancient memories. He may not have seen a recent anti-alcohol campaign that played on another sex symbol – the circle and arrow that denotes masculinity. In this campaign, the arrow drooped. The message ran to the effect that alcohol can reach your parts.

JINGLE BELLS

The way that symbols both survive and change – and are clearly a kind of language we need – is neatly shown by some recent research on a well known figure, whose identity you should try to guess from the following:

There is no doubt that, in deepest Lapland, Finland and parts of northern Russia, one of the high points of the year was the harvesting of a 'magic mushroom' which stimulates in particular sexual prowess. Known in the west as Fly Agaric, it is the toadstool that (unlike *Phallus impudicus*) you most usually see in fairy-tale

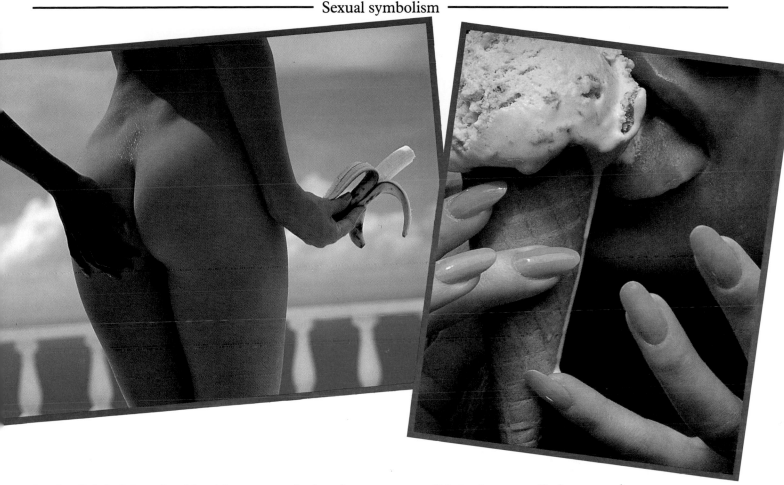

books. It is bright red, with white spots and trimmings. Collectors of the fungus were priests, known as shamans – distinguished, usually elderly men with beards. They travelled with reindeer.

The reindeer were as swift to discover the amazing effects of Fly Agaric as their owners. When the shaman passed water on the snow, the reindeer hastened to drink the still-drug-enriched results. Intoxicated in their turn, they indulged in odd behaviour.

Father Christmas, dressed in his toadstool colours of red and white, is still accompanied by cruising reindeer around December, from the baking depths of Australia to the snowy wastes of Canada.

PAGAN SYMBOLS

The idea that such a homely, even sanitized figure as Father Christmas comes weirdly and symbolically from a Lapland sex cult invites disbelief. But no one denies that the eggs and bunnies of Eastertime – the other great Christian festival – predate that faith by far. Ancient Egyptians revered the sexual prowess of the hare. Easter eggs have been part of the magically sexual revival of springtime for thousands of years.

AROUND THE MAYPOLE

Today, we live like ghosts in a world of these half-remembered, half-understood symbols. We no longer dance round the maypole, but we remember that folk

once did (and, more dimly, guess it was once some phallic symbol that the dancing girls surrounded). Oysters, we seem to recall, have a reputation as aphrodisiacs. Did we read somewhere that this rested partly on the resemblance of an open oyster to a vagina? Or do we recall, maybe subconsciously, that all fish have symbolized the power of swift sexual reproduction in any society on Earth.

EARLY SYMBOLS

The earliest Christians seized on that powerful image of the swimming fish and scratched it on the walls of catacombs as a shorthand code. The letters IHS still appear in hundreds of thousands of stained glass windows worldwide and they stand not for In His Service but for the Greek letters meaning Fish.

PURITY SYMBOLIZED

Some symbols have entirely lost their sexual connotations. When a medieval artist depicted the virgin with a unicorn resting its single horned head in her lap, he and his viewers knew that the unicorn stood as a symbol of purity. When he painted the virgin in an almond-shaped lozenge, he shared with most the knowledge that the almond (from its association with the first blossom of Spring) also denoted unsullied virtue. In an age without printed words and little literacy, symbols served as language instead.

It has been suggested that the deliberate use of painted, gaping lips in advertising is meant as a 'genital echo' – they resemble the labia when a woman is aroused.

PIERCED TO THE HEART

It was never, of course, a universal language. The Westerner sees the heart as the most potent symbol of life and love. The Easterner locates the seat of life in the belly. That is why the Japanese bent on self-destruction aims at the belly (hara) with the death thrust (kiri). The Westerner aims at the heart (usually missing, since the power of symbolism locates it on the left breast some way from its true, nearly central site). But in the West, the heart's power as a symbol has diverted millions of dollars into show-piece heart transplant surgery, when most doctors agree that less fashionable organs deserve more attention.

SYMBOLIC DRAMA

There are other symbols – now half forgotten but still steeped in sexual potency – that lurk and whisper to us. The frenzy that follows even the most minor new addition to the British Royal Family on the way to the altar shows our need to refresh ourselves at the fairy-tale source of romance that royalty represent.

OF PRINCES AND PRINCESSES

As any student of European newspapers and magazines will know, such 'love' for royal figures goes hand in glove with a curious desire to expose, even attack and destroy them. For every story that adulates the female royals, another will suggest that they are starving themselves to death, dying of cancer, or divorcing. But what is being played out here is a symbolic sexual drama that any ancient Greek, Sumerian or Dark Age Briton would understand at once.

Sacrificing kings (or, in a de-masculinized society, princesses) is the most central rite of sexual symbolism.

Each year, nature dies and each year nature is reborn. For some reason, the human race has decided that if it rounds on Elvis Presley, Princess Diana or William Rufus (the one that got shot by an arrow) the sacrifice will work, and the land will be renewed.

THE TWENTIETH CENTURY

Probably, some symbolists argue, we have chosen to feed virgins (or similarly powerful symbols like androgynous pop stars) for sacrifice on the same principle that ancient Greek myth threw virgins off the rock to keep the Minotaur content (he, you will recall, was the powerful, bull-headed beast that was caged in a technologically superior maze). Arguably, today's counterpart of the Minotaur's maze is the nuclear reactor (a labyrinthine building that holds a secret power at its core) – a raging bull that does not want to be let loose but nevertheless exudes sexual strength.

Ancient Greek myth solved that problem symbolically. Today we have the Chernobyl disaster. Is it fanciful, entirely, that symbolism's ancient language has been brought into play to ward off the nuclear threat? Can newspaper stories about such sex symbols as Princess Caroline have anything to do with the fact that the news story alongside is about the end of the world and that the advertisement on the same page shows a new, sexy, car?

REVELATIONS

Like the bower birds, we are a fanciful species. In Russia, in 1986, there was a big boom in sales of the Bible. It seems that, symbolically, the Book of Revelations told what would happen when a certain star exploded. The star was called Wormwood. The word for wormwood is, in Ukrainian, Chernobyl.

EROTIC POSTCARDS

Erotic postcards are nearly a hundred years old. They are a curious mix, ranging from the witty and saucy to the beautiful and highly explicit

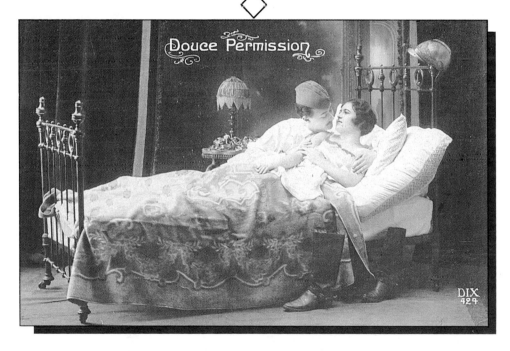

It seems to be part of human nature to enjoy erotic pictures of one sort or another, as most civilizations and periods of history can demonstrate. But in western societies, although erotic art has existed for centuries, it has remained mainly the preserve of the educated and the wealthy.

This is probably why the saucy postcard, when it appeared in the early part of this century, enjoyed such enormous popularity. It was witty, inexpensive, and best of all, available to everyone.

The postcard itself was invented in the 1860s, but photographic view cards did not appear until the 1890s. Cheap postage and the development of photographic and printing techniques led to a mania for collecting postcards, and special albums were widely available by the turn of the century.

THE BEGINNING

Germany at first cornered the market with their chromolithographs – coloured prints made from polished stones – but France soon developed collotype printing, a process that enabled photographs to be reproduced on postcards. Views, great occasions, stars of the theatre and famous paintings were all eagerly sought after, and soon a demand grew for more sophisticated subjects.

The Victorian era had been a period of overbearing respectability and strict repression of personal sexu-

Many erotic postcards were bought by mail order from Paris. During the 1914–1918 war soldiers even sent them as love letters.

Above and far right The very early erotic photographs were classic, innocent, often awkward and sometimes extremely humorous.

Natural and unashamedly naked, the erotic models of the 1870s and '80s catered predominantly for repressed male fantasies.

ality. Perhaps for that reason the beginning of the Edwardian years marked a dramatic change. What could be more natural, therefore, than widening the scope of cards to include erotic subjects.

SENTIMENTAL SEX

Sex and sentimentality were the main themes of these new collectables, and although they conformed to the postcard size of 14 × 9 cms (5½ × 3½ inches), they were not designed to be popped into a letterbox unless firmly sealed in an envelope.

Colour photography was still in its infancy, but the erotic or sentimental effects of these black and white images were often enhanced considerably by careful hand-tinting with aniline inks.

Although many erotic postcards originated in London, the main source was Paris from where they could be obtained by mail order. A magazine entitled *Rabelais* (issue of 1902) offers 'suggestive postcards for Art lovers' such as *Ardent Kisses*, *The Cigarette*, *Butterfly Hunting*, and *Alone at Last*, 18 centimes black and white and 21 centimes coloured.

RESTRICTED CIRCULATION

A catalogue in the Restricted collection of the British Library in London announced 'strictly confidential' sets of cards from Paris including *In the Nunnery*: 'the nun is well shaped, its forms are standing out prominently, the secret charms of an irreproachable freshness, the eyes blazing with unsatiable desires. Add to this a sexton who knows how to handle the holy-water sprinkler and to ring the bell during the divine service.

Twenty views for thirty shillings or seven dollars.'

Not everyone was prepared to admire the sexton's peculiar skills, however, as is shown by the many vain efforts at censorship. On August 22nd 1900, the police raided shops all over Paris and seized 80,000 'objectionable' postcards.

RESPECTABLE OR PORN?

A wide range of subject-matter is covered by the term 'erotic postcard'. At one end is the 'respectable' card depicting a painting or sculpture of one or more nude women as might be seen in the contemporary art exhibitions at the Royal Academy in London.

Especially popular were cards featuring nude models posed in imitation of famous images from the past, such as Greek statues of Aphrodite or *The Rokeby Venus* by Velázquez in London's National Gallery.

PASSING TRADE

At the other end of the scale is the hard-core pornography that found its main outlet among soldiers and sailors and became associated with busy sea-ports such as Marseilles and Port-Said.

Another set of cards in the British Library entitled *The Belle of Castillane* offers a girl whose 'beautiful knickers with lace insertion and embroidery excites alone men's admiration, revealing still prettier scenes underneath. She is seen in lusty indulgencies with a young gentleman, a debauchery is going on, and at the very moment when both their sperm is fired off, she indicates her sweet enjoyment by frantically beating a Tambourine.'

Between the two extremes is the most common type of card, usually sentimental or amusing, which is still avidly sought in junk shops by today's collectors. The publishers and photographers were almost exclusively male, working with a male clientele in mind, and so the imagery is very definitely geared towards men.

Male homosexual themes, like postcards catering exclusively for the tastes of women, were very rare, the exception being the photographs of Baron Von Gloeden showing nude Sicilian boys posing as the ideals of Classical youth, for contemporary laws made this a dangerous subject and the market limited.

LESBIAN IMAGES

There were, however, no laws against lesbianism, and suggestive images of women fondling each other held especial fascination for men in those days, just as they do today. A French set of about 1900 shows a maid helping her mistress to track down an insect which is stinging her under her clothes. The situation gives free rein to male fantasies about lesbianism.

Indeed, male fantasy is the staple diet of these postcards. Women posing alone, either in the nude or in the process of various stages of undressing, and women catering to the pleasures of men are the most usual subjects, together with a rather more limited range of props.

SPURS TO FANTASY

Underwear is one such prop. Representing the last barrier, it invites speculation as to what lies beyond. Others include a letter from a lover, dogs or cats fondled by the woman and representing the absent male, flowers sent by the lover and a mirror to enhance the voyeuristic flavour.

The male voyeur could sometimes find an Oriental scene depicting a Pasha's harem or a slave market which provided for the fantasy of owning several women. There were also cards featuring celebrated 'femmes fatales' such as Mata Hari (executed as a spy in 1917), Caroline Otero (mistress of Edward VII and other royalty) and Theda Bara (among the most famous of the early cinema vamps) which implied that the man's role was one of willing slave.

SEX SYMBOLS

Obvious symbolism was continually used, from cigarettes to sticks of asparagus, from gushing fountains to spurting champagne bottles, from guns, waves, arrows, and Zeppelin airships to swords entering scabbards and trains disappearing into tunnels. These all pre-dated Freud, but their messages were clear.

During the First World War, the importing of Continental cards was halted. England, France and Germany all produced cards depicting women accompanied by men in uniform as part of their unofficial war efforts.

COMIC SEASIDE CARDS

The production of erotic postcards continued after the war, but their popularity declined. The one exception was the comic seaside card, drawn by a host of specialists led by Donald McGill. These curiously innocent scenes of event-filled holidays gain their effect from the double meanings in their bylines, a trick often used in turn-of-the-century cards. A girl lies in the bath holding a rather startled cat and tells us 'I always wash my pussy with scented soap'. Replaced by magazines and films, the comic seaside card is all that remains of the erotic postcard.

SEX REVOLUTIONARIES

They made enemies, caused ructions and were considered scandalous.
But as pioneers, the sex revolutionaries paved the way to
a greater understanding of human sexuality

While other cultures and other ages have been uninhibited about some aspects of sexuality, it is our own age which has seen the most widespread discarding of sexual taboos and conventions.

No single 'movement' can take the credit for the overall loosening of sexual attitudes, but certain individuals do stand out in Western society as pioneers of a new awareness. Each of the following has, in his or her own way, made a breakthrough towards the growing confidence and boldness about sexual matters which characterize the 20th century.

SIGMUND FREUD 1856–1939

The sedate, bourgeois society of Vienna, where Freud spent most of his life, was an unlikely setting for the revolutionary ideas and psychoanalytic theories he introduced. These were that fears and phobias are often related to repressed sexual desires.

Working first as a neurologist, Freud studied hysteria and hypnotism in Paris, and began his investigations into the human mind. Setting up as a private consultant in Vienna in 1886, he was increasingly absorbed in the treatment of neuroses. Experiments with electrotherapy were a failure, and he learned hypnotic techniques to make patients relive emotions experienced during physical traumas which they had forgotten, but which were often the cause of their neuroses.

Moving from hypnotism to 'free association', in which patients were encouraged to say whatever came into their heads, Freud became aware that there is an unconscious sector of the mind, which struggles to remain hidden, and which is made up of desires and wishes that are often sexual in nature.

His investigations with both adults and children led him to the belief that, from the earliest age, infants were sexual beings who experienced sexual desires and sought sexual gratification. Whereas previously it had been taken for granted that sexuality started at puberty, Freud shocked the establishment by insisting that from as early as two years this generalized sexuality became focused on a specific object.

Freud claimed that in most cases this object was a parent – boys focused predominantly on their mothers,

Sigmund Freud shocked the bourgeois society of Vienna with his theories. He claimed that from infancy human behaviour is motivated by sexual desires and the need for sexual gratification.

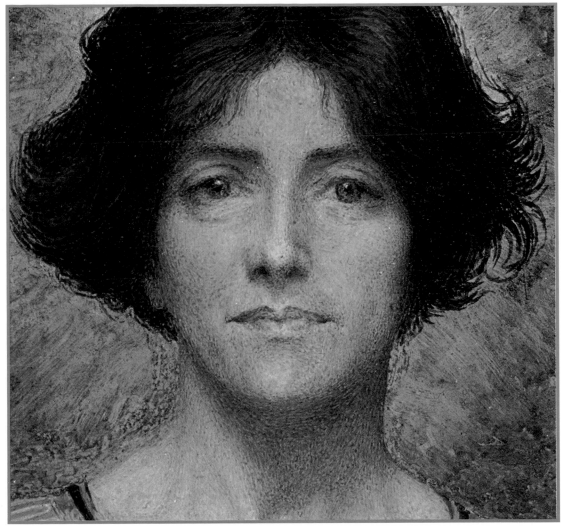

Marie Stopes strove hard to take the fear and anxiety out of lovemaking by establishing the use of birth control as an accepted part of sexual life.

while girls were more likely to focus on their fathers. (He called this the Oedipal phase, after the mythological Greek prince who became his own mother's lover.) And because society's rules forbade such emotions, this and other sexual manifestations were repressed in early childhood.

According to Freud, this repression could lead to hysterical states in later life, which might be expressed as an irrational anxiety or even as physical paralysis in certain circumstances, with no apparent organic cause.

MARIE STOPES 1880–1958

The daughter of an academic father and a mother with strong feminist leanings, Marie Stopes had the sort of self-confidence that was rare in young English-women during the reign of Queen Victoria. She was a brilliant scholar, winning a double degree at London University and a doctorate a year later, and becoming the first woman member of the Science Faculty at Manchester University.

The sexual inadequacies of Marie Stopes' first husband led to the annulment of the unconsummated marriage, and the beginning of her life-long involvement in the sexual problems of couples.

Marie Stopes looked upon sex as something to be enjoyed without fear or guilt. In 1918 she published *Married Love*, in which she encouraged young couples to throw the inhibitions and repressions of Victorian upbringing out of the window, so that the joys of sexual relationships could be fully appreciated.

Despite, or perhaps because of, the outrage caused by this book, it became a runaway bestseller. She received hundreds of letters from young marrieds who agreed with her theories, but were in great need of straightforward contraceptive advice. Therefore, the same year she brought out *Wise Parenthood* which gave detailed advice on the use of a range of contraceptive methods, from caps, pessaries and condoms, to coitus interruptus (withdrawal) and the 'safe' period.

The world had obviously been waiting for Marie Stopes, for the two books sold millions of copies in

thirteen different languages. They appealed to ordinary men and women, and contained none of the evasions and euphemisms of the 'respectable' sex manuals. Young couples in 1920 were impatient of the older generation's coy puritanism. And Marie's forthright enthusiasm and practical advice were exactly what they wanted.

In 1921, with her second husband, Marie Stopes opened a birth control clinic in London. The giving of contraceptive advice was described as 'a monstrous crime' by one public health doctor, and vociferous opposition came from both the medical profession and the Catholic Church. But Marie saw contraceptive campaigning as an aid to sexual fulfilment. She carried on writing best-selling books on sex and contraception. And after World War II she continued with her birth-control work in the Far East.

MARGARET MEAD 1901–1978

As an anthropologist Margaret Mead explored the social structures, family relationships, and adolescence patterns in some tribal societies which were, at the time, relatively untouched by western industrial influences.

She lived for long stretches in the communities she was studying, gaining insights which she wrote up brilliantly in books that were, accessible to the general public. These books enabled readers to look at their own societies from an entirely new viewpoint.

Margaret Mead, raised by an enlightened mother and grandmother, understood from an early age that women were given a raw deal in western societies. By demonstrating that what is customary in one cultural grouping may be wholly unacceptable in another, she was able to undermine the long-held male opinions that there are certain unalterable laws in relationships between the sexes, and that universal custom upholds the practice of treating women as inferiors.

She wrote *Coming of Age in Samoa* in 1928, and *Growing up in New Guinea* in 1930. *Sex and Temperament in Three Primitive Societies* (1935) was particularly concerned with the sexual basis for women's position in society. In *Male and Female* (1950), she compared the sexual attitudes of modern Americans with those of Pacific Islanders. Her 40 books, over 1000 articles and monographs, and large collection of tapes and films, make anthropology accessible to the non-academic, enabling us to cast a more understanding eye over our own society's sexual and moral attitudes.

D H LAWRENCE 1885–1930

Lawrence treated sex more frankly and honestly than any previous English novelist. *Lady Chatterley's Lover*, his most controversial novel, became the centre of a court case, nearly 30 years after the writer's death, which marked a watershed in publishing history. To Lawrence the ordinary niceties of polite society were a strait-jacket. He saw the human personality imprisoned by social rules which prevented its true expression. Sexual expression was an important part of his philosophy, and he considered its denial to be a major cause of misery.

Born in Nottingham to a coalminer father and a mother who was ambitious for her sons to rise above their origins, Lawrence was an intensely emotional and sensitive man. He poured out a prolific stream of novels, poems, plays and essays while travelling all over the world, vainly trying to discover the ideal environment in which to settle down.

His wife, Frieda, who accompanied him on his journeyings, had left a husband and three children to live with Lawrence. Thus his own life mirrored the disruption of social morality that featured in his writings.

Sons and Lovers, Lawrence's first major work, deals with the theme of possessive motherhood (echoing his own background) and is a pioneer of English psychological fiction. The theme of the search for a love that is free from possessiveness recurs throughout his novels. *The Rainbow* (1915) and *Women in Love* (1920), demonstrate Lawrence's desire to join spiritual aspirations with animal sensuality. His characters often demonstrate one or other of these qualities, and are shown to be flawed.

He blamed modern industrial society for the imbalance in people. *Lady Chatterley's Lover* (1928) presented, in the gamekeeper, Oliver Mellors, the complete Lawrentian hero for the first time, combining sensuality and sexual potency with intelligence and creativity. Sexual love, graphically described in the book, becomes a means of salvation for his aristocratic mistress from the sterility of her own marriage. Banned

Margaret Mead shown with a young Samoan girl during her field work in 1926. The trip resulted in Mead's first major work – Coming of Age in Samoa.

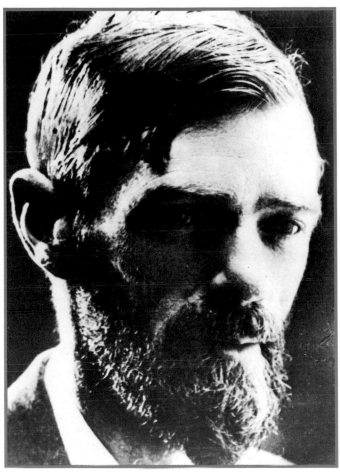

Even 30 years after his death, D H Lawrence's work was causing a stir. His novel, Lady Chatterley's Lover, *was the subject of an obscenity trial that made publishing history.*

from unexpurgated publication in Britain for many years, *Lady Chatterley's Lover* finally appeared under the Penguin imprint after a lengthy obscenity trial. Lawrence would have enjoyed the victory.

GERMAINE GREER

An innovator in the feminist movement, Germaine Greer has managed to combine academic skills with a talent for publicity and for upsetting all the self-appointed guardians of public morality.

Born in Australia, she was educated in a convent, and Melbourne and Sydney Universities before coming to Britain. It was the Swinging Sixties era when she studied at Cambridge, and went on to teach English at Warwick – the rebellious decade of instant magazines, zany, sexy clothes, and a more serious undercurrent which severely questioned establishment values in all spheres, including sexual propriety.

With other expatriate Australians, Germaine Greer contributed to the anarchic *OZ* magazine, appearing topless on the cover in a jokey take-off of a groupie unzipping a pop musician's trousers. In 1963 she was married for just three weeks. She wrote for *Private Eye*

under the nom-de-plume 'Rose Blight, gardening correspondent'.

In 1970 Germaine Greer published *The Female Eunuch*, her immensely successful attack on conventional marriage and attitudes towards women. In it she attacks the stereotypes that have plagued women for centuries, the way girl children are conditioned to be subservient and 'feminine', the fixed sexual roles of masterful male and passive female, and the middle-class phenomenon of the 'nuclear family', isolated by its own rules. The book is at one and the same time erudite, funny, passionate and angry, and its many reprints have made it a key work in the growth of feminist awareness.

Germaine Greer has continued to produce both academic work and feminist propaganda. On screen and in print she was the most skilful of the pundits who emerged in the sixties, and she continues to use the media to her own advantage in order to put across the message that women should strive for a better deal than the introverted drudgery of the western, middle-class marriage unit.

ALEX COMFORT

Alex Comfort's name is forever identified in the public's mind with *The Joy of Sex*, an illustrated 'gourmet guide to love-making' that made its first

Germaine Greer's The Female Eunuch, *which attacks the stereotype roles of 'masterly male and passive female', has become a key work in the growth of feminist awareness.*

appearance in 1972, to be followed by a number of reprints, updates and sequels. People are usually surprised to discover that Dr Comfort was a long-established, highly revered biologist many years before the 'Joy' books, an academic with brilliant and extensive qualifications. Apart from his academic work he has also published novels, plays and volumes of poetry.

The secret of *The Joy of Sex*'s success is its immediacy and lack of mystery. Sex manuals have appeared at regular intervals over the last century, but the message has always been hidden behind learned vocabulary and stilted, mechanical instructions. Suddenly here was a book that answered all the questions, used normal, every-day language, and was copiously illustrated with clear, sensuous drawings that featured real people doing real things to one another, instead of the usual scientific diagrams with numbered arrows.

Books of detailed illustrations had been available before, but were nearly always classified and sold as pornography. By producing *The Joy of Sex* as a large-format, high-quality publication, Alex Comfort and his colleagues overcame the reticence and secretiveness that had tended to accompany the purchase of books about sex.

Publication coincided with a period when the public was becoming much bolder about exploring sexuality, and the book, which has even been given out on prescription by some physicians, remains a bestseller.

Alex Comfort, who has worked most of his life as a physiologist interested in the problems of ageing, welcomed the chance to work as editor on *The Joy of Sex*. As he says in his introduction, 'Love is too seriously joyful a matter to be left to the solemnities of academics, moral authorities, and the porno trader, all of them basically anxious people.'

QUENTIN CRISP

Quentin Crisp 'came out' as a homosexual long before the era of Gay Rights and crusading self-revelation. His autobiography, *The Naked Civil Servant*, at once details a remarkably bold and eccentric character, and gives an intimate insight into the world of the gay man in London's seedy underworld of the 1930s and 1940s.

Having realized at an early age that he was a homosexual, Quentin Crisp made no compromise with a generally censorious and often violent society. They could take him as they found him, with heavy make-up, camp speech and effeminate mannerisms. His street companions were often male prostitutes as he hung around Soho and central London, and Crisp himself went on the game as the opportunity offered itself.

Homosexuality became a cause, and he acted as one of its most overt champions. He dressed and made up to increasingly bizarre standards. He details in *The Naked Civil Servant* how he lost jobs, and suffered persecution, humility and brutality because of his appearance. Yet he never wavered in holding out for his right to act as the personality he knew he was. As he

Eccentric and effeminate, Quentin Crisp was a champion of homosexuality long before it was ever a cause. Despite being persecuted for his appearance he has always refused to conform – and to live a lie.

says, 'From the age of 28 I never did for long anything that I didn't want to do – except grow old.'

NANCY FRIDAY

One of the last sexual myths to survive into our relatively enlightened age was the idea that sexual fantasies were a mainly male phenomenon. Society had reluctantly acknowledged that women enjoyed sex, but the idea that they fantasized about it was improper – and threatening to men's self-image.

Nancy Friday dispelled the myth once and for all in her book *My Secret Garden* (1973). Deciding to break the 'conspiracy of silence' that made many women ashamed of their sexual fantasies, she began her work by putting advertisements in British and US newspapers, inviting women to send in their fantasies.

Women of all ages and backgrounds responded in their thousands, many of them relieved to unburden themselves of what they had long considered to be an unnatural and guilty secret. Nancy Friday followed up the letters with hundreds of interviews, and the book contains an enormous range of detailed, richly imagined fantasies experienced by women when alone and when with lovers.

THE
EASTERN
WAY

The proverbial passion of the Latin lover and sexual finesse of the French are obvious examples of how we invest an identifiable group with certain qualities. These characteristics, real or otherwise, are part of our mythology, providing us with a ready-made ideal of sexual prowess. Yet the fact remains that for many centuries it has been the East that has shown those who wish to pursue it the way in matters of love. The cultures of the Near East, of India, and of China and Japan, sophisticated long before Europe and North America, offer us a whole world of practical instruction. Books such as The Perfumed Garden, The Kama Sutra, *the Chinese Pillow Books, and many other works devoted to the arts of love explore to the full both the physical and emotional aspects of human sexuality. The centuries-old wisdom enshrined in these books is no instant key to sexual skill and does not offer facile solutions to our problems. Furthermore, the language in which they are written, even in the best translations, has often proved an obstacle to the ordinary reader. Yet for all that they represent an invaluable distillation of generations of experience and deserve a wider understanding. In this chapter you will find in a digestible form the teachings that are the Eastern Way to sexual fulfilment.*

THE CHINESE WAY OF LOVE

To the Ancient Chinese, making love was almost an art form. Their sexually explicit 'pillow books' are as practical as they are poetic

It is easy to be misled into thinking that sexual enlightenment is a western invention – a 20th century phenomenon that has suddenly and miraculously opened the eyes of the civilized world. What is often forgotten is that more than three and a half thousand years before the so-called 'sexual revolution' there existed in China a civilization characterized, among other things, by a remarkably sophisticated attitude to sex.

THE 'JOY' OF SEX

Studying the Chinese way of love is as rewarding as it is fascinating. Although the philosophy on which it is based sounds strange to western ears, underlying the quaint and the mystical are commonsense principles which betray a profound and sympathetic understanding of human nature.

Most importantly, the Chinese way underlines the 'joy' of sex, stressing time and again that it is an art to be mastered by both parties in the interests of their mutual enjoyment.

In this sense, at least, it has as much to offer the western couple exploring their own sexuality as it did their eastern counterparts of ancient times.

PUTTING THINGS IN PERSPECTIVE

Much of the accumulated wisdom of the Taoists was recorded in 'pillow' books. These were as candid in their many illustrations as they were comprehensive in their coverage of the subject. To western eyes, such

The Dragon in Flight
Lady Yin lies on her back with her legs raised. Lord Yang parts her feet and, pulling them over his shoulders, lowers his Jade Stem into her Golden Pavilion. Because Lady Yin's feet point upwards, the position is said to be suggestive of a flying dragon.

Cicadas Mating
Lady Yin lies face down on a couch, her right leg raised, her left leg straightened out and her Golden Gully pointing upwards. Lord Yang takes up a position behind her and buries his Heavenly Dragon Pillar deep inside her Receptive Vase.

books might easily be seen as pornographic. To the Chinese, however, they were simply recipes for living, to be consulted as frequently – and in much the same way – as a favourite cookbook.

The language of the books may be flowery but we can learn much from the Taoists' teaching and incorporate it into our lovemaking.

We do not, however, need to take all the teaching too literally. Certainly, there is no medical evidence to support the Taoist theory of a physical transference of energy during intercourse, nor that ejaculation is physically draining once the resolution phase has passed. Likewise, it is wrong to think that orgasm is absolutely essential in lovemaking – it is perfectly possible to enjoy each other's bodies without climaxing, or, indeed, without penetration. Both are important dimensions of lovemaking – not the be-all and end-all.

To the Taoists, the act of lovemaking had a deep significance which went far beyond the need to produce children. Yet, inbred in the philosophy is the view that good sex is essential for both partners if they are to live a long and happy life. Quite possibly it evolved from a basic realization that having sex could be enjoyable – and once the mystical concepts and language are stripped away, enjoyment is what Taoist sex is all about.

AN ENLIGHTENED SOCIETY

The Taoist pillow books displayed a remarkably liberated attitude to most forms of sexual activity, though deviations from straight male/female intercourse were invariably discouraged on philosophical grounds.

About the only sphere of activity conspicuous by its absence was sado-masochism. Surrounded by the savagery of everyday life, the Chinese felt violence had no place in the bedroom.

TAOISM AND SEX

The Chinese way of love has its origins in Taoism – a part-religious, part-philosophical movement which established a firm foothold in Chinese cultural life by 2000 BC.

To the Taoists, everything had an equal and opposite reaction. When something advances, something else must fall back. When something grows, something else must shrivel. Night must always follow day.

The forces responsible were given names – Yin, the passive, negative, nourishing force, and Yang, the active, positive and consuming force.

When it came to human beings, the Taoists recognized the presence of both Yin and Yang. Men, being by nature more assertive, were thought to contain a relatively large amount of Yang, while the more passive nature of women was the result of their higher proportion of Yin-force, hence the names

Lord Yang and Lady Yin used for male and female lovers.

The balance of Yin and Yang was always believed to be precarious. The way to correct this imbalance, according to Taoist belief, was for a man to take some of a woman's Yin force, and for her to take some of his Yang force – which could only be achieved by intercourse.

Crucial to Taoist teaching was the idea that the longer inter-

course was prolonged, the greater the flow of Yin and Yang between one partner and another. The two forces were thought to be at their most potent at the exact moment of orgasm. But whereas a woman's Yin essence (as embodied in the vaginal fluid) was believed to be infinite and inexhaustible, a man's Yang essence (his semen) was considered to be definitely finite in quantity and was thus to be conserved.

Cunnilingus and fellatio were actively encouraged as means of rousing the Yin/Yang spirit to full potency.

Masturbation was discouraged, or regarded as silly, on the grounds that it wasted precious Yin/Yang energy. (Nocturnal emissions also worried the Taoist Masters, who feared they were caused by female spirits bent on draining a man of his Yang energy.)

Anal intercourse was permissible as long as no Yang essence was lost. It was thought to be an inferior source of Yin energy.

Sex aids were largely regarded as beneficial as long as they caused no physical harm to either partner.

Kissing was considered an extremely important part of lovemaking, but was thought to be unseemly in public.

Pornography was not really recognized. In no sense did the Taoist Masters see the illustrations in their pillow books as lewd or pornographic images. Their main purpose was designed to excite the readers to partake in the Delights of the Couch.

Homosexuality was accepted in both sexes, although it was regarded as unproductive because it resulted in the interaction of two equal, rather than opposite, forces.

Bisexuality was also accepted, although it was believed that if bisexuals had children then there was a strong chance that the offspring would turn out to be hermaphrodite.

HAPPY, HEALTHIER SEX

Although, on a philosophical level, having sex was a sacred act, in more down-to-earth terms it was a struggle between the sexes.

It was also a sort of battle of the bedchamber, in which the assertive force of the male sought to subdue the passive – but equally powerful force – of the female.

Yet, notwithstanding the sexism implicit in some of its teachings, Taoism is about fulfilment.

Without really understanding why, the Taoist philosophers knew instinctively that happy, healthy sex between a man and a woman was to the mutual advantage of both. And in their pillow books, they sought to make this as clear as possible, as well as providing clear instruction on how the theory could be put into practice.

ART OF THE BEDCHAMBER

The Taoist pillow books were unanimous in their insistence that only if a man and a woman were both equally aroused, would the outcome of a confrontation succeed. According to Taoist master Tung Hsuan, 'If a man moves and a woman does not respond, or if the woman is roused and the man does not comply, then the sexual act will not only injure the man but harm the woman.'

The Chinese recognized that retiring to bed in the wrong mood was the most common cause of impotence.

The Tiger in the Forest
Right: *Lady Yin kneels down and lowers her head on to her hands. Lord Yang inserts his Swelling Mushroom into the Vermilion Gate and thrusts vigorously for one hundred strokes.*

THE MOOD FOR LOVE

The oldest surviving sex treatise was written by Huang-Ti, The Yellow Emperor, about 2,500 years BC. It was written in the form of questions and answers. When the Yellow Emperor inquired of his goddess-instructress, The Wise Maiden, as to how the right mood for love could be induced, she advised him to follow the 'Five Natural Humours of the Male'.

The first 'natural humour' was to be relaxed and unassuming, the second to be generous of spirit, the third to be controlled in breathing, and the fourth to be serene in body. The fifth humour – a desire for solitude brought on by feelings of loyalty – was the only legitimate excuse a man could give for the failure of his Jade Stem to stiffen.

The Floating Turtle
Lady Yin lies on her back, like a turtle floating on the water.
Lord Yang raises her legs, gently brings her feet up to his ears
and then passes his Jade Stalk into her Open Peony Blossom
to achieve the Clouds and the Rain.

SEX AIDS

Contained in the famous Taoist pillow books are numerous recipes for potions to help improve sexual performance. One of the most celebrated is the 'Bald Chicken Drug', so called because when one well known user accidentally fed it to his cockerel, the poor bird's sexual appetite became so voracious that he pecked bald the heads of his equally unfortunate hens while mounting them.

Among the many mechanical aids which fell into common usage was a variation of the Penis Ring — a circle of jade or ivory which was slipped around the male member and held in place by a silken waistband. Like its western equivalent the 'Goat's Hair', this was believed to help maintain erection and to act as a clitoral stimulant.

Other frequently documented aids included the 'Tinkling Bells' — small metal balls inserted under the foreskin to improve penile dimensions — and the 'Burmese Bell' — a pair of hollow balls placed in the vagina and designed to produce erotic sensations when accompanied by movements of the thighs and hips.

THE CHINESE LANGUAGE OF LOVE

Much of the appeal of the ancient Chinese pillow books lies in the colourful language used by the authors

Intercourse
The Clouds and the Rain
The Mists and the Rain
Delight of the Couch
The Mountain of Wu

Orgasm
Bursting of the Clouds
The Great Typhoon

Male sexual organ
Male Peak, Stalk or Stem
Jade Stem, Stalk, Root
Coral Stem
Heavenly Dragon Pillar
Turtle Head

Red Bird
Swelling Mushroom
Secret Pouch (scrotum)

Female sexual organs
Jade Gate or Pavilion
Cinnabar or Vermilion Gate
Open Peony Blossom
Golden Lotus
Receptive Vase
Coral Gate
Magic Field
Pearl on the Jade Step (clitoris)
The Jewel Terrace (clitoral area)
Golden Gully (labial cleft)
Examination Hall (inner labia)

The Swinging Monkey
Lord Yang lies back and Lady Yin lowers herself on to his
lap. She slides her Jewel Terrace over his Red Bird, and as
the excitement mounts, she impales herself on him.

THE WOMAN'S MOOD

The Wise Maiden proceeded to advise The Yellow Emperor to be guided by the Five Responses of the Female.

First, when she became flushed the man should approach her. Then, as her nipples rose and beads of perspiration appeared on her nose, he would know his advances were welcome.

As her mouth opened, her breathing quickened and her hands trembled, he should take it as a sign to thrust forward. When her Golden Gully became profusely lubricated he should let himself be carried away by the current. And finally, as her thighs relaxed and she appeared to lose all strength, he would know that it was time to pause before resuming the attack.

In addition to this highly practical instruction, the pillow books took care to stress the need for careful dress, a convivial atmosphere and strict personal hygiene in the run-up to a love session.

FOREPLAY

If all was well with both partners, the next stage was foreplay. This held great importance for the Taoist Masters, who believed that only if the Yin and Yang forces were stirred slowly into action could they be expected to reach full potency.

In the case of a new or inexperienced partner, Master Tung Hsuan counselled tenderness, consideration and restrained exploration, accompanied by soft caresses, reassuring words and gentle kisses. In this way, he promised that 'a thousand charms would be unfolded and a hundred sorrows forgotten'.

After these initial embraces came more intimate touching, with the woman fondling the man's Jade Stem and causing her own Yin essence to flow in the process.

But even though by now both partners could be thought ready to unite, Tung Hsuan advised 'further dalliance' before penetration was attempted.

The man should allow his Jade Stem (penis) to hover over the Cinnabar Gate (vagina) while kissing the woman lovingly and gazing down at her Golden Gully. He should stroke her breasts and stomach while allowing his Male Peak to flick the sides of the Examination Hall (labia) and caress the Jewel Terrace (clitoral area). And if necessary, he should kiss and lick the Pearl on the Jade Step (clitoris) to ensure that the Yin essences were thoroughly stirred before the Clouds and the Rain (intercourse).

THE THRUST OF THE JADE STEM

Master Tung Hsuan was quick to point out that when it came to penetration, a man must never cling to one style just for his own convenience.

Among the possible courses of action open to him at the start were:
☐ To plunge into the Jade Pavilion of his partner,

employing a sawing motion, as if opening an oyster
☐ To thrust upwards against the Golden Valley, splitting the rock to reveal its precious contents
☐ To grind the Jade Stem against the Jewel Terrace like a pestle grinding into a mortar
☐ To move the Yang Peak slowly and steadily, as rhythmically as the breeze
☐ To plough the Male Thruster through the Precious Field and into the Far Valley beyond
☐ When the Yin was fierce, to crash down on the Cinnabar Cleft like two great rocks battering each other.

With penetration successfully completed, Tung Hsuan then had the following advice:
☐ Swing the Jade Thrusting Root to left and right like a warrior charging through the enemy's ranks

Standing Bamboos
*Lady Yin stands, placing one foot on the edge of a couch.
Lord Yang stands in front of her and slowly penetrates her
Golden Lotus with his Coral Stem. The Standing Bamboos
bend – as if blown by the wind – and the couple lie down to
find the Delight of the Couch.*

☐ Sweep along, then pause, like a great sail caught in
the wind.

As the Jade Pavilion achieved full lubrication, so the
man should plunge ever deeper, slanting to left and
right, sweeping in a circular motion, and alternating
deep thrusts with shallow strokes. Cries from Lady Yin
begging for her life were to be ignored, although Tung
Hsuan was more reasonable in his suggestion that
pauses should be taken periodically.

PROLONGING THE PLEASURE

The Taoist belief in the need for man to conserve his
Yang-essence as much as possible, while still promoting
a 'Bursting of the Clouds' (orgasm) in his partner,
placed a heavy burden on the male sexual performance.
Tung Hsuan wrote that 'to retire from the field of battle
in a state of miserable detumescence suggests that the
Yin spirit has vanquished the Yang spirit'. To dispel the
'Hundred Anxieties' of the nervous male lover, he
advised quick penetration with much thrusting.

Then, as the Last Moment was approaching, he
counselled the man to close his eyes and concentrate his
thoughts, to press his tongue against the roof of his
mouth, bend his back and stretch his neck. The man
was to follow this by opening his nostrils wide, squaring
his back and drawing breath, so preventing ejaculation
and causing the Yang-essence to 'advance inward'.

The Phoenix in Flight
*Lady Yin lies back, bringing back her feet as far as she can.
Lord Yang then encircles her thighs, presses his Jade Root into
her Coral Gate and thrusts vigorously from left to right. The
movements made in this position should resemble those of a
Phoenix flapping its wings.*

☐ Allow the Male Peak to play like a horse leaping
through a stream – first up, then down
☐ Float and sink, like a duck on a lake
☐ Peck like a sparrow, first shallow, then deep
☐ Move slowly, like a snake entering its hole
☐ Move swiftly, like a rat chased into its burrow
☐ Hover like an eagle, swooping on its prey

THE INDIAN WAY OF LOVE

Of all the ancient treatises on the art of love, the Indian Kama Sutra *has had perhaps the greatest impact on western society*

Since its translation into English in the 19th century, it has found its way on to the bookshelves of countless people, becoming a byword for all that is mysterious and exotic in the field of sexual relationships.

But popular misconceptions of the *Kama Sutra* abound. In reality, it is far from being the motley collection of ligament-straining positions, outdated practices and bizarre recipes for aphrodisiacs which on first reading it can appear to be.

Nor is the information contained within it hopelessly bound up with the prevailing religious attitudes of the time when it was written.

THE JOYS OF LOVEMAKING

The *Kama Sutra*, together with its lesser-known companion volumes the *Khoka Shastra* and the *Ananga Ranga*, represents the cumulative experience of a thousand years of sexuality as practised by one of the world's greatest civilizations. And like their Chinese counterparts, the Taoist pillow books, these manuals reveal an intuitive understanding of the joys and problems of lovemaking which time has done little to change.

THE INDIAN WAY

In accordance with the ancient Hindu philosophy and teaching, the Indian sex manuals view lovemaking within the broader context of male/female relationships. The implication is that while sex itself is an art to be studied, practised and mastered, it cannot be divorced from the other aspects of *kama* – the World of the Senses – which Hindus consider forms such an important part of existence.

This attitude comes across clearly in the *Kama Sutra*. Only one section is devoted to the technicalities of lovemaking, the others dealing with how to find, attract and keep a mate, how to behave with courtesans,

as well as how a man should cope with the problem of being attracted to the wife of another man.

Throughout the treatise, there is heavy emphasis on the need for personal cleanliness, care in dress and behaviour, and a knowledge of the Arts. Also stressed is the importance of getting to know the preferences of one's partner and how to respond to them.

INDIAN LOVEMAKING

On the subject of lovemaking itself, the authors take an encyclopedic approach, their chief aim being to record

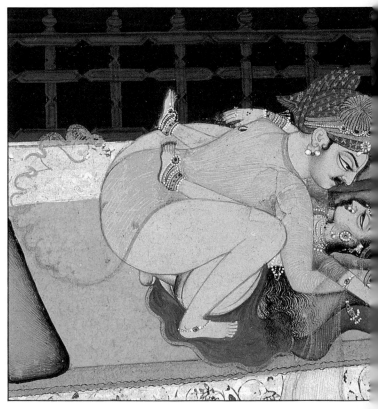

THE HINDU PHILOSOPHY OF LOVE

According to Hindu belief, the soul or *Karma* of Man is an indestructible force which is reincarnated from one life to the next.

The level at which this reincarnation will take place depends on how correctly the Karma's possessor has lived his or her previous life, the aim being to reach the highest level and be released from this cycle of rebirth into a paradise of 'Eternal Nothingness'.

Thus, a life lived in exemplary fashion promises elevation to a higher level in the next one, while a dissolute and immoral existence results in a down-grading of one's Karma that must be made good in later incarnations.

This emphasis on correct behaviour is underlined by the Hindu's *Three Great Aims* in life. The first and most important Aim, *dharma*, is to improve one's spiritual well-being by living life according to the religious, social and moral laws of society.

But only slightly less important are *artha*, the accumulation of wealth and material security, and *kama*, the stimulation and satisfaction of the senses through activities such as the Arts, eating and drinking, and lovemaking.

In short, Hinduism not only recognizes sexual activity as an important part of human existence, but also considers it one of the routes to a full and rounded spiritual life.

The embrace
Indicating the mutual love of a man and a woman, an embrace may be practised at any time – but particularly before they make love.

the practices of the day. Only rarely do they pass moral or religious judgements, and even then it is with the proviso that at the height of passion the rules of love seldom know any bounds.

Kissing, embracing and foreplay are described in considerable detail, including sections on scratching, biting and striking. While these sections have been frequently misinterpreted as an incitement to sadism, they are no more than an attempt to formalize and control the more aggressive side of sexual behaviour, and to place it in its proper context.

THE POSITIONS

'Straight' intercourse is dealt with exhaustively and comprehensively, although the celebrated '64 positions' are rather less imaginative than their Chinese equivalents. Most consist of slight variations on familiar themes, while others require almost superhuman suppleness of the limbs.

In addition – and in common with other ancient sex manuals – there are numerous references to aphrodisiacs and sex aids. Most concern an Indian obsession – incompatibility of size between the *lingam* (penis) and the *yoni* (vagina).

UNDERSTANDING THE MANUALS

Since they are products of an essentially male-dominated society, the *Kama Sutra* (and its later companion volumes) takes an inevitably sexist and patronizing view of the role of women.

However, this applies more to the sections on general behaviour than to the one on lovemaking itself. Here, the roles of men and women are clearly defined and given equal importance, which makes them as relevant today as when they were first written down.

Misunderstandings may arise over the way in which sexual techniques and practices are rigidly classified, often by references to the practices of different ethnic groups within the Indian sub-continent.

The important point here is that the authors were trying to define stereotypes (and the behaviour typical of them) in much the same way as an astrologer lists the characteristics of the 12 signs of the zodiac.

By doing this, the writers of the *Kama Sutra* hoped to make it easier for readers to pinpoint the sexual characteristics and preferences of their own partners.

THE KAMA SUTRA IN ACTION

The section of the *Kama Sutra* which deals with lovemaking begins with advice on how to approach a lover, followed by instruction on kissing and foreplay, and then the positions and techniques for intercourse. Oral sex is treated separately, on account of its rather special position.

THE EMBRACE

According to the *Kama Sutra*, when lovers meet, their bodies may touch lightly, rub against one another, 'pierce' each other (invade one another's 'personal space') or be pressed against a nearby solid object such as a wall.

From here, the encounter progresses to one of the four classic embraces of lovers.

Standing, the couple may be entwined – *The Twining of the Creeper* – or else the woman may grip the man with one foot off the ground and the other on his foot – *The Climbing of a Tree*.

Lying down on a bed, the lovers can entwine their limbs passionately around one another in the *Mixture of Sesamum Seed with Rice*. Or, the woman can sit on the man's lap in the embrace of *Mixing Milk with Water*.

The authors then mention variations in which the couple concentrate on close contact between their foreheads, breasts, and lower bodies. Implicit in the advice is that close bodily contact (as opposed to direct genital stimulation) is an essential preliminary to a satisfying bout of lovemaking.

THE KISS

While the authors of the *Kama Sutra* take care not to lay down a strict order for the various actions of love-making, they are at pains to stress the importance of correct and varied kissing.

The forehead, eyes, cheeks, lips, throat, inside of the mouth and breasts the most kissable areas, and the arms, thigh joints and navel are important.

Kisses themselves are classified both by intensity and according to the different roles played by the lips, tongue and teeth. As well as what is now known as the 'French kiss' – appropriately called *The Fighting of the Tongues* – there are descriptions of more playful petting kisses in which one lip only is kissed, or where the tongue is held in reserve.

More intriguingly, the authors describe a kind of loveplay in which one partner, having failed to obtain a kiss, feigns indignation and turns away – only to try again when their lover's guard has dropped. Called *The Wager and the Quarrel*, the game appears to recognize that finding love, losing it and then finding it again is a sequence of events which never fails to add a thrill of excitement to lovemaking.

The passage on kissing ends with a verse illustrating the *Kama Sutra*'s underlying message, namely that while the male and female roles in lovemaking may be different, they are both of equal value and importance:

'Whatever things may be done by one of the lovers to the other, the same should be returned by the other.'

SCRATCHING, BITING AND STRIKING

While deliberately blurring the distinction between foreplay and behaviour during actual intercourse, the *Kama Sutra* devotes no less than three separate chapters to the roles during lovemaking of marking with the nails, biting and striking.

Although it has been suggested that the chapter on striking places undue importance on the sado-masochistic aspects of love, and even that it advocates the brutalization of women, to see it in these terms is to miss the point.

For as well as making it plain that what holds for one partner must hold equally for the other, the authors stress that such things must only be done if they give pleasure to the recipient. This means that, while recognizing that pain has a part to play in sex, they quite rightly observe that what may be pleasurable for some is painful for others, and that much of the skill in

The kiss
When one partner turns the face of the other by holding their chin and then kisses them, it is called a 'turned kiss'.

lovemaking lies in knowing just how far to go to please your partner.

MARKING WITH THE NAILS

The armpits, throat, breasts, lips, thighs and buttocks are listed as being those parts of the body which are most suited to marking.

The marks themselves, like kisses, are classified by intensity and also by the shapes which they make on the body.

At one end of the scale are light, tickling scratches which leave no mark. Called *Soundings*, their primary purpose is to titillate in the run-up to intercourse.

VISIBLE SIGNS OF LOVE

At the other extreme are deep, visible marks such as the *Peacock's Foot* – made with all five fingers, and cited in the *Kama Sutra* as 'requiring great skill'.

On the subject of nail-marking in general, the authors comment, 'The love of a woman who sees the marks of nails on the private parts of her body, even though they are old and almost worn out, becomes again fresh and new.'

Scratching
When love becomes intense, the nails may be used to scratch the lover's body. This is practised by those of a very passionate nature.

THE INDIAN SEX MANUALS

The *Kama Sutra* is the most celebrated of the Indian sex manuals. It is thought to have been written between the first and fourth centuries AD. Although the work is attributed to the sage Vatsyayana, he himself quotes from the writings of several earlier authors, including the Brahmin scholar Svetaketu and the sage Babhravya.

The *Khoka Shastra* appeared in the 12th century and is the work of the scholar Khokkoka. Less liberal and more concerned with purely marital sexual relations than the *Kama Sutra*, it reflects the attitudes of medieval – as opposed to ancient – India.

The *Ananga Ranga* of Kalyaanamalla was written in the 16th century and achieved importance primarily because it was translated into Arabic, after which it had considerable influence on Muslim sexual attitudes. Not as comprehensive as the *Kama Sutra*, it nevertheless elaborates on many of the classifications and techniques of the earlier work, and contains numerous references to aphrodisiacs.

The *Kama Sutra* was translated into English in the 19th century under the auspices of the 'Kama Shastra Society'.

The two men responsible were Sir Richard Burton, an ex-Indian Army officer and adventurer, and F F Arbuthnot, a retired Indian civil servant. Both maintained a passionate interest in erotica from the subcontinent. The book was distributed privately by the Society during the translators' lifetime.

BITING

As with kissing and scratching, the *Kama Sutra* classifies love-bites both by intensity and method.

The *Hidden bite* is made gently with the teeth and results in no more than slight reddening of the skin.

The *Swollen bite* is made by pinching the skin to give a more pronounced mark.

Nipping the skin with two teeth is called the *Point*, and a series of nips the *Line of Points*.

More passionate are the *Coral and the Jewel*, the *Broken Cloud*, and the *Biting of the Boar*, all of which are made by sucking in the skin and using the teeth and lips together to produce familiar 'love-bite' marks.

Recommended areas for biting include the cheeks, throat, shoulders, arm-pits, breasts and thigh joints. The authors point out that when biting is included as part of foreplay, a bite from one partner should be returned with one of double the force by the other:

'Thus if men and women act according to each other's liking, their love for each other will not be lessened even over a period of one hundred years.'

STRIKING

The *Kama Sutra* likens lovemaking to a quarrel, in that when the passions are aroused there must be room for physical expression. The shoulders, head, space between the breasts, back, buttocks and sides of the body are quoted as the areas most appropriate for striking, which may be done with the back or palm of the hand, the fingers or the fist.

The authors draw a close parallel between the blows themselves and the sounds made in response to them. These, they say, should be 'expressive of prohibition, sufficiency, desire of liberation, pain or praise'.

The inference is that moans and cries not only heighten the moment of passion, but also serve as a guide whereby one partner can discover what the other likes most.

THE ACT OF CONGRESS

When it comes to intercourse itself, the *Kama Sutra* lays heavy emphasis on the various possible positions. The authors considered that these provided the variety necessary for a continually satisfying sex life, and saw them as a means of compensating for any incompatibility in size between the partners' sexual organs.

POSITIONS FOR LOVE

Most space is devoted to variations on the missionary position, with the man's action remaining the same, and the woman ringing most of the changes.

The Widely Open position Here the woman arches her back, lowers her head and stretches her legs apart

The Yawning position She raises her thighs and keeps them wide apart

The Clasping position The legs of both partners are stretched out and wrapped around one another

The Pressing position This starts with the Clasp, after which the woman squeezes the man with her thighs

The Mare's position Here she holds his *lingam* (penis) inside her *yoni* (vagina) while in a Clasp.

The last three positions can be adopted either with the woman on her back or with both partners lying side by side.

Other variations include:

The Yawn The woman places her legs on the man's shoulders

The Rise She raises both legs straight up

Woman playing the man
When she sees that her lover is fatigued, the woman should lay him down on his back and give him assistance by acting his part.

The Press She draws in her legs and presses them against his chest

The Half Press Only one leg is drawn in this way against the man's chest

The Splitting of the Bamboo Having adopted the Yawn, the woman stretches out first one leg and then the other

The Crab's position She folds her legs against her stomach

The Packed position The woman's thighs are folded over one another

The Lotus position The woman's legs are fully folded (for Yoga devotees only).

Two standing positions are described:

Supported congress The man presses the woman against a wall or pillar and uses this for support

Suspended congress She hangs from him with her arms wrapped around his neck and her legs coiled around his waist.

Then come the rear entry positions. Apart from a brief comment that the woman should kneel on all fours, these rely on both partners having considerable knowledge of zoology, since they are described only by name. They include the *Congress of the Cow, Dog, Goat,* *Deer* and *Cat*; the *Mounting of the Horse* and *Ass*; the *Jump of the Tiger*; the *Pressing of the Elephant*; and the *Rubbing of the Boar.*

Passing references are also made to anal intercourse and intercourse between a man and two or more women.

THE WOMAN ON TOP

The authors suggest that the female-superior (woman-on-top) position be employed either as a variation in its own right, or when the man tires before his partner is satisfied. On these occasions they advise the woman to 'do the work of a man'.

LOVEMAKING TECHNIQUES

The *Kama Sutra* states plainly that it is a man's duty to please a woman, and that this cannot be achieved successfully unless he gauges her disposition.

When the woman is ready, the man has the following options at his disposal:

☐ Moving forward – straightforward penetration of the yoni

Congress
Above centre *When the woman raises her thighs and keeps them wide apart for her partner to enter her, it is called the 'yawning position'.*

Ending congress
Above *After making love, the woman may lie in her partner's lap with her face towards the moon and he can show her the different stars.*

☐ Churning – holding and moving the lingam in the yoni
☐ Piercing – penetrating from above and pushing against the clitoris
☐ Rubbing – penetrating from below the yoni
☐ Pressing – pushing the lingam hard against the yoni
☐ Giving a Blow – removing the lingam from the yoni and then striking the yoni with it
☐ Blows of the Boar and Bull – rubbing the lingam against one or both sides of the yoni
☐ Sporting of the Sparrow – moving the lingam rapidly in and out of the yoni.

When the woman takes the initiative she may also try:
☐ The Top – turning round on top of the lingam
☐ The Pair of Tongs – grasping the lingam, drawing it into the yoni and squeezing it
☐ The Swing – swaying from side to side.

ORAL LOVEMAKING

The *Kama Sutra*'s attitude to oral sex is strangely contradictory. On the one hand the authors infer that it is 'not proper' and that because of it, 'men of good quality . . . become attached to low persons'. On the other, fellatio in particular is described in remarkable detail – albeit the job of eunuchs and courtesans.

Cunnilingus is mentioned only briefly, the practitioner being advised to follow the instructions for kissing. Also described is the *Congress of the Crow* – the equivalent of the '69' position. In the *Auparishtaka* or 'Mouth Congress' eight distinct actions may be attempted:
☐ Nominal congress – the lingam is simply taken into the mouth and caressed
☐ Biting the Sides – the end of the lingam is taken between the fingers and pressed lightly with the lips and teeth
☐ Outside Pressing – lips are used on the end of the lingam in a sucking action
☐ Inside Pressing – the same is done, but with the lingam inside the mouth
☐ Kissing the lingam
☐ Rubbing the lingam with the tongue
☐ Sucking the Mango Fruit – a more vigorous version of Inside Pressing
☐ Swallowing Up – here the whole of the lingam is drawn into the mouth.

THE ARABIAN WAY OF LOVE

The Arabs' intuitive understanding of lovemaking, and belief that sex is a gift to be enjoyed by both men and women, is reflected in The Perfumed Garden, *a fascinating eastern sex manual*

In the 16th century, at a time when the Arab civilization could rival any in the world in terms of culture and learning, a renowned scholar named Sheikh Umar ibn Muhammed al-Nefzawi was commissioned by his ruler, the Grand Vizir to the Bey of Tunis, to write a manual on the arts of love.

The result, entitled *The Perfumed Garden*, is among the most celebrated of all the eastern sex manuals, and contains a wealth of practical advice for the aspiring lover within its sensual, poetic pages.

But like its predecessors, the Chinese and Indian love epics, *The Perfumed Garden* does more than simply catalogue the arts of love. It also sings their praises, preaching the message that a happy and rewarding sex life is among the richest of experiences.

THE ARAB WAY

Sheikh Nefzawi was a profoundly religious man, and devoted much space in his writings to the praise of God and the Prophet Muhammed. But in contrast to the Christian Church of the day, which regarded sex as an unavoidable evil, Nefzawi, as a devout Muslim, saw no conflict of interests.

In *The Perfumed Garden* he reflects the prevailing Muslim view – that sex is a gift from God and that it is both man's right and duty to enjoy it. The Arabs had inherited from the East the conviction that sex education is about prolonging pleasure for both parties and avoiding the monotony which inevitably leads to infidelity. Thus, in their eyes, a knowledge and mastery of the arts of love was a prime requirement for a happy (and hopefully also monogamous) marriage.

This view is summed up by a commentator on the Koran who wrote: 'For Christianity, celibacy is the strictest religious ideal, even monogamy is a concession to human nature. For Muslims the ideal is monogamy; the concession to human nature is polygamy.'

THE PERFUMED GARDEN

The book is essentially an instruction manual for men on how to please women, and as such the roles of the two sexes are rigidly defined.

But even so, *The Perfumed Garden* makes fascinating reading. The chapters on technique demonstrate an intuitive understanding of the problems of lovemaking from both sides of the fence, while the passages on what men find attractive in women (and vice versa) are full of illuminating and often amusing insights into male preferences.

Added to this, the numerous references to maladies

The first position
The woman lies back, and with her thighs slightly raised, her partner places himself between her legs, then enters her.

associated with sex – and the many 'recipes' for curing them – betray some of the commonest and most deep-seated anxieties suffered by the sexual man.

Conspicuously absent from *The Perfumed Garden* is any instruction on oral sex, although Nefzawi must have known of its practice and does indeed make several obscure references to it in the stories padding out his basic text. Perhaps he took the *Kuma Sutra*'s view – that oral sex is a 'lower' form of intercourse, not, under normal circumstances, to be practised by a man and wife, and therefore unsuitable for inclusion in a manual claiming to promote happy sexual relations within marriage.

Neither is there any description of homosexuality (either male or female), or more bizarre practices such as bestiality and sado-masochism, although again, references to them in his stories prove that Nefzawi was aware of their existence.

REDRESSING THE BALANCE

True to the spirit of Oriental and Indian sexual practice, Sheikh Nefzawi is at pains to stress the importance of foreplay as a preliminary to intercourse.

In doing so, he recognizes a phenomenon which research in the West has since confirmed – namely, that on average, a woman takes up to three times as long as a man to reach orgasm through direct genital stimulation.

Given that Nefzawi's ultimate aim is for a man and a woman to climax simultaneously, his instructions can therefore be seen as a way of redressing Nature's imbalance. By advising the man to administer kisses and caresses which will stimulate the woman both physically and mentally, the Sheikh hopes to give her the head start she requires in the race to orgasm.

'Thus it will be well to play with her before you introduce your member and accomplish the coition.

'You will excite her by kissing her cheeks, sucking her lips and nibbling her breasts.

'You will lavish kisses on her navel and thighs, and titillate the lower parts.

'Bite at her arms and neglect no part of her body. Cling close to her bosom, and show her love and submission.

'Interlace your legs with hers, and press her to your arms, for as the poet has said: "Under her neck my right hand has served her for a cushion And to draw her to me I have sent out my left hand which bore her up as a bed".'

Nefzawi goes on to liken a woman to a fruit . . . 'which will not yield its sweetness until you rub it between your hands. Look at the basil plant. If you do not rub it warm with your fingers it will not emit any scent. It is the same with a woman. If you do not animate her with your toying, intermixed with kissing, nibbling and touching, you will not obtain from her what you are wishing. You will feel no enjoyment when you share her couch, and you will waken in her heart neither inclination nor affection, nor love for you. All her qualities will remain hidden.'

The learned Sheikh also quotes from another teacher on the subject:

'Those things which develop the taste for coition are the toyings and touches which precede it, and then the close embrace at the moment of ejaculation!

'Believe me, the kisses, nibblings, suction of the lips, close embrace, the visits of the mouth to the

The second position
In another man-on-top position, the man raises the woman's legs and lifts her buttocks up towards him before he penetrates her.

The third and fourth positions
Two more variations of the missionary position where the pace and mood have increased and the degree of penetration is greater.

nipples of the bosom are the things to render affection lasting.' The advice is still as useful today.

THE CRUCIAL MOMENT

In the sure knowledge that a woman cannot fail to be aroused by such overwhelming expressions of desire, Sheikh Nefzawi feels it appropriate to instruct his male readers on how they might tell that she is ready to be entered.

'If you see a woman heaving deep sighs, with her lips getting red and her eyes languishing; when her mouth half opens and her movements grow heedless; when she appears to be disposed to go to sleep, vacillating in her steps and prone to yawn; know that this is the moment for coition.'

THE ELEVEN POSITIONS

The section of *The Perfumed Garden* dealing with positions for intercourse is among the most comprehensive of all the eastern sex manuals.

As well as describing the eleven positions most commonly practised in the society he knew, the author also gives many details of positions suited to the disabled, and to couples of substantially different physique, thereby re-affirming his overriding belief that sex is a gift handed down from God, to be mastered and enjoyed by everyone.

THE POSITIONS

Nefzawi prefaces his description of the eleven classic Arab positions with a passage adapted from the Koran: 'Women are your field. Go upon your field. Go upon your field as you like.' To this he adds: 'According to your wish you can choose the positions you like best, provided, of course, that coition takes place in the spot destined for it, that is, in the vulva.'

But later in the chapter, as if to answer any charges of sexism laid against him, Nefzawi states: 'It is well for the lover of coition to put all these manners to the proof, so as to ascertain which is the position that gives the greatest pleasure to both combatants. Then he will know which to choose for the tryst, and in satisfying his desires retain the woman's affection.'

The First Position 'Make the woman lie upon her back, with her thighs raised, then, getting between her legs, introduce your member into her. Pressing your toes to the ground, you can move in her in a convenient, measured way. This is good if your member is long.'

The Second Position 'If your member is a short one, let the woman lie on her back, lift her legs into the air so that they be as near her ears as possible, and in this posture, with her buttocks lifted up, her vulva will project forward. Then put in your member.'

The Third Position 'Let the woman stretch herself

upon the ground, and place yourself between her thighs. Then, putting one of her legs upon your shoulder and the other under your arm near the armpit, get into her.'

The Fourth Position 'Let her lie down, and put her legs on your shoulders. In this position, your member will just face her vulva, which must not touch the ground. And then introduce your member slowly into her vagina.'

The Fifth Position 'Let her lie down on her side, then lay down yourself beside her on your side, and getting between her thighs put your member into her vagina. But note that sidelong coition can result in rheumatic pains and sciatica.'

The Sixth Position 'Make her get down on her knees and elbows, as if kneeling in prayer. In this position the vulva is projected backwards. You then attack her from that side and put your member into her.'

The Seventh Position Place the woman on her side and squat between her thighs, with one of her legs on your shoulder and the other between your thighs, while she remains lying on her side. Then you enter her vagina and make her move by drawing her towards your chest.'

The Eighth Position 'Let her stretch herself on the ground, on her back with her legs crossed. Then mount her like a cavalier on horseback, being on your knees, while her legs are placed under her thighs, and put your member into her vagina.'

The Ninth Position 'Place the woman so that she leans with her front, or, if you prefer it, her back upon a low divan, with her feet set upon the ground. She thus offers her vulva to the introduction of your member.'

The Tenth Position 'Place the woman near to a low divan, the back of which she can take hold of with her hands. Then, getting under her, lift her legs to the height of your navel, and let her clasp you with her legs on each side of your body. In this position, you plant your member into her.'

The Eleventh Position 'Let her lie upon her back on the ground with a cushion under her posterior. Then, getting between her legs and letting her place the sole of her right foot against the sole of her left foot, introduce your member.'

THE SIX MOVEMENTS

The Perfumed Garden lists six classic movements to be practised, where possible, during intercourse:

The Bucket and the Well The man and the woman push and retire alternately, mimicking the movement of a bucket being lowered and withdrawn from a well.

The Mutual Shock After entry, both the man and woman withdraw a little, without dislodging the man's member. They then both push tightly together and start the sequence over again.

The Approach The man moves in his accustomed way and then stops. The woman then mimics these

The fifth position
*A front entry, side-by-side position – but beware. Nefzawi
warns that this can lead to rheumatic pains and sciatica – for
both partners.*

The sixth and seventh positions
*Two rear entry positions. Either the woman kneels and raises
her buttocks or she can remain lying on her side for the man to
penetrate her.*

movements herself. The couple continue in this way
until they both reach orgasm.

Love's Tailor The man, with his member only partially
inserted, practises a series of quick in-out movements
before plunging it in up to the hilt. (Nefzawi notes that
this is only suitable for men who can control ejaculation
satisfactorily.)

The Toothpick in the Vulva The man drives his
member up and down and from left to right inside the
woman. (Recommended for those with a 'very vigorous
member'.)

The Boxing-up of Love The man penetrates the
woman up to the hilt of his member and then executes
vigorous movements without letting it slip even a
fraction.

Nefzawi regards this as 'the best of all movements'
and the one best-suited to the position of the Pounding
on the Spot (which he says is a woman's favourite).

THE ART OF KISSING

The Sheikh has more to say on the subject than merely
listing coital techniques. He regards kissing during
intercourse as absolutely essential, and even suggests
that those positions which make it impossible are less
than satisfactory as a consequence.

Concerning the kiss itself he writes:

'The best kiss is the one impressed on humid lips
combined with the suction of the lips and tongue . . . It
is for the man to bring this about by slightly and softly
nibbling his partner's tongue, when her saliva will flow
sweet and exquisite, more pleasant than refined honey.'

THE END OF THE AFFAIR

The period immediately following the climax of both
partners is seen by Nefzawi as critical, and he has some
important words to say on the subject:

'And after the enjoyment is over, and your amorous
struggle has come to an end, be careful not to get up at
once, but withdraw your member cautiously.

'Remain close to the woman and lie down on the
right side of the bed (significant for Muslims) that
witnessed your enjoyment.

'You will find this pleasant, and you will not be like
the fellow who mounts the woman after the fashion of
the mule, without any regard to refinement, and who,
after the emission, hastens to get his member out.'

THE IDEAL MAN

According to *The Perfumed Garden*, the man 'who
deserves favours is, in the eyes of women, the one who is
anxious to please them. He must be of good presence,
excel in beauty among those around him, be of good
shape and well-formed proportions. True and sincere in
his speech with women, he must likewise be generous
and brave, not vainglorious (boastful), and pleasant in
conversation.'

By contrast, the man who, when making love, tries
to enter without foreplay, is quick to ejaculate and beats
a hasty retreat afterwards, merits nothing but derision.

Equally despicable is the man 'who is false in his
words, who does not fulfil the promise he has made,
who never speaks without telling lies, and who conceals
from his wife all his doings – except his adulterous
exploits.'

THE IDEAL WOMAN

Of the ideal woman, Nefzawi requires that she 'assists
(her husband) always in his affairs, and is sparing in
complaints and tears. She does not laugh or rejoice
when she sees him moody or sorrowful, but shares his
troubles and wheedles him into good humour until he is
quite content again. She does not surrender herself to
anybody but her husband, even if abstinence would kill
her. She hides her secret parts, and does not allow them
to be seen. She is always elegantly attired, of the utmost
personal propriety, and takes care not to let her
husband see what might be repugnant to him. She
perfumes herself with scents, uses antimony in her
toilets (a primitive deodorant) and cleans her teeth
with *souak* (a mouth-freshening wood bark).' He
sees women's main faults as ugliness, nagging, and
maliciousness.

THE INDIAN POSITIONS

In *The Perfumed Garden*, the author gives details of 25 positions which he states to be of Indian origin. Almost certainly these are derived from the *Kama Sutra* and the *Ananga Ranga*, both of which had been translated into Arabic and had gained wide recognition in the Muslim world by the 16th century.

The Stopperage
The woman lies on her back with a cushion under her buttocks. The man then pins her thighs back against her chest and places his hands under her shoulders. (Since this constricts the vagina, it is recommended only for the less well endowed.)

Frog fashion
Lying on her back, the woman folds her legs so that her heels are as close as possible to her buttocks. The man then places her knees under his armpits as he enters her.

With the toes cramped
The man squats in front of the woman who is lying on her back. She then wraps her legs behind him and he wraps his arms around her neck, using his toes for leverage.

With legs in the air
The woman lies on her back between the man's outstretched legs. He then lifts her legs together into the air as he enters her.

He-goat fashion
Rear-entry with the woman on her side. The man stretches out the woman's lower leg and rests the upper one on his shoulder.

Archimedes' Screw
The man lies on his back with the woman astride him. She uses her hands to move up and down, without letting her stomach touch his.

The Somersault
The woman, wearing a pair of trousers (or nowadays tights) half-removes them and traps her arms in the legs. She then rolls backwards on to her back, and the man enters her while kneeling.

The Ostrich's tail
The woman lies on her back and the man kneels in front of her. She then wraps her legs around his neck while he lifts the lower part of her body from the bed.

Fitting on of the sock
With the woman on her back, the man kneels in front and part-inserts his member using his thumb and forefinger to open the vaginal lips. After a while, he enters her properly.

Reciprocal sight of the posteriors
The man lies on his back and the woman sits astride him, her back to his face. She then leans forward to view his buttocks while he views hers.

The Rainbow arch
The woman lies on her side, and the man, also on his side, enters her from behind. She grasps his feet to form a 'human arch'.

The alternate movement of piercing
The man sits with the soles of his feet together and draws them as near

The eighth position
It is easy to see why Nefzawi likens this position to a cavalier on horseback. The man has the option of leaning forward or sitting erect.

to his body as possible. The woman then sits on his feet facing him. After he has entered her, the man grasps the woman around the waist, using his feet to move her.

Pounding on the spot
The man sits with his legs stretched out, while the woman sits astride him with her legs around his waist and her arms around his neck. He then helps her to rise and fall upon him.

Coitus from the back
The woman lies on her stomach and raises her buttocks with a cushion so that the man can enter from behind. (Nefzawi quotes this as being 'the easiest of all methods'.)

The tenth and eleventh positions
Two more variations of the man-on-top position. The woman supports herself by gripping the end of the bed or clasping the man with her legs.

Belly to belly
The man and woman stand face to face, with his legs inside hers, one a little in front of the other. The couple hold each other by the hips.

After the fashion of the ram
The woman crouches on her knees with her forearms on the ground. The man enters from behind.

Driving the peg home
The man stands, while the woman wraps her legs around his waist and her arms around his neck, at the same time propping herself against a wall.

Love's fusion
The man and woman lie side by side facing each other and cross their upper legs over the sides of each other's bodies — the woman first, then the man.

Coitus of the sheep
The woman kneels on hands and knees and the man enters from behind, drawing her thighs to him.

Interchange in coition
The man lies on his back and the woman kneels in front of him. She then lifts his thighs, presses them back against his body, and draws his member into her while using her toes for leverage.

The race of the member
The man, lying on his back, draws back his legs until his knees are level with his head. The woman then sits facing him and impales herself on his erect member, using her thighs and her knees to generate movement.

The Fitter-in
The man and woman sit facing each other on the points of their buttocks. He then places his right thigh over her left and she does the same. After entry, the couple rock backwards and forwards, holding each other by the upper arms and using their feet for leverage.

The one who stops at home
The woman lies on her back and the man on top of her. She then raises her buttocks as high off the bed as possible, and down again, while the man supports her with cushions. All the time, his member must remain full inside her until the climax.

The coition of the blacksmith
The woman lies on her back and draws her knees as far back as possible towards her chest. The man, after he has entered her, then periodically withdraws and slips his member between her thighs.

The Seducer
The woman lies on her back, while the man sits between her legs. He then raises and separates her legs, placing them under his arms or over his shoulders, and grasps her by the waist.

THE JAPANESE WAY OF LOVE

Japanese erotica is raw and sensual — but never without beauty.
A sensitive couple can learn much from its lovemaking techniques

To people in the west, Japan and Japanese erotica have a peculiar mystery of their own. While much of the erotic prose and poetry remains to be translated, there is an abundance of erotic art that is explicit almost to extremes. And what is clear from the paintings is that the Japanese had a detached and frank attitude to sex from which we can learn much.

Japanese culture is fascinating in many ways, but when it comes to sex it is quite astonishing.

A FREE AND OPEN NATURE?

Naturally, the realities of life being what they are, it would be wrong to imagine that Japan existed in a state of constant sexual frenzy, with random copulation the principal daily activity and sex the main, if not the only, motivating force in people's lives. But, comparing old Japan with the Christian tradition, with its emphasis on the fundamentally sinful nature of sex, it is hardly surprising to discover that the inhabitants of old Japan tended to have a lot more fun in bed than did their European contemporaries.

EARLY SEX MANUALS

All of this pleasure-seeking world is captured by the early *ukiyo-e* artists, and the picture of uninhibited sexuality that emerges is unparalleled. The most explicitly erotic of the countless prints, scrolls and book

All can be done to another with lip service
For a woman to use her mouth and tongue on her lover's penis is sometimes considered to be the supreme love-gift. The sensations that she gives can be exquisite and sensual either as foreplay or as a form of intercourse which is complete in itself.

Choose the woman whose hands speak
Masturbation, whether mutual or as a gift from one partner to another, happily crosses the barrier from shunga print to a lover's bedroom. Hands can be used either to bring a partner to orgasm or as part of sensual foreplay.

illustrations are called *shunga*, or 'spring drawings'.

Shunga is unique because, unlike all other Oriental erotic art, it has neither a religious nor philosophical basis. It simply represents life as the artists observed it – just as they observed and recorded other Japanese activities.

Of course, the subject matter is as erotic as it could be, and the shunga prints are, in turn, as erotic as they can be, because part of their purpose was to be sexually stimulating. Indeed, some prints show the subject putting aside the shunga he or she has been aroused by, in order to enjoy the real thing.

Shunga books served quite naturally as sex-education manuals for a very long time. As late as the 1930s, some of Japan's more traditional department stores kept up the charming custom of tucking away a shunga volume in the corner of chests of drawers purchased for prospective brides.

AN EFFECTIVE TECHNIQUE

There are many remarkable features about shunga prints, but two are striking on first glance. First, the lovers are rarely naked. That could hardly be put down to prudishness, given the content of the pictures. The Japanese simply thought that sensuous, loose-fitting clothing heightened sexual attraction.

Also, this focussed attention on the genitals, which is the second thing that strikes the viewer so forcibly on first glance.

The sexual organs are grossly exaggerated – the vulvas gaping wide and often dripping, the pubic hair luxuriant, the penises massively swollen, heavily veined and bristling with hair.

The reason for this is that the artists wanted to

emphasize the sexual act itself, rather than the participants as individuals.

A FRANK APPROACH

The subject matter of the prints makes clear the completely uninhibited and unrestrained Japanese approach to sex. There are often two or more women making love to one man, or to each other, since lesbian sex was considered perfectly natural. Sometimes, a third party watches or listens to the sounds of the lovers from an unseen position, becoming aroused in the

The resin oozes from the pines
The 'spoons' position, where the man enters his partner from behind, allows the man undisturbed freedom to caress his partner's body. For the couple who are not in a hurry, this is the most relaxing position of all.

process. Women are frequently observed masturbating with a dildo, lying or sitting back with the dildo strapped to a foot. Dreams and fantasies, sometimes involving sex with animals or mythical creatures, are freely portrayed.

DIFFERENT POSITIONS

The shunga prints present sex in an almost inexhaustible variety of ways. One classic book illustrates the 48 positions considered practicable or possible for heterosexual couples to enjoy.

Naturally, many of these positions are only minor variations on others, but they indicate the ingenuity of a people who were eager to explore the very furthest shores of their sexual capacity with their partners.

Other books are given over completely to the pleasures of male homosexuality, which was common-place. Young actors did a brisk trade in the tea houses of the Yoshiwara, where they were especially popular with Buddhist priests and visiting Samurai warriors.

Boys were considered at their best in their early teens, when their anus was still hairless. They were fondly referred to as 'bamboo shoots' – tasty only when young.

SEX AND ANIMALS

Bestiality did not figure largely in the Japanese scheme of things, but it was not forbidden. In the Yoshiwara – the pleasure districts of Edo, now Tokyo – there were displays of sex between women and stallions, and these were not banned until 1863. When they were banned, it was not on grounds of morality but for safety – after a stallion broke loose and killed a passer-by.

SEX AIDS FOR WOMEN

The Japanese had nothing to learn from the modern porn shop when it comes to sex aids. There were plenty of books illustrating sexual implements, giving tips on how to make a dildo (*harigata*) and how to use one to best effect.

Carrots and mushrooms came highly recommended, but the most favoured vegetable dildo was a Japanese variety of radish, like a parsnip. It was carved and painted to resemble a penis, and was 'guaranteed to be more satisfying than a man'.

Such advice was accompanied by prudent warnings. Beware, they pointed out, that the head of the mushroom does not become so swollen by the heat of the vagina that it breaks off and gets stuck inside. Similarly, the delights of the radish had to be weighed against the possible hazard of splinters.

THE SEX INDUSTRY OF EDO

Edo boasted a sex shop called *Yotsume-ya*, which displayed an incredible range of sex aids. There were dildos of every shape and size and material, including

beautiful and costly examples made of tortoiseshell that were designed to meet the requirements of the most discriminating noblewoman.

Double dildos were a great favourite among the ladies of the Court, whose movements in the outside world were restricted to one excursion every six months. Hollow metal spheres that contained one or more metal balls were also popular – lodged in the vagina, they vibrated pleasingly on the slightest movement.

SEX AIDS FOR MEN

Yotsume-ya carried a good range of sex aids designed specifically for men. There were outsize hollow penises (perhaps for those who felt a little inadequate by shunga standards). There were rings with small buttons attached which were intended to increase friction during intercourse. And there were even different types of artificial vulva available, including a very expensive one carved from a cantaloupe melon and modelled on the vulva of a 14-year-old girl.

LOVE DRUGS

Aphrodisiacs, potions and pastes abounded. One particular drug made great claims to overcome impotence. It was smeared on paper, and the paper was wrapped around the unresponsive penis. The penis was then inserted into the vagina, and as the drug melted it caused the penis to swell. It is not recorded what became of the paper at this point.

All her mouths attract kisses
The man who intimately uses his lips and mouth can give his partner a lovemaking experience that can be both unique and absorbing. With his hands free to explore the rest of her body, he can tease and tantalize – and finally bring her to orgasm.

COURTESANS AND GEISHAS

The courtesan and the geisha have always held a unique place in Japanese society. To the rest of the world, a whore is just a prostitute, varying only in her skills and the amount of money she charges. The geisha is different because the rest of the world has no equivalent. The training that both sets of women underwent shows an attention to detail that western eyes find fascinating.

THE COURTESANS

The *oirans*, as the female occupants of the brothels, or 'green houses', were called, began life with a similar training to the geishas, although with a very different end in mind. As children, they learned to sing and dance and the complex ritual of the tea ceremony. Then, around the age of 12, they entered a 'green house', under the strict supervision of one of the experienced *oirans*, who acted as an older sister figure – both protector and tutor.

While the young girl continued with her general education, aimed at making her grow up into an intelligent and agreeable companion, she now embarked on learning the particular skills of her future job.

This on-the-spot training began with careful observation of her friend and tutor at work. She would either peep through cracks in the partition blinds that served as room-dividers, or more directly through a half-open door. From such a vantage point, she would be able to take in every detail as her tutor displayed the rich range of her sexual repertoire. In particular she would note the male response to her tutor's expert technique, from arousal to orgasm.

THE PATH TO SUCCESS

By the age of 15, she was considered ready to take up her vocation, and her debut was of critical importance to her. She had to find a client whose complete satisfaction with her was demonstrable – shown by his generosity and the frequency of his visits.

The quicker he did this the quicker she achieved senior status, which meant a room of her own and perhaps a novice or two whom she in turn would begin to train.

A LIFE OF LUXURY

One way or the other she would soon find her level. If she was exceptionally gifted at her task she would find herself living in the utmost splendour, pampered by wealthy clients and often able to wield considerable influence, like the powerful mistresses of European tradition.

If she was not up to the mark, her prospects were bleak. She would find herself drifting 'down market' in

Watering the spring grass
The lover who tenderly uses his hand to caress his partner's clitoris can control the pace and timing of orgasm for her. A tender kiss on the lips softens the sensations, turning foreplay into a complete experience in itself.

the carefully graded world of the 'green houses'. Or worse, she might drop right through the bottom of that pecking order. There would be nothing left but to head for the provinces, there to take her chances with less demanding rustics' approach to prostitution.

THE GEISHA

The courtesans of the Yoshiwara and similar pleasure districts of Japan's major cities were of course prostitutes, but of a rare order, possibly the most skilled and sophisticated prostitutes ever known.

The geisha was, and is, something very different. The concept of the geisha has no equivalent in other societies, and it is therefore harder to understand.

Japanese culture has always been extremely male-centred. To understand the geisha, one must imagine a world in which the relationship between the sexes is completely one-sided in a way that it has never been in the West, even in times of the greatest repression for women.

A UNIQUE SERVICE

The geisha existed, and is still very much in evidence in modern Japan, to provide men with all those non-sexual pleasures of the sociable sort, including even intellectual stimulation. As it was deftly put, 'The virgin excites the ardour of your penis, the geisha gives it a little wit and much wisdom.'

In Edo, the geisha to-be began learning her craft from the age of ten. She was taught to make up her face in the distinctive creamy white, thus highlighting the vermilion lips and delicate black eyebrows.

ESSENTIAL SKILLS

She was decked out in a gorgeous kimono, and then painstakingly instructed in carriage and movement, the skills of the hostess such as flower arranging and the elaborate tea ceremony – indeed everything one would expect from a good finishing school for young ladies. And it did not end there. The child was taught classical dance and music, so that she would eventually be able to entertain her clients. She received a literary education so that she would be able to converse intelligently.

A PRIZED CONFIDANTE

Once launched in the world, the geisha might fly very high. As an accomplished hostess and a soothing presence, she might find herself influential as a negotiator or mediator in political or commercial disputes.

Her discretion made her privy to confidences, and the workings of the minds of influential men. She might easily marry well. While generally she was not exploited sexually as a geisha, advancing age or some misfortune might cause her to cross the divide into prostitution.

Enter the deep waters
For any couple, rear entry allows a raw urgency to enter their lovemaking. It allows the man complete control while the woman can concentrate on the act itself, perhaps immersed in her own fantasies.

SEXUAL PLEASURE

While so many of the words the Japanese wrote about lovemaking remain, as yet, untranslated, what is available – together with the extraordinarily explicit erotic art – offers a feast of instruction to western eyes and ears.

For where western poets celebrated love and romanticized women, the Japanese tradition was quite different.

Since they felt no need to jusify their feelings and they believed that sexual pleasure provided its own rewards, they wrote about it – with wit and imagination, but without a trace of shame or sentiment.

LOVEMAKING TECHNIQUES

There is a beauty in the way that the Japanese wrote that loses nothing in translation. While they described a whole variety of sexual techniques, they paid particular attention to the value of foreplay:
'Knowledgeable gardeners always begin
By watering the spring grass'.

A man who holds the secrets of arousing his partner will ultimately reap the rewards for himself:
'If you know how to approach her,
She will mix every night
Her honey with your milk'.

ORAL SEX

Unlike the Indians, who disdained oral sex but went to great lengths to describe it in detail, the Japanese recognized it both as a means of foreplay and as an end in itself:
'Everything can be done with lip service,
Even love'.

The descriptions and advice are appropriate, but the language lends cunnilingus a charm all its own:
'If the cup is deep,
Plunge your tongue into it several times'.

In a male dominated society, it is not surprising that fellatio was written about with undisguised gusto:
'If she sucks the grains of rice
Of which your sake is made,
It will only be the better for it'.

LOVEMAKING POSITIONS

The advice on sexual positions could be direct:
'If you plant your knife
In a tuft of spring grass,
Push it in as far as the root'.
Or it could be couched in metaphor as this description of rear entry shows:
'While awaiting the seed,
The woman is like the earth,
She likes to be turned over'.

Yet the techniques were not entirely devoid of emotion and consideration. The Japanese lover rec-

THE SHINTO RELIGION

The original religion of Japan was *Shinto*, and while the more sophisticated religion of Buddhism arrived in Japan (via India) as early as the 6th century, and the Taoist influence from China even earlier, the old Shinto cult proved to be highly resilient. Buddhism may have supplanted Shinto as the national religion, but in doing so it took aboard many deeply held Shinto beliefs. Even today, every Buddhist temple has an associated Shinto shrine.

Shinto has been described as the most comfortable of religions. From the standpoint of sexual enjoyment it would be hard to match. Shinto was largely based on the cult of the phallus and weird and wonderful carved phalluses still adorn Shinto shrines. According to Shinto, all physical pleasures are divine gifts to be enjoyed to the full.

Sexual pleasure is the greatest of all – and therefore should be indulged in as frequently as possible, as well as in the most exciting manner possible.

This idea is not clouded with notions of romantic love nor anything of that sort. It is to sex what the attitude of the gourmet is to food, without waistline worries.

In its pure form, undiluted by Buddhist restraint or the practicalities of social organization, Shinto provides a charter for absolute sexual abandon and experiment.

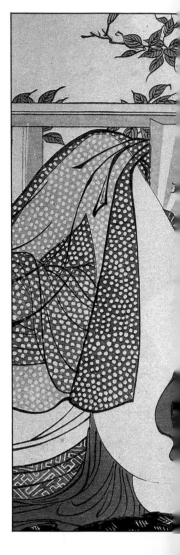

ognized the value of afterplay, if only as a means of ensuring his own pleasure later on:
'Sowing seed is nothing if one neglects
The garden thereafter'.

However, they also recognized that a polite lover does not deny his partner post-coital bliss:
'On board the floating world of pleasures'
The good sailor does not dream of going ashore again'.

THE WOMAN'S POINT OF VIEW

The man whose sexual performance is less than satisfactory is given short change by Japanese women:
'Sooner the moist and warm leather of a good *bariagata*
Than the penis of a blunderer'.

The man's penis is seen not just as a sexual implement but almost as a soothsayer:
'If you do not know why he loves you,
His penis will tell you.
If you do not know why you love him,
It will tell you that too'.

THE DEFICIENT LOVER

For the husband who fails to take his wife's sexual needs seriously, there follows this chilling advice:
'Rather than my husband's cow's milk,
I would sooner have that of the rough and ready man
Who awaits me in the stable'.

And in a world where physical bravery and prowess were esteemed above all other manly qualities, the man with ill-proportioned dimensions was treated with contempt and derision:
'If his penis reaches down to the ground,
Maybe it is less thick than long'.

The floating world of pleasures
The missionary position is the most popular – and versatile – of all. It allows tender sensual lovemaking where lovers can both watch and caress each other and, as the tempo increases, have the freedom to move as they wish.

Her honey and his milk
From time to time, a woman can use her partner's body to bring herself to orgasm. She can use her breasts to brush his face as she controls the pace of their lovemaking and moves towards orgasm.

THE PLEASURES OF THE 'GREEN HOUSES'

The name *Yoshiwara* means 'meadow of good fortune', and for the men of Edo it was surely that. It was a clutter of tea houses and restaurants, bath houses and craft shops. But its principal inhabitants were court-esans and prostitutes of different grades, and geisha. The courtesans were called 'night-time cherry blossoms in full bloom', and they sat, exquisitely costumed, in trellised windows of what were called 'green houses'.

While that may conjure up in the modern mind some seedy red-light district, it would be very wide of the mark. Imagine instead a casual, even tranquil, atmosphere, without hassle or hustle, where a man could while away a pleasurable evening.

SEX AND THE ANCIENT WORLD

Was life in the Ancient World just a succession of wild orgies? Was there an accepted sexual role for men and women — and how strict were the laws governing their actions?

Among those early civilizations that we know about, it is clear that a woman's sexual role was, for the most part, far more limited than a man's. She was usually considered the property first of her father and then of her husband.

Once she married, her function was simply to bear children and to tend to the home. The husband might seek his sexual pleasure with his concubines or perhaps with one of the many types of prostitute available. The wife had no such opportunity.

There were, however, some strange exceptions. In certain societies, even respectable women were bound to sleep with men other than their husbands — for religious reasons, to provide for their dowries, or as an initiation into marriage.

A WOMAN'S LOT

But most aspects of an ordinary woman's life in the Ancient World were fairly restricted. Only successful courtesans and a tiny minority of very powerful aristocratic women could exercise some choice in their sexual dealings with men.

Within each society, and at different periods, the laws relating to marriage and divorce, and to what was considered to be sexually permissible, varied greatly.

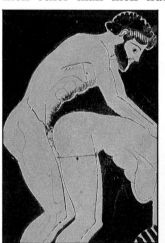

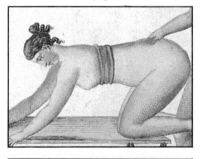

The woman dominating this erotic scene from an Egyptian tomb suggests that her social status brought with it a certain amount of sexual freedom.

A WIFE'S DUTY

The early Hebrews, for example, had complex laws which laid down who might marry whom, and what the duties of each partner were within a marriage. For a Hebrew wife, this included the obligation to show her husband affection, notwithstanding the fact that she might have to share him with one or more of his secondary wives or concubines.

There were strict laws against prostitution, adultery, and what was termed 'sexual perversion'. A woman who committed adultery could be stoned to death. Divorce was permitted, although it could only be brought about by the husband – the wife had no say.

Children were considered a gift from God, and a Hebrew woman who became a mother was held in great respect. Large families were thought of as a blessing, and the Hebrews were probably unique among early civilizations in forbidding the practice of infanticide (killing your children).

In many societies, infants might be simply left to die or be killed as a means of controlling the population, of reducing the numbers of girls who would need dowries, or of disposing of a sickly or handicapped child.

EGYPTIAN INCEST

The early Egyptians also allowed their men secondary wives and concubines. But an Egyptian wife appeared to have one advantage over the Hebrew one – she could divorce her husband if she chose.

However, she also suffered from a considerable disadvantage: if her husband was convicted of a crime, she and her children were also punished, often by being made slaves.

Whereas the Hebrews and many other societies had strong taboos against incest, the Egyptian royal family was famous at certain periods for its incestuous marriages. These were often between half-brother and half-sister, and their aim was to strengthen the family's claim to the throne.

GREEK MISTRESSES

Ancient Greek marriages were officially monogamous – but this did not mean that husbands felt obliged to concentrate their attentions on their wives. Marriages were arranged by families for convenience.

The attitude of many men may be reflected in the words of Demosthenes (c.384–322 BC), the famous Athenian orator, who writes, 'Mistresses we keep for pleasure, concubines for daily attendance upon our persons and wives to bear us legitimate children and be our faithful housekeepers.'

Women in Athens were very much in the position of slaves without political or legal rights. They were subject to the absolute authority of their male next of kin, and led a secluded life – usually confined to the women's quarters.

An Athenian wife dined infrequently with her husband and certainly never if he had company – so there was little opportunity to meet men other than her relatives.

According to Xenophon, a Greek historian (c.430–354 BC), a wife was expected to spin, weave, make clothes, bear children, manage the servants, budget sensibly and run the household wisely. If necessary, she should be prepared to have intercourse with her husband at least three times a month until an heir was provided.

If by any remote chance a wife did manage to make contact with a man and commit adultery, her husband

71

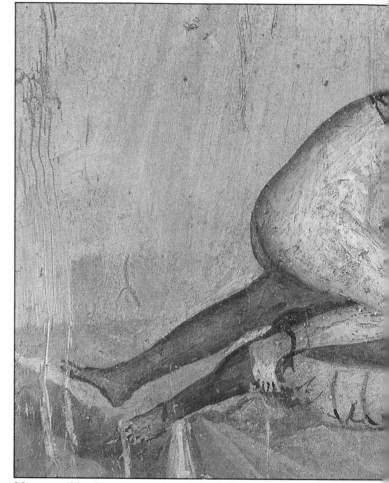

was forced to repudiate her or lose his civic rights. He was allowed to deal with the lover as he wished.

A Greek husband could divorce his wife without cause, but she could only divorce him in extreme circumstances, which did not include his own adultery.

ROMAN MARRIAGE

The fate of women in early Rome was equally hard. Before marriage they were totally under their father's control, and could be married to whom he wished. If they remained single, they could be sold as slaves.

Once married, they passed completely into their husband's power or were under their father-in-law's ruling, if he was still alive.

In one early form of marriage, common among ordinary people, the bride might be bought for a symbolic amount such as a few peppercorns.

In another type of marriage, observed only by the powerful upper class, there was a solemn religious ceremony, which was considered binding. Divorce from this marriage was almost impossible.

Gradually, a third form of marriage – a civil marriage – which offered greater flexibility became popular. All that was needed here was that a man and a woman should live together for a year as husband and wife in order to be considered married.

However, if a woman wished for any reason to postpone the 'marriage' all she had to do was to absent herself from the house on three consecutive nights before the year was up. The couple might then, if they wished, start to qualify all over again by living together.

The more wealthy families began to take more interest in their daughters' marriages. They started to provide them with dowries and retain some control over their fate. Children could become engaged at seven and legally married when the girl was 12 and the boy 14.

Marriages were seen as benefitting the respective families and the state, not an individual preference.

By the first century BC, during early Imperial Rome, the position of a wife was certainly preferable to that of her counterpart in Athens at that time. She was far less secluded, and played an active role in the whole family life.

With the abandonment of the religious ceremony for marriage, divorces became easier for both men and women to obtain. However, if a marriage was cancelled, the dowry had to be paid back – which might cause financial difficulties to the husband's family.

ADULTERY AND DEATH

Although divorce became easier, the punishment for women who committed adultery remained harsh. Under the Emperor Augustus, who reigned before Christ's birth and during his childhood, a father who discovered that his daughter had committed adultery was entitled to kill both her and her lover. Her husband could only kill the lover, but he had to divorce his wife or be punished.

Many wealthy Romans acquired villas in fashionable Pompeii, which was later destroyed by a volcano. Murals found among the ruins tell us something of their pastimes.

Prostitution has been around since the early Hebrews and Egyptians. The Greeks and the Romans had state-run brothels and prostitutes licensed to offer a range of sexual services.

A special court was set up to deal with adultery cases. The lover, if he had not been killed by either father or husband might lose half his property, be penalized and exiled.

The adulterous woman, who would be unable to remarry, might lose half her dowry, a third of her property and also be banished – far away from her lover.

Adultery by a husband was not considered such a crime until several centuries later – but if it took place in the matrimonial home or with a married woman anywhere, his wife was immediately entitled to divorce him.

POPULATION PROBLEMS

The Romans had worried about their falling birth rate for some centuries and the Emperor Augustus tried to remedy the situation by passing laws aimed at

benefiting the fertile and penalizing the childless.

Widows were ordered to remarry within two years of their husband's deaths and divorced women had to remarry within 18 months.

Bachelors were not permitted to receive legacies, and young couples without children could only receive half of any bequest. Couples with sufficient numbers of children were rewarded.

All this may well have had an effect in increasing sexual activity between husband and wife. However, it had little effect on the birth rate itself.

SEX WITH STRANGERS

Some sexual customs in early civilizations seem startling today. For example, in ancient Babylon, each woman was obliged once in her life to visit the temple of Mylitta, the goddess of love, and there sleep with a stranger.

According to Herodotus, a Greek historian who wrote more than 400 years before Christ, women sat in the holy enclosure of the temple while men moved among them making their choice. Once a silver coin had been thrown in a woman's lap by a man, she had a sacred duty to go with him. After she had had intercourse, her obligation to the goddess was fulfilled and she could return home to continue with her ordinary life.

Herodotus writes that beautiful women were soon released but ugly ones were forced to wait for up to three or four years in the enclosure. Similar sexual customs, he adds, also took place in parts of Cyprus.

TEMPLE PROSTITUTES

Perhaps even more bizarre was a custom among the ancient Armenians. The most important members of the tribe consecrated their daughters while still virgins to the goddess Anaitis. These young girls would serve as temple prostitutes for a considerable time.

Unlike the Babylonian women, they could choose whom they had sex with, and usually preferred someone of their own rank. Once their term of prostitution was over, they would have no trouble in finding a suitable husband.

Temple prostitutes were common in many societies. It was believed that they acted as intermediaries between the worshipper and the gods or goddesses.

They were also a useful source of revenue. Some were attached to a temple for life and some for a short term. In Ancient Egypt, the daughters of the nobility also spent a period of time as temple prostitutes. They were offered to strangers and the fees paid to the temple treasury.

Prostitution to collect dowries for marriage was not uncommon in the Ancient World. According to Herodotus, it was a custom in Cyprus for young girls to be sent to the seashore on certain days to sell their sexual favours.

In some early societies, the task of deflowering the

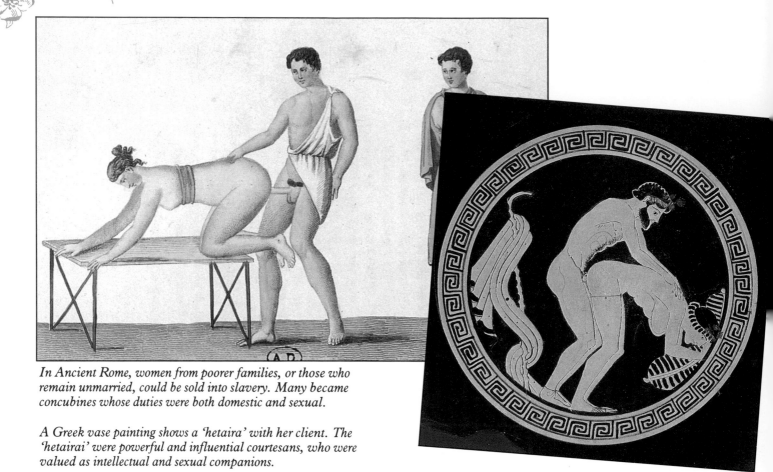

In Ancient Rome, women from poorer families, or those who remain unmarried, could be sold into slavery. Many became concubines whose duties were both domestic and sexual.

A Greek vase painting shows a 'hetaira' with her client. The 'hetairai' were powerful and influential courtesans, who were valued as intellectual and sexual companions.

bride was accorded to a stranger. The Nasmonians, however, had a more exhausting ritual, as Herodotus reports. The bride on her wedding night had sex with each of the male guests in turn.

STATE PROSTITUTION

The Greeks and Romans had an entirely practical attitude to prostitution. Adultery was seen as the great evil, as it broke up the family. But prostitutes catered for the natural desires of men – and prevented the need for adultery.

State-run brothels were introduced in Athens around 600 BC. Brothels were inspected and owners taxed.

Prostitutes were quite open about their activities. They were stationed in various quarters of the city, wearing little or no clothing, so that the customer could see what he was getting. They were available to anyone who could pay the low prices, although customers were also expected to give them a present.

In Rome, prostitutes were supposed to wear certain clothes and dye their hair a particular colour. They were to inform an official of their name, age and birthplace and how much they intended to charge clients. In return, they were put on a register and given a licence.

In both Athens and Rome, there were groups of women who only practised prostitution part-time, and who occupied a higher rung in the social ladder than most prostitutes. These were the female entertainers – usually foreign dancers, musicians or acrobats. The more successful were highly sought after and could amass considerable wealth.

CONCUBINES AND COURTESANS

Concubines were another group of women used for sex. They were slaves who combined both sexual and domestic duties. As they were owned by their masters, they could be sold or given on loan to others. Also, at the top end of the social scale, there were the mistresses or courtesans who chose their patrons with care. In Rome, courtesans often came from the upper classes and had chosen their profession deliberately – either for money or from inclination. They were talented women, sought after as much for their company as the sex they might provide.

Even more famous were their Greek counterparts known as the 'hetairai'. These were cultured, educated and witty women who provided companionship, affection and intellectual stimulation, as well as sex. They could not simply be bought, but would select a lover who would pay for their upkeep while he was in favour. And unlike most ordinary women of ancient civilizations, they were often highly influential and the power behind the leading men of their time.

SEX MANUALS

Sex manuals have existed for more than 20 centuries. But why do people need to read them if sex is the most natural thing in the world?

In the animal kingdom, creatures simply seem to couple without any thought or instruction. It comes naturally to them. Idealists believe that there was a similar golden age for humans, when we simply made love without feeling the need for guidance. Perhaps the need for sex manuals and other forms of sexual instruction is yet another element of the price we have paid for civilization. For most of us, however, the sex manuals offer an insight into the sexual lives of past civilizations as well as valuable information on sexual techniques.

A secondary purpose may well be to assist adolescents who are embarking on the voyage of sexual discovery.

PILLOW BOOKS

As the oldest civilization, it fell to the Chinese to produce the first sex manual. The oldest surviving work was written in 2500 BC by the Yellow Emperor, Huang-Ti. It took the form of a dialogue between the Yellow Emperor and a goddess-instructress called the Wise Maiden.

Using this device the sexual needs of both men and woman were explored, so that the reader – of whichever sex – would better know how to satisfy their partner.

Although the language of the pillow books is liberated, and their recipes for prolonged intercourse and mutual satisfaction anything but puritanical, they did reflect the religious thinking of the day. Men were advised sometimes to withhold ejaculation. This way the semen's vital Yang power was retained while the man strengthened himself by taking Yin power from the vaginal fluid, thought to be inexhaustible.

THE INDIAN EXPERIENCE

Hindu philosophy acknowledged the importance of lovemaking to *Kama* – the world of the senses – and saw it as one of the routes to spiritual paradise. It became an integral part of their religion and the Indians produced several of the most poetic and explicit sexual manuals ever written.

The ancient *Kama Sutra* and the medieval *Khoka Shastra* are two exquisite works of literature and deal with the art of kissing and the rituals of lovers' meetings as well as the various sexual acts themselves.

Although they are religious books, they are not moralistic. The *Kama Sutra* examines exhaustively the various positions and techniques of lovemaking – and is

Two erotic Chinese paintings from the late 19th century. The woman's bound feet (right) were thought to be highly erotic. Bulging stomachs (below) were a sign of spiritual tranquillity, and were not considered distasteful.

At a time when Indian sex manuals were filled with sexually explicit scenes, the European attitude was still very prudish. This Indian erotic painting features, ironically, a European man making love to an Indian girl.

a considerable work of scholarship. It also gives advice on how to acquire a wife, how to treat her, ways to deal with other people's wives and with courtesans and the art of making oneself attractive to others.

The *Khoka Shastra* describes physical types, and defines women by their age, temperament, disposition, and origins. It discusses embraces, kisses, lovemarks, love blows, love cries and sexual positions. Not only does it tell a man how to woo a bride, it also describes relations with strange women, love-spells and recipes.

Both the *Kama Sutra* and the *Khoka Shastra* were invaluable guides to inexperienced men who wanted a long and mutually satisfactory married life and who sought spiritual enlightenment through the medium of sex.

JAPANESE MANUALS

The earliest Japanese sex manuals had no religious or philosophical dimensions. In fact, they dispensed with words altogether and simply instructed the student of sex by the use of *Shunga*, or sexually explicit drawings.

The scenes depicted were uninhibited and part of their purpose was to arouse – as well as inform – the viewer.

The *Shunga* were not primarily aimed at men. They were often bought by prospective brides and remained the primary medium of sexual knowledge in Japan into the 1930s.

ARABIAN NIGHTS

The classic Arabian sex manual, *The Perfumed Garden*, was written in the 16th century and borrows much from the *Kama Sutra* and the *Ananga Ranga*, another Indian classic. Both of them were widely available throughout the Islamic world at that time.

But *The Perfumed Garden* does much more than cover the same ground again. It delves into such diverse subjects as the deceits and treacheries of women and

the causes of and cures for impotence. It gives prescriptions for increasing the dimensions of small penises and making them splendid. It even advises on how to keep the underarms and sexual parts of women sweet-smelling and how to tell the sex of a foetus.

Not only is its subject matter more extensive, *The Perfumed Garden* reveals a completely different attitude to sex. It does not see it, as the Indians do, as a road to spiritual enlightenment akin to practising yoga. It considers it to be a celebration of sensual pleasure in its own right.

The Perfumed Garden gives a prescription for an earthly paradise of the flesh.

HOW-NOT-TO MANUALS

Ironically, in the late 19th century when the *Kama Sutra* and *The Perfumed Garden* were first being translated into English, the English themselves were writing sex manuals which advised young people not to have sex under practically any circumstances.

They forbade masturbation, premarital sex, extramarital sex and, in some cases, recommended that sex within marriage should be restricted to once a month. Women were not expected to have orgasms – in fact, there is no mention of the female orgasm.

Curiously, no-one in the United Kingdom appeared to see the contradiction between the publication of the uninhibited oriental treatise simultaneously with their puritanical English counterparts.

To them, it seemed necessary to understand how debauched the Indian and the Arab people were to appreciate how naturally superior the Englishman was – even though the streets of Victorian London were packed with brothels and whores.

At the same time, young Britons were to be 'kept pure from the desires of the flesh to preserve their strength and their moral right to rule the Empire'.

These attitudes lasted long into the 20th century. Professor Hall's *Adolescence*, published in 1911, describes masturbation as 'an evil' which seems to 'spring from the Prince of Darkness'.

Geldenhuys's *The Intimate Life* (1952), warns engaged couples that they 'have no licence to perform the sex act before marriage' and that by 'going astray, it is his mother's sex that a man dishonours'.

In 1900, Dr L B Sperry, author of *Confidential Talks with Husband and Wife* recommends delaying the honeymoon for a few months after marriage so that the husband can 'show himself a man, instead of self sensualist or careless and ungovernable brute'.

TOWARDS ENLIGHTENMENT . . .

Sex manuals reflect the values of the society they are written for. And as sexual attitudes changed over the course of the years, the manuals slowly changed too.

The force behind the change was science. At the end of the nineteenth century, Sigmund Freud began to investigate the human subconscious and found it full of uncontrollable sexual desires, while Henry Havelock Ellis and Richard von Kraft-Ebbing studied and classified the vast range of human sexual expression.

But it was contraceptive campaigner Marie Stopes who began to translate their academic findings into practical advice in the 1920s. In her popular books she began to explore the crucial element in sexual pleasure – female satisfaction.

As the ancient oriental sex manuals explained in detail, the art of love only begins when the man is prepared to delay his own fulfilment and lavish attention on the female to ensure that she maximizes her pleasure from sex too.

. . . AND LIBERATION

Yet it was fiction that carried the banner of sexual freedom until the 1960s. Liberated youth sought out the works of D H Lawrence, Henry Miller, Frank Harris and Anaïs Nin.

When the widespread use of the contraceptive Pill first freed women from the risk of unwanted pregnancy, a new atmosphere of freedom was born. After protracted law suits Lawrence and Miller were published freely.

LIBERATED SEX MANUALS

In the 1970s, a spate of new, liberated sex manuals appeared on the bookshelves.

The most influential of these was Alex Comfort's *The Joy of Sex* which has sold between 80,000 and 100,000 every year since its publication in 1972. Its sequel *More Joy of Sex* (1975) was also a success.

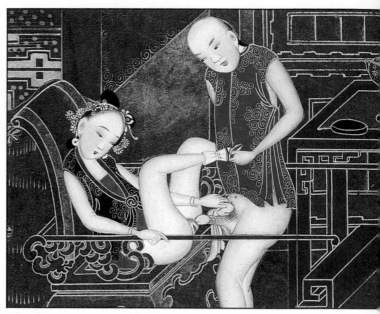

The Chinese saw sexual fulfilment as a means of gaining spiritual fulfilment. Their sexual imagery was frank and uninhibited, as in this 19th century lacquer painting.

Although Comfort adopts the French names for sexual positions, rather than the Hindi or Arabic, he conveys much the same attitude towards sex as the *Kama Sutra* and *The Perfumed Garden*. He positively exhorts people to try everything.

In 1973 there followed *The Sensuous Woman* by 'J' which encouraged women both to enjoy sex and drive their lovers wild with pleasure.

During the early 1980s the quest for female orgasm became a dominant theme, with Helen Gurly Brown's *Having It All* appearing on the bookshelves and the discovery of the G Spot, named after Dr Grafenberg, the first modern physician to describe it.

HOW TO USE SEX MANUALS

The uses of sex manuals are varied:

☐ **They can calm your fears.** If you think you have a sexual problem or have some simple worry that may turn out to be nothing at all, it is helpful to be able to set your mind at rest by consulting a sex manual. Many aspects of sex are still shrouded in ignorance and even the most sexually secure people may not want to embarrass themselves in front of their family doctor.

☐ **They can be used to improve your sex life.** If you or your partner are inhibited about some point, reading about it in a sex manual can often help. And if the missionary position is the only one you have ever used, seeing all the other variations spread out across a page can help you choose.

☐ **They can also make enlightening reading.** The *Kama Sutra*, *Khoka Shastra* and *The Perfumed Garden* are classics in world literature and are worth reading if only for their poetic value. And they provide a fascinating insight into cultures where the joys of lovemaking are seen completely differently.

☐ **They can be used as a 'gourmet' guide.** Left on the bedside table, a sex manual can be dipped into whenever you fancy something a little more adventurous.

☐ **They can be used as a turn-on.** Even the authors of the most clinical manuals realize that people are titillated by reading about sex. And you can use a sex manual – particularly an illustrated one – as a device to arouse you before making love.

But the most important thing you will learn from reading a sex manual is that you are not alone in what you think and what you do. Whatever your tastes, you will find that the subject has been covered.

ADVANCED CHINESE LOVEMAKING

To the Ancient Chinese masters, lovemaking should be a unique experience – every time. Their techniques allowed almost every conceivable variation

To the Taoist philosophers who shaped the attitudes of the Ancient Chinese, sex was not something to be 'got over with quickly' or whispered about behind closed doors. It was an art – to be studied, practised and perfected at every available opportunity.

For most of us, hurried and anxious in almost everything we do, there is much to be learned from this relaxed and refreshingly liberated view of lovemaking.

THE PLEASURE PRINCIPLE

The essence of the Taoist attitude to sex, as stated by numerous masters of sexual technique in their celebrated pillow books, is that making love stimulates the flow of life-giving Yin/Yang energy between a man and a woman. This in turn makes it a highly desirable occupation, and one to be engaged in whenever – or wherever – possible.

The catch is that both partners have to be truly satisfied for the energy flow to have any real benefit. And the Masters are not slow to point out that the chief responsibility for ensuring this happens rests with the man.

Consequently, their basic advice on lovemaking contains a wealth of material on how to set the scene for love, how to make love in a way that is pleasurable for a woman, and how a man can control himself until his partner has herself experienced a climax.

At the same time, however, the Chinese Masters are not so naïve as to think that sexual technique is something a couple can learn overnight. Nor do they assume that becoming 'good' at sex automatically guarantees a continually happy sex life.

The Leaping White Tiger
Lady Yin kneels forward, lifting her buttocks to show her Recreation Chamber. Like a tiger from the forest, Lord Yang leaps upon Lady Yin, pushing his Iron Implement into the Coral Gate.

INFAMOUS LADIES – MISS ACE

Around the turn of the century, Miss Ace was renowned as the number one prostitute in Shanghai. Li Chung, a young writer who had saved his money for months in order to visit her, recounts in *Shanghai Stories* a blissful night spent in her company.

Upon entering her chamber, Miss Ace noticed how the young man stared at her pubic triangle. She thus carefully arranged herself on a couch with her legs apart and offered him a mag- nifying glass to inspect the object of his desire further.

After gentle words of encouragement, the pair moved to the bed, whereupon Miss Ace 'guided the young man's Monk into her Temple' and battle commenced. Her famous grip of the Jade Stem caused Li Chung's motions to become more and more vigorous, and soon her placid smile was re- placed by moans and whimpers. She was so delighted by his per- formance that she then invited him to spend the night with her free of charge.

Miss Ace, however, still had a trick of her own to try. After several more battles, she attached her wrists and ankles to four leather collars sus- pended from the ceiling – a position which left her to swing gently back and forth through the air at the 'mercy of her opponents'. Her helpless- ness gave Li Chung the greatest pleasure of all.

Awakening the Sleeping Beauty
Lady Yin lies as if asleep. Lord Yang teases her with a thousand kisses, lightly touching the Pearl on the Jade Step. Then awake, Lady Yin urgently engages in battle with Lord Yang's Swelling Mushroom.

Their recipe for success is to combine practice – from which grows confidence, and hence better tech- nique – with a little healthy experimentation to keep the flames of passion well and truly burning. And although the precise and methodical way in which they state their case in the pillow books is sometimes more reminiscent of a car workshop manual, the conclusions they come to are really no different from those of contemporary sex therapists – namely, that a sexual relationship has to be worked at by both partners if it is to remain exciting.

MAKING ADVANCES

'To retire to the bedchamber in the wrong mood is the commonest form of impotence.' This advice, given by the legendary Wise Maiden to the Emperor Won Hung Lo more than 5000 years ago, is as worthy of note today as it was then. If one, or both, partners feel uncom- fortable in their surroundings, neither will be in the mood for relaxed lovemaking.

The pillow books suggest setting the scene with some care. In Ancient China, erotic wallhangings, subdued lights and scented sheets were all employed to create a romantic atmosphere in the bedchamber, thereby stimulating its occupants' desire to make love.

Translated into a modern context, this means think- ing about simple touches like subtle lighting, plenty of pillows or perhaps glossy satin sheets – all of which can transform an ordinary bedroom into a warm, inviting love nest.

Soothing background music helps too, and with a

modern hi-fi you can go one better than the wealthy
lovers of the Orient, who frequently had a maidservant
stand nearby reciting poetry while they made love.

BREAKING DOWN THE BARRIERS

While never underestimating the power of surroundings to induce the right mood for love, the Taoist
Masters were cleverer than to think that this alone
would be enough to launch couples into lovemaking
with abandon.

In their teachings they accept that one or even both
partners might, for various reasons, feel hesitant or
inhibited. And to overcome this situation they suggest
that couples, before even touching each other, place a
pillow book on the bed and look through it together.

In this way, the more hesitant partner – in Ancient
China, probably a shy young bride – can arouse themselves (the illustrations in the Chinese sex manuals were
highly erotic, even by today's standards) without any
feeling of pressure to do so.

The Masters go on to point out that if the less-
inhibited partner is at all sensitive, they will quickly
realize which images and stories appeal to their lover,
and will then feel encouraged to begin caressing them.

Thus by Taoist reckoning, there is nothing strange
in the fact that many couples today use erotic books and
magazines or 'blue' videos to help them into a loving
mood prior to foreplay. Nor would the Masters question
for a second that reading or watching erotic material not
only relaxes and arouses a shy partner – it also makes it
easier for lovers to express what turns each other on.

TOUCH SENSITIVE

The pillow books recommend that a couple move on
from this stage of subtle excitement of the senses to
more direct stimulation only when both have let each
other know they are fully aroused.

Accepting that frequently a woman takes longer to
reach a state of readiness for intercourse, the pillow
books make it plain that it is a man's duty to first take
the lead in a session of foreplay.

Massage is considered particularly beneficial in this
respect. Starting with general caresses and the
whispering of sweet words, a man is then advised to
move on gently to kissing the breasts and Jade Step
(clitoris) until he feels the time is right to begin his
'assault on the Jade Pavilion' (vagina).

In anticipation that it is the man who needs encouragement, the pillow books mention the power of
fantasy and fetishism to accelerate the onset of desire.
At the time they were written, for a man to glimpse the
traditional leggings that bound the feet of Chinese

women was thought enough to send him into a frenzy of desire.

Similarly, today, for a woman to give her partner a tantalizing view of her stockings and suspenders remains a time-honoured way of arousing his ardour.

THE ACT OF LOVE

Since sustained, pleasurable intercourse in which both partners experience a climax is the ultimate goal of Taoist sexual teaching, it is hardly surprising to find that the pillow books contain a wealth of instruction on the different positions for love. Ranging from the

The Tandem Ducks in Flight
Lord Yang sits back upon the bed with Lady Yin sitting lightly on his stomach. She gently coaxes his Turtle Head until it is ready for battle and guides it with both hands into her Receptive Vase.

The following tips, given by the Taoist master Te-Hui in a piece entitled 'How to Choose a Woman', offers some interesting advice. He believed that a woman's character could be judged from careful observation of the following:

☐ **Buttocks** High and protruding — the woman will be demanding and hard to satisfy.
Flat as a featureless plain — she was not created for love and should labour in the kitchen.
Narrow — she will seldom have orgasms.
Drooping over the back of the thighs — she will be lazy and passive.

☐ **Pubic hair** Black like the feathers of a glossy bird — a strong and obstinate woman.
Brown with golden tints — an easy-going and generous woman.
Fine, silky and short — a quiet and retiring female.
A really thick growth sweeping down and under — a woman with the abandonment of a waterfall.
Patchy and arid like vegetation on hill tops — a woman lacking warmth and sentiment.

The Bouncing Infant
Lord Yang lies on his back, his Jade Stem swollen. Lady Yin opens her Golden Lotus, captures Lord Yang's Heavenly Dragon Pillar and falls and rises until the coming of The Great Typhoon.

GAMES OF PLEASURE

common-sense to the downright hazardous, their purpose is, of course, to keep that all-important spark of vitality going.

But the Taoist Masters realized that experimentation in lovemaking had another important benefit too. When a couple set out together to explore each other's bodies in a playful, relaxed way, the pressure to 'perform' is removed and both partners can let their senses take over.

As might reasonably be expected of books written in a society where power was invested in men to the virtual exclusion of women, the Ancient Chinese sex manuals do have a tendency to concentrate on positions in which the man plays the dominant role. Yet it is possible to adapt both the games and the sexual positions described in these manuals so that either partner can play the role in which he or she feels most comfortable, which is more in keeping with today's practices.

The Goat Butting a Tree
Lord Yang retires to his most favoured chair. He draws Lady Yin towards him until her Golden Gulley hovers over his Red Bird. He butts her fiercely until they both find the Bursting of the Clouds.

THIRTY POSITIONS

As well as describing the four basic positions – the missionary, woman-on-top, rear entry and side entry – Most Noble Tung's sex guide 'Art of the Bedchamber' lists 30 different positions which couples should regard as more advanced. The author goes on to suggest that lovers follow them in sequence, then experiment further with variations of their own.

Teasing, flirting love games leading to joyful union are very much part of the Taoist lovemaking philosophy and indeed, Most Noble Tung actively encourages lovers to indulge in lighthearted play.

☐ **Awakening the Sleeping Beauty** Here, Lady Yin lies quite still, with eyes closed, pretending to be asleep. Lord Yang undresses her slowly, yet her body remains limp and lifeless. His gentle kisses and caresses fail to have any effect so he begins to fondle her breasts and the Pearl on the Jade Step (clitoris).

Lady Yin becomes more and more aroused until she springs up to meet Lord Yang's Iron Implement as it strikes passionately at the Jade Gate.

☐ **Blind Man's Buff** This is another playful romp in which both partners are blindfolded and search for each other around the bedchamber. When Lady Yin is caught, intercourse takes place while her blindfold remains in position.

☐ **The Bouncing Infant** After the chase, one of the positions most enjoyed by Lord Yang is the 'Bouncing Infant' – Lady Yin sits astride the erect Jade Stem and bounces up and down in a carefree, playful way.

LOVE IN A COLD CLIMATE

Most Noble Tung expands on his 'love games' theme by taking the action outdoors. The 'bamboo grove' (garden) was considered by the Ancient Chinese to be a delightful place for lovemaking.

☐ **Floating Porpoises** This intriguing aquatic adventure ideally takes place in a private swimming pool, although the sea or a quiet lake would do just as well. Lord Yang floats on his back while Lady Yin lies on top of him. They both 'doggie paddle' in order to remain afloat and their movements cause their sexual organs to come into contact and rub together.

Eventually penetration is achieved, and from then on the couple rely on the motion of their lovemaking to prevent them from sinking.

☐ **The Lady submitting to the Leaping White Tiger** This offers plenty of scope to lovers of outdoor sex. Here, Lady Yin is bent low over the extended, almost ground level, branch of a tree with her head resting on her folded arms. Lord Yang then approaches her Vermilion Gate from the rear.

IN DEEPER

In order that the Yin/Yang essences might mingle in the most harmonious way during the 'Bursting of the Clouds' (orgasm), the pillow books are particularly fond of suggesting, in colourful illustration, numerous positions which allow for maximum penetration by the male.

☐ **The Crossed Pine Branches** The lovers are both seated with their legs up on the bed. Lady Yin sits on Lord Yang's feet with her legs extended over his, her feet placed on his stomach.

As the couple's desire increases, they draw forward together. Lady Yin's legs separate and the Jade Stem penetrates the Jade Gate.

☐ **The Tandem Ducks in Flight** Lord Yang then lies back facing upwards for the position. Lady Yin sits on his stomach facing his feet and begins to gently caress the Jade Stem. When it is fully erect, she uses both hands to guide it into the Golden Gully.

☐ **The Kicking Mule** This is a rather complicated position, but one which offers maximum penetration if performed properly.

Lady Yin positions herself in the centre of the bed, with Lord Yang above her. He places his left hand under her head, and his right hand under her right leg.

Lord Yang then inserts the Jade Stem while raising her head and leg together, and continues raising and lowering to the rhythm of his thrusts.

☐ **Two Swallows with a Single Heart** Here Lady Yin is presented lying on her back with Lord Yang above her. He pushes her legs apart sideways as far as they will stretch until they resemble a bird with open wings.

Lord Yang then leans on to the Vermilion Valley and plunges forward.

☐ **The Goat Butting a Tree** This takes place away from the bed with Lord Yang seated in his favourite chair. He draws Lady Yin on to his lap, her back towards him. While she looks down at his erect Male Peak, he pushes her down and inserts it fiercely. He then holds her in this position for a series of butting movements until they simultaneously reach 'Bursting of the Clouds'.

☐ **Over the Rainbow** For energetic lovers, this position offers perhaps the deepest penetration of all. It should only be attempted when both partners are fully aroused, and preferably after trying out the simpler positions first.

Lord Yang kneels on the bed and sits back on a cushion placed under his thighs. Lady Yin sits astride his knees and leans back, her head touching the bed with her body arched like a rainbow. Lord Yang then grips her by the hips, striking upwards with the Iron Implement and caressing the Pearl on the Jade Step while Lady Yin remains arched backwards.

The Kicking Mule
Lady Yin lies back, Lord Yang above her. Taking her head in his left hand and her right leg in his right hand, Lord Yang enters the Open Peony Blossom and lifts Lady Yin to the rhythm of his thrusts.

ADVANCED INDIAN LOVEMAKING

To the Indian masters of the art of lovemaking, a thorough knowledge of the senses, the right atmosphere and a leisurely seduction led to perfect sexual harmony

A thousand years ago the Indians, like the Chinese, possessed an awareness of human sexuality which we in the West are only just beginning to come to terms with.

To us, sex is all too often marred by feelings of guilt, anxiety or simply lack of imagination. To the Indians, it was no more, no less than a basic human privilege – to be practised, mastered and enjoyed in the interests of leading a happier, more fulfilled life.

The ancient Indian sex manuals – the *Kama Sutra*, the *Khoka Shastra* and the *Ananga Ranga* – make no secret of the fact that sex is not something you learn overnight, or even several nights. The authors of these celebrated books were well aware that lovemaking embraces almost all aspects of human existence – from what you eat, to the way you decorate your bedroom – and that only by taking such things into account can anyone hope to become a master of the art.

USING IMAGINATION

Just as important, to their mind, was the ability to sense what turns a person on and then exploit it so that their enjoyment of sex might be heightened.

But the Indians also realized that sex between a couple – however understanding they might be of each other's needs – can quickly become dull and predictable unless both partners make a concerted effort to inject variety and imagination into the way they make love. And on this subject, as on many others, they have a wealth of advice for lovers keen to re-live the thrill and excitement of their first few weeks together.

THE ART OF SEDUCTION

The Indians set great store by creating an atmosphere which is conducive to lovemaking. Soft lights, comfortable surroundings and sweet music are all considered essential for establishing the right kind of mood. And, more intriguingly, the authors of the *Kama*

Sutra recommend having other people around in the early stages of courtship – to divert the lovers' attentions and stop them feeling too self-conscious.

By 'other people', the authors were no doubt thinking of servants – who, they assumed, could then be dismissed at the appropriate time. And although today, you cannot 'dismiss' friends quite so easily, there is still a lot to be said for starting off a romantic evening in company so that you avoid the anxiety which one-to-one situations can sometimes provoke.

Overcoming shyness was something that the Indians, in a society where arranged marriages between teenage girls and older men were common, knew plenty about. And their advice on the subject is just as relevant for the less bashful couple whose day-to-day cares tend to inhibit genuine displays of romantic affection.

In the *Kama Sutra*, the author, Vatsyayana, recommends that a man begins by embracing a woman in the way she likes best, but for a short time only.

He then goes on to suggest that while the man is seated beside his loved one, holding her gently by the arm, he offers her a sweet or tasty morsel of food. This he places seductively in her mouth, lightly caressing her lips with his fingers, so that at once a more intimate – although still innocent – contact is established.

THE GAME OF LOVE

As things progress, the man should steadily become more adventurous and intimate with his caresses, but kneel at his lover's feet so that at no time does she feel threatened.

Nor should he become discouraged or anxious – in other words 'pushy' – if she makes no verbal response. For as Vatsyayana says, quoting an old Indian sage: 'All girls hear everything that is said to them by men, but sometimes themselves do not say a single word.'

On the woman's side, her coyness and reticence are seen as a necessary part of the 'game' whereby a man's passions are aroused and eventually satisfied, but not so quickly that he soon becomes bored.

Before long, the *Kama Sutra* promises, this subtle loveplay will result in increased confidence and understanding between the couple. But rather than rush head-long into lovemaking, it advises the man to touch his loved one intimately – or better still wash her in the most private of places, 'accidentally' brushing against her genitals and the inside of her thighs – before making any more obvious advances.

CONFIDENCE

As Vatsyayana himself puts it: 'A man acting according to the inclinations of a girl should try to gain her over so that she may love him and place her confidence in him.

Embracing was considered to be one of the most important elements of foreplay, as the authors of the Indian sex manuals believed it encouraged feelings of security and relaxation between partners.

A man does not succeed either by implicitly following the inclinations of a girl, or by wholly opposing her.'

Implied throughout is the idea that the best things in life are definitely worth waiting for – that seduction is not something to be rushed. And the *Kama Sutra* warns most strongly that if the woman in question is particularly shy, then the whole process may have to be measured in days rather than minutes or hours.

ESSENTIAL PRELIMINARIES

Recognizing that a woman is often slower to become aroused than a man, and that lovemaking in such circumstances can be positively unpleasant for her, the

Indian authors devote large sections of their works to the business of foreplay. They make it quite plain that while the man should take the initiative, he must be sensitive at all times to his partner's wishes, and should put her pleasure before his own.

AROUSAL

The *Ananga Ranga*, which like the *Kama Sutra* has a passion for classifying things, lists the most important elements of foreplay as embracing, kissing, scratching, biting and caressing of the hair.

On the subject of the embrace, which it says should be accompanied by frequent kissing, the *Ananga Ranga* recommends several positions – all designed to promote light, 'accidental' contact between the partners' erogenous regions.

INTIMATE PRESSURE

Touching of heads, say the authors, allows a couple to feel close and loving, while grasping each other around the waist encourages feelings of security and relaxation. But far more delightfully arousing is the brushing of hardened nipples, confined by a blouse or dress, against a man's chest, or the deliberate pressing of a straining groin against a woman's undergarments, exposed by the riding up of her dress.

Creating the right atmosphere for loving was thought to enhance the quality of sex. Sweet smelling flowers and heady perfumes in the bedroom helped to pleasure the senses of both partners.

MASTERING THE ARTS

Gaining a thorough knowledge of Kama — the World of the Senses — was one of the Three Great Aims of any self-respecting Hindu man, although there was some disagreement over how much it was safe for a woman to know.

The *Kama Sutra* takes a fairly liberal attitude, considering the time it was written, and lists 64 points summarizing what every woman should know of the science of Kama (or Kama Shastra).

Named among the 64 are most of the visual arts, as well as reading, writing and poetry, together with music and sciences such as mathematics and chemistry. Sports, hobbies and practical crafts such as carpentry and needle-work are also mentioned, as is the law, warfare and languages.

But there are also some more intriguing ones, the significance of which is best left for the reader to puzzle out. They include:
- ☐ Playing on musical glasses filled with water.
- ☐ Making lemonades, sherbets and acidulated drinks.
- ☐ Making parrots, flowers, tufts, tassels and similar playthings out of yarn or thread.
- ☐ A knowledge of mines and quarries.
- ☐ Teaching parrots and starlings to speak.
- ☐ The art of speaking by changing the form of words — for example by changing the endings or by adding unnecessary letters.
- ☐ The art of obtaining other people's property by the use of spells and incantations.
- ☐ Practice with a sword, single stick, quarter staff and bow and arrow.

Kissing – one of the most intimate acts between lovers – was an art to be practised and perfected. The tongue was used to simulate the role of the penis being thrust into the one partner's mouth in slow rhythmic movements. Chewing and biting of the lips was also recommended. Kissing was also used as the ideal way of awaking a sleeping partner, with the pressure of the kiss being intensified until the sleeper awoke. If the advice in the Indian sex manuals is followed, a simple kiss can be turned into a feast of delight.

KISSES FOR FOREPLAY

The *Ananga Ranga* recommends that certain kisses should accompany this early phase of foreplay. Three are particularly interesting.

In the *Ghatika*, or 'neck-nape' kiss, the woman covers her lover's eyes with her hands and then, closing her own eyes, thrusts her tongue into his mouth in a series of deep, slow rhythmic movements which are intended as a parody of the act of intercourse itself.

In the *Uttaroshtha*, or 'upper-lip' kiss, she takes his lower lip between her teeth and then chews and bites it gently. He, meanwhile, does the same with her upper lip.

Most agreeable of all, however, is the *Pratibodha*, or 'awakening' kiss. Here, one of the couple, on finding the other fast asleep, presses their lips to them and gradually increases the pressure until they awake.

THE POWER OF THE FINGERNAILS

Bizarre as it might sound to some western ears, the ancient sex counsellors of India were firm believers in the power of the fingernails – tickling, scratching, and in some cases marking quite deeply – to titillate and arouse during foreplay. And in the *Ananga Ranga* alone, there are pages devoted to describing how – and even when – lovers' nails may be used to best effect.

Among the times thought best for scratching are when both partners are engrossed with desire, when the woman is angry, when the couple are about to separate or go on a long journey and when the couple have just lost a great deal of money.

The scratches themselves range from light, dabbing movements on the breasts, back, buttocks and thighs, to deeper marks – for example the 'Peacock's foot', in which the man grasps one of his lover's nipples between thumb and forefinger and uses the other three fingers to score marks on her breast.

The lighter scratches are designed only to produce a delicious shuddering sensation in the recipient. The deeper ones must, warns the *Ananga Ranga*, be used with caution at the heights of passion – and then only with the recipient's full consent.

BITING

Much the same goes for biting, another foreplay technique favoured by the Indians, although in this case, the lips, cheeks, neck and breasts come in for the most attention. And here too, there is a strict code of

WHAT EVERY MAN SHOULD KNOW

The *Kama Sutra* contains plenty of useful hints for the modern man-about-town, including suggestions on how to decorate his bedroom.

As well as a bed – soft, and covered with a clean white cloth, plus garlands and bunches of flowers – our young man is advised to invest in another couch, with a stool at the head upon which to place the 'fragrant ointments of the night'.

Other essentials include a pot for spitting, a box containing ornaments, a lute hanging from a peg made of an elephant's tooth, a drawing board, a pot of perfume, some books, a round seat, a toy cart, a board for playing dice and – a birdcage!

practice to stop things getting out of hand – where a man is doing the biting, the authors state that when the woman utters a sharp, high-pitched sound, he should take it as a sign to stop.

The most favoured bite of all, and one said to require 'great practice' to perfect, is the *Pravalamani-dashana*, or 'coral bite' – a protracted and passionate union of a man's teeth and woman's lips, in which sucking, nibbling and nipping all play their part.

Alone among the ancient civilizations, the Indians exhibit a great fascination with hair, and the *Ananga Ranga* lists four ways in which the erotic possibilities of this part of the body might be explored.

HAIR PLAY

First, the man may clasp his lover's hair with two hands, the palms open. From here, he can then draw her towards him, sliding his hands around behind her head. As passions mount, write the authors, the man should grasp a knot of her hair tightly while embracing her. Then as the couple come together, they can run their fingers through each other's hair, ruffling and pulling it as they do so before moving on to lovemaking.

TOWARDS PERFECT HARMONY

Like modern-day counsellors, the authors of the Indian sex manuals realized that there is no greater threat to a happy sexual relationship than boredom and predictability. And since promoting marital fidelity was their primary concern, it is hardly surprising that they devote so much space to different positions for actual lovemaking.

Above left *A variation of an Indian standing position – if the man kneels down, his partner can easily wrap one leg around his waist as he penetrates her. Kneeling makes this position less tiring.*

Far left *In this sitting position, the man is cross-legged and his partner descends on to his penis and wraps her legs around his waist.*

Left *Fingernails had their place in Indian loveplay. Grasping one of the woman's nipples and scratching her breasts was a favourite ploy.*

To quote the *Ananga Ranga*: 'The chief reason and the cause which drives the husband to the embraces of strange women, and the wife to the arms of strange men, is the want of varied pleasures and the monotony which follows possession. There is no doubt about it. Monotony results in sufficiency, and sufficiency in a distaste for further congress.'

While the manuals all assume that an inexperienced couple is likely to spend most of their time trying out variations of the classic 'missionary' position, the *Ananga Ranga* in particular goes on to describe others – sitting, standing, rear-entry and female superior (woman-on-top) – so that more jaded palates might continue to have something to excite them.

SITTING POSITIONS

Most sitting positions involve the man sitting cross-legged on a rug with his lover perched on his lap facing him.

From here it is possible for him to draw her legs up under his arms and manoeuvre her over his erect penis – either from side-to-side or back-to-front. At the same time, he can clasp her shoulders or embrace her neck, kiss and bite her, or (if he's strong enough) raise and lower her with his arms.

A slightly different approach is for the man to sit with his legs wide apart, and then, once he and his lover are joined, to press them hard against her thighs.

STANDING POSITIONS

When it comes to standing positions, the *Ananga Ranga* has three suggestions. One (described as requiring considerable strength in the man) is for him to raise his partner to waist height, supporting her with his elbows placed under the crook of her knees, while she hangs on by throwing her arms around his neck.

Marginally less exhausting is for the woman to clasp her legs around her lover's waist and her arms around his neck.

In either case, if the couple then prop themselves against a wall, this permits powerful thrusting and deep penetration.

For the third standing position, the man need raise only one of his partner's legs to his waist, letting her use the other to support herself. This is reputed to be 'particularly enjoyable' for younger women.

REAR-ENTRY LOVEMAKING

On the subject of rear-entry positions, the *Ananga Ranga*'s two suggestions are perhaps a little unimaginative – although the first, being 'In the Manner of the Bull', had great religious significance for Hindus. In fact, the bull's position consists simply of the woman kneeling on all fours, while the man squats behind her and draws her to him.

And the second, the 'Elephant Posture', is equally basic, the woman in this case lying flat on her stomach.

FEMALE SUPERIOR

More interesting by far for advanced lovers are the woman-on-top positions, many of which were practised and perfected by some of India's most celebrated courtesans, and which had men throughout the subcontinent clamouring for their favours.

In the 'Contrary Position', the man lies outstretched on his back on the bed, and his lover lies on top, flat on her stomach. Once he has entered her, she then arches her back a little, presses her hands into his waist, and uses these as leverage to swing her hips in a circular motion.

In the position 'Like a Large Bee', the woman sits astride the man and lets him enter her. She then closes her legs in front of her, grasping his penis tightly, leans backwards on her arms and begins a series of churning movements made from the waist.

Most advanced of all is the position of the *Gopala-girl* ('She Who Milks the Cow'). With the man on his back, the woman sits crosslegged above him, seizes his penis, and thrusts it into her. She then moves her waist up and down, advancing and retiring, while at the same time constricting her vaginal muscles to squeeze her lover's penis.

Likewise, the authors offer advice on how the woman should appear towards her lover during this form of lovemaking, lest she risk bruising his presumably fragile ego. They tell her to '. . . smile gently and show a kind of half-shame, making her face so attractive it cannot easily be described.'

The *Ananga Ranga* says that, once learned, the art is never lost, and that henceforth her lover 'will value her above all women. Nor will he exchange her for the most beautiful *Rani* (queen) in the three worlds, so lovely and pleasant to man is she who constricts.'

Left and below right *Although the* Kama Sutra *considered oral sex to be an unnatural act, the authors went to great lengths to describe it. Today, it is thought by many couples to be an important part of their sexual repertoire and a gentle and highly arousing form of lovemaking.*

Above Far left and left *Rear-entry and woman-on-top positions both featured in the* Kama Sutra *and the* Ananga Ranga. *'In the Manner of the Bull' the woman kneels on all fours while her partner enters her from behind. In the 'Contrary Position' the woman lies on top of her partner.*

ADVANCED ARABIAN LOVEMAKING

Expert lovemaking requires devotion and dedication. To those who practise the art, the Arabian masters offer a unique variety of sensations

The Arabian tradition of erotic writing owed much to earlier works of the Chinese and Indian masters. But, by the sixteenth century – when Europe was just emerging from the Dark Ages – Arab scholars were providing instructions in the varied arts of love with an earthiness and zest.

That sex should be frequent, prolonged and cul-minate in orgasm for both partners was the order of the day. This was based on two precepts – that the ecstasy of orgasm symbolized union with God and that an imaginative and varied sex-life keeps husband and wife together in happiness.

MANY DIFFERENT WOMEN

The chief reason for the separation between the married couple, and the cause which drives the husband to the embraces of strange women, and the wife to the arms of strange men, is the want of varied pleasures, and the monotony which follows possession. 'There is no doubt about it . . . I have shown how the husband, by varying the enjoyment of his wife, may live with her as with 32 different women, ever varying the enjoyment of her, and rendering satiety impossible . . .' wrote Kalyana Malla in the Indian *Ananga Ranga* that was translated into Arabic and freely circulated among scholars.

This belief is the recurring theme in the classic work of Arabian erotic literature, *The Perfumed Garden*. The author, Sheikh Nefzawi, makes it plain that lovemaking – as the greatest pleasure – should be studied and practised at every opportunity.

TOWARDS SIMULTANEOUS ORGASM

Sheikh Nefzawi believed that every 'act of combat' should end in orgasm for both partners. To achieve this end, much of *The Perfumed Garden* is concerned with ways to excite a woman, to teach a man to delay pene-tration until she is fully aroused and to control his ejaculation until the woman has come – or preferably, enjoy simultaneous orgasm.

Reporting on a conversation with a woman regard-ing the pleasures of lovemaking, the Sheikh gives her reply. 'Believe me, the kisses, nibbling, suction of the lips, the close embrace, the visits of the mouth to the nipples and the sipping of the fresh saliva, these are the

Pounding on the spot
This was a position favoured by women as they could control the depth of penetration and the pace of the lovemaking, thus increasing their opportunities for orgasm.

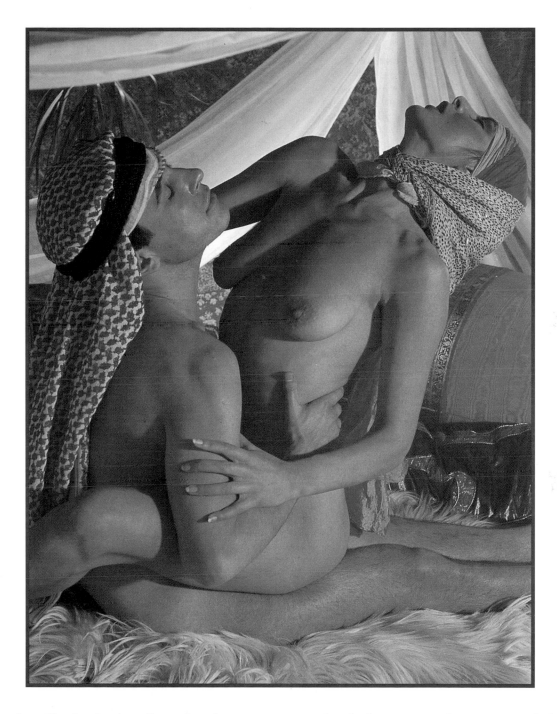

things to render affection lasting. In acting thus, two orgasms take place simultaneously, and enjoyment comes to the man and woman at the same moment. The man feels the womb grasping his member, which gives to each of them the most exquisite pleasure. Then do all you can to provoke a simultaneous discharge of the male and female fluids – here lies the secret of love.'

MALE PLEASURE

The woman who could contract her vaginal muscles tightly around a man's penis was highly prized in Arabian society, and it is the contraction of the vaginal

muscles during orgasm that was regarded as creating the highest pleasure for a man.

The perfect ejaculation was regarded as fast and abundant and should be 'milked and sucked from the member by the suction pump of the vagina'.

THE SEARCH FOR PERFECTION

In his extensive descriptions of lovemaking positions, Nefzawi attempted to link the positions to the needs and physical characteristics of the lovers.

Of the 25 positions that he derived from his readings of Indian scripts he stated that 'the majority of them do

OBSERVATIONS USEFUL FOR MEN AND WOMEN TO KNOW

In attempting to explain clearly the differences in sexuality, desire and performance in love-making, Sheikh Nefzawi understood that all people are individuals and that both physically and emotionally there were some people who were not matched. His observations were a product of the time and society in which he lived and he introduced them in the form of questions and answers between a reporter and a wise woman – advice that had been used for thousands of years.

In what part of a woman's body does her mind reside?
Between her thighs.

And where is her enjoyment?
In the same place.

And where is the love and hatred of men?
In the vulva. To the man whom we love we give our vulva, and we refuse it to the one we hate.

Which virile members are preferred by women?
Women are most eager for coitus.

Which are the men preferred by women?
Not all women have the same conformation of the vulva, and they also vary in their manner of making love, and to their love and aversion for things. The same exists in men, both with regard to their organs and their tastes. It has been observed that little women love coitus and have a stronger affection for the virile member than large women. Only long and vigorous members suit them. There are also women who love the coitus only on the edge of their vulva, and when a man wants to get his member into the vagina, they take it out and place its tip between the lips of the vulva.

As to the desire of men for intercourse, they are also addicted to it more or less according to their different temperaments. The difference is that the desire of women for the virile member is stronger than that of the man.

not yield enjoyment, and give more pain than pleasure!'

However, he goes on to acknowledge that the Indians had 'advanced further than we in the knowledge of the investigation of coitus and that all the positions should be tried to find the one that suits both partners best'. And when the perfect manner is discovered to use it every time 'for every woman likes one in preference to all others for her pleasure'.

Furthermore, he firmly believed that the majority of women preferred the position called Dok el arz, or pounding on the spot, because in this position in which the woman sits astride the man, her orgasm is a certainty.

THE TWENTY-FIVE POSITIONS

Even though Nefzawi had distilled the extensive list of Indian lovemaking positions into 25, he still states that he believed that some of them were difficult to obtain and 'their only realization of it consists in words and design.' Yet he gives detailed instructions to how many of them can be achieved.

Of the 25 positions, seven are variations of the woman-on-top, nine man-on-top, three rear entry, three side-by-side, two standing and one of death-defying athleticism.

The stopperage
This was considered ideal when the man cannot achieve a full erection. With the woman's knees pulled towards her chest, her vulva is easily accessible. With a full erection, penetration is deep.

WOMAN-ON-TOP

The Sheikh believed that all woman-on-top positions would bring satisfaction for the woman.

Pounding on the spot The man sits down with his legs stretched out. The woman then sits astride his thighs, supporting herself on her hands, crossing her legs behind the man's back. She positions the entrance to her vagina opposite his penis and guides it into the entrance. She now places her arms around his neck and he holds her sides and waist. He helps her to rise and fall upon his penis. Nefzawi also says that the woman must assist in this work. No doubt he recognized that if the woman could control the depth of penetration and the pace of lovemaking, her chances of orgasm were increased.

The screw of Archimedes The man lies stretched out on his back. The woman sits on his penis, facing him, and holds herself upon her hands to make sure that her stomach does not touch his. The movement of the woman is up and down, and if the man is fit he can assist her from below. Nefzawi believed that kissing during lovemaking is important and adds the note, 'If in this position she wants to kiss him, she need only move her arms along the bed.'

The tail of the ostrich
A difficult position for the woman to maintain for a long period of time as only her head and shoulders remain in contact with the bed. But penetration can be quite deep, though any movement is restricted.

Legs in the air
Not a particularly comfortable position for the woman to maintain for any length of time, but it is useful if her vagina has stretched after childbirth – closing her thighs means her partner's penis is gripped more tightly.

The double view of posteriors The man lies stretched out on his back, and the woman sits down on his penis, facing away from him. The man presses her sides between his thighs and legs while she supports herself on the bed with her hands as she rises and falls on the penis. The position is so-called because if the woman 'lowers her head, her eyes are turned towards the buttocks of the man'.

Alternate piercing This is another position where the woman is exhorted to help in the movements, even though she has little control. The man sits upright on the floor and puts the soles of his feet together. By lowering his thighs to the floor or couch, he can draw his feet towards his penis. The woman sits on his feet, clasps his sides between her thighs and holds her arms around his neck. The man now draws his feet, and her vagina, closer to him and enters her. He moves his feet backwards and forwards, making sure never to withdraw his penis entirely. Nefzawi's advice to the woman is 'to make herself as light as possible, and assist as well as she can in this come-and-go movement. Her co-operation is, in fact, indispensable. And for the man, if he apprehends that his member may come out entirely, he takes her round the waist, and she receives no other impulse than that of the feet of the man. This should accelerate mutual orgasm.'

Interchange in lovemaking This is an active position for the woman, the basic idea being that the woman fulfils the traditional part of the man and the man is passive like a woman. The man lies on his back and the woman kneels between his thighs. She lifts his buttocks until his erect penis is opposite her vagina, and then guides the penis inside her with her hands. 'The woman's feet should rest upon a cushion to enable her to keep her vulva in concordance with his member' is Nefzawi's advice to the lovers.

The race of the member The man lies on his back with cushions raising his shoulders, but with his buttocks firmly on the bed. He draws up his legs until his knees are level with his face. The woman now sits down on to his penis. Strict advice to the woman is 'she must not lie down, but keep seated as if on horseback – the saddle being the knees and stomach of the man'. In that position she can, by the play of her knees, work up and down and down and up. If the couple have little sense of balance, it is acceptable for the woman to put her knees on the bed and hold on to the right shoulder of the man. This also allows the man to make more active movements.

The fitter in This is a position that allows little movement for either partner, and is basically a face-to-face sitting position. The woman sits on the points of her buttocks and the man does the same. The woman puts her right thigh over the man's left thigh, and he puts his right thigh over her left thigh. The woman guides the man's penis into her vagina. By taking turns to lie back slightly, the swaying movements cause small butting movements of the penis.

Frog fashion
Designed for comfort, the woman lies on her back with the
man sitting close to her – at the point of orgasm, the man can
pull his lover close.

WOMEN OF EXPERIENCE

The Perfumed Garden informs us that 'there are women of great experience who, lying close with a man, can elevate one of their feet vertically in the air, and upon that foot a lamp is set full of oil, and with the wick alight. While the man is ramming them, they keep the lamp steady and burning, and no oil is spilled. Their lovemaking is no way impeded by this exhibition but it must require great practice on the part of both'.

MAN-ON-TOP POSITIONS

The stopperage As this position can be painful for the woman, Nefzawi only recommends it if 'the man's member is short or soft'. In probability, he was also recommending it for the man who is making love for the third or fourth time during a lovemaking episode and, perhaps, for the man who has drunk too much alcohol.

Place the woman on her back with a cushion under her buttocks. The man kneels between her thighs and then presses them against her chest as far as possible. The man can now place his penis in her vagina. At the moment of ejaculation the man should draw the woman towards himself.

Frog fashion The woman lies on her back and pulls her legs back until her heels touch her thighs. The man sits close to her with his penis opposite the entrance to her vagina. When his penis is inserted, the man places the woman's knees under his armpits and holds her upper arms to draw her towards him at the moment of orgasm.

The toes cramped The woman lies on her back with the man kneeling between her thighs. The man lifts the woman's buttocks so that she can cross her legs over his back. He then lifts her until she can hold her arms around his neck.

Legs in the air In this position the woman keeps her thighs closed, thus 'making a tighter comfort for any man's member.' The woman lies on her back and the man raises her legs until they are vertical. The man continues to hold up the woman's legs while he encircles her with his thighs and places his penis in her vagina.

The tail of the ostrich The woman lies on her back and the man kneels in front of her. He lifts up her legs until only her head and shoulders remain in contact with the bed. He enters her vagina and holds on to her buttocks. Movement is created by his pushing and pulling on her buttocks.

Fitting on a sock Although Nefzawi includes this as a lovemaking position, it can be regarded as more of a teasing lovemaking action, perhaps thought suitable for a woman who does not lubricate profusely or one who suffers from vaginal contractions. The woman lies on her back and the man sits down between her legs. The

The manner of the bull
This was considered by Nefzawi to be the easiest of all methods of lovemaking. Penetration is not very deep, but the couple are touching along almost the entire length of their bodies.

The double view of posteriors
An excellent position for the bottom-centred man as he can view and caress his partner's anus while she rises and falls on his penis.

The toes cramped
This is for close-contact lovemaking. Penetration can be exceptionally deep and as the couple are locked in a tight embrace, they can kiss and caress each other.

man places his penis between the lips of her vulva and fits them over the tip with his thumb and forefinger. The man's movements are then regulated to rub the penis until the woman's vagina is moistened (Nefzawi states 'by the liquid emitted from your verge' – a reference to prostatic fluid that leaks from the penis before ejaculation). When the woman was prepared for penetration Nefzawi advises 'put it into her full length'. Perhaps the Sheikh also had this technique in mind as a possible recourse for the man who suffered from premature ejaculation.

The one who stops at home There are two essential props for this position – a soft bed and two cushions. The woman lies on her back and the man lies on her with a cushion in each hand. When his penis is in her vagina, she raises her buttocks as high off the bed as she can. The man raises himself, but keeps his penis deep inside her. The woman then lowers herself to the bed again. These movements continue with only the genital areas of each lover being in contact.

Intercourse of the blacksmith Again this is not so much a new position but really a technique of using the penis. It is named not for the legendary prowess of those who followed the blacksmith's trade, but as being descriptive of the way a blacksmith works metal. The woman lies back with a cushion under her buttocks and her knees raised towards her chest. She guides her lover's penis into her vagina. The man begins with in-

out movements, then suddenly withdraws his penis and glides it for a moment between her thighs, before re-entering her . . . 'as the smith withdraws the glowing iron from the furnace in order to plunge it into cold water'.

The seducer In this energetic position the woman begins by lying on her back, while the man sits on his legs between her legs. He lifts her up and separates her thighs and places her legs under his arms. He then holds her waist or shoulders and pulls her on to his penis. He then pushes her back and forth.

REAR ENTRY POSITIONS

Lovemaking positions in which the man pentrates the woman from behind were not described in great detail in Arabian literature. This is probably because of the great belief that mutual kissing during lovemaking was essential to sensual enjoyment for both the man and the woman. Nefzawi even suggests that it is extended foreplay and kissing which 'distinguishes man in the art of love from the beasts of the field'. Significantly, the positions carry the names of animals.

The manner of the bull The woman lies on her stomach, her buttocks raised by cushions. The man approaches from behind, stretches along her back and inserts his penis. Nefzawi concludes that 'this is the easiest of all methods'.

After the fashion of the ram The woman kneels and takes her weight on her forearms. The man kneels down behind her and penetrates her vulva which is standing out as much as possible. For stability and leverage, it is suggested 'he will do well in placing his hands on the woman's shoulders'.

Intercourse of the sheep The woman supports herself on her hands and knees. The man approaches from behind and lifts her thighs until her vagina is level with his penis. He then inserts his penis and the woman places her head between her arms.

SIDE-BY-SIDE

Not particularly recommended by Nefzawi, side-by-side positions were believed to cause rheumatism and sciatica. He lists three, two of which are rear entry, the other face-to-face.

He-goat fashion The woman crouches on her side and stretches out the leg on which she is resting. The man squats down behind her thighs and lifts her upper leg until it is over his back. He inserts his penis and takes hold of her shoulders.

The rainbow arch The woman lies on her side and the man lies alongside her, facing her back. He penetrates her vagina and lays his hands on the upper part of her back. The woman then takes hold of his feet and draws them up as far as possible. This is said to resemble the form of an arch.

Love's fusion The man lies on his left side, the woman on her right. The man stretches out his lower leg and raises his upper leg until it is level with her vagina. He then places her upper leg on his side. 'Introduce your penis and move as you please.'

FOR THE FIT AND ATHLETIC

Nefzawi describes two standing positions and one quite extraordinary act of agility called The Somersault.

Belly-to-belly. The man and woman stand upright facing each other. The woman opens her thighs and the man moves forward to place his feet between hers. The partners then hold firmly on to each other's hips and the man penetrates the woman. The movement recom-

mended by Nefzawi is for the man to push a little and then withdraw a little. The woman then does the same. For this classic 'knee trembler', Nefzawi advised the man to keep one foot slightly in front of the other in order to maintain perfect balance.

Driving the peg home The woman holds on to the man's neck and clasps his waist with her thighs. It is suggested that she steadies herself by leaning against a wall and 'thus suspended the man insinuates his pin into her vulva'.

The somersault This position is best described in Nefzawi's own words. 'The woman must wear a pair of pantaloons, which she lets drop upon her heels. Then she stoops and places her head between her feet, so that her neck is in the opening of her pantaloons. At that moment, the man, seizing her legs, turns her upon her back. Then, with his legs curved under him he brings his member right against her vulva, and, slipping it between her legs, inserts it.' Nefzawi also comments, with some incredulousness, that 'it is alleged that there are women who, while lying on their back, can place their feet behind their heads without the help of pantaloons'.

OF SMALL MEN AND TALL WOMEN

Sheikh Nefzawi recognized that many of the positions he described were not suitable unless both partners were of perfect proportions and fitness. He therefore gave extensive advice for the lean man and the fat woman, sex during pregnancy, the problems of an obese man with a thin wife and how a very small man and tall woman can enjoy coition. He states that 'there are only three positions in which the actors in love can kiss while in action'.

☐ **The first position** The woman lies on her back with a thick cushion under her buttocks, and a similar one under her head. She then draws up her thighs as far as possible towards her chest. The man lies on his partner, introduces his penis, and then takes hold of her shoulders and draws himself up towards them.

☐ **The second position** The man and woman lie face-to-face on their sides. The woman slides her undermost thigh under the man's side and puts the other one over his. Then, she arches her stomach out, while his penis is penetrating her vagina. They hold each other's neck and the woman crosses her legs over his back and draws him in close.

☐ **The third position** The man lies on his back, with his legs stretched out. The woman sits on his penis and stretching herself down over him, pulls her knees up to the height of her stomach. Holding his shoulders, she pulls herself up and presses her lips to his.

Nefzawi says that these positions can be tiring, but, for reasons best known to himself, the Sheikh recommends them to 'artists and designers of books'.

EXOTIC SEX AROUND THE WORLD

We live in a world of sex for sale and in this chapter we look at some of the innumerable forms that it takes when it is seen purely as a commodity. Our survey takes us from glamorous movie personalities, through prostitutes and the uninhibited performers in live sex shows, to the shadowy figures who provide the cold comfort of telephone sex services.

But for the rest of us too, sex takes different guises depending on what part of the world we live in. Throughout history, regional differences have existed in matters of morality — towards homosexuality, incest, and bestiality, for example — and on the practical level certain lovemaking positions have come to be associated with particular areas of the world. The simplest illustration of this is the traditional, but increasingly eroded, distinction between countries where the 'missionary' position predominates and those where penetration of the woman from behind has always enjoyed at least equal appeal.

The chapter also examines those subjects which for most people remain clouded in half-truths — aphrodisiacs, sexual taboos, transvestism, and fetishism. It discusses too our varying attitudes to nudity and to the question of what is beautiful, and investigates the ways in which sexual morality has evolved over the past hundred years.

APHRODISIACS

Rightly or wrongly, oysters have long been regarded as an effective aphrodisiac, while eating ground rhino horn or a wolf's penis has been in and out of fashion over the centuries. Do these old methods work, or will 20th century science provide the elixir of love?

More than 900 supposed arousers of sexual desire, known as aphrodisiacs, have been recorded, yet it seems that only some of them have stood the test of time. Indeed, a list of all aphrodisiacs would also be a testament of the gullibility of man in his desperate bid to discover the fabled elixir of love.

All manner of concoctions have been dreamed up and consumed over the centuries – the testes of an ass, the intestines of birds, fresh semen, menstrual blood, the penis of a wolf, hedgehog and musk – as well as onions, wild cabbage, pineapple and nettle seed.

One stimulant highly esteemed in Mediterranean countries since Biblical times is the root of the mandrake *(Mandragora officinarum)*.

While the mandrake's powers as an aphrodisiac have now fallen somewhat into disrepute, it used to be thought that the more the root resembled the human form – especially if it had appendages that looked like testes – the more prized and expensive it was.

It was very fashionable to use as aphrodisiacs any organic matter – animal or vegetable – that resembled the genitals of a man or woman. Hence, beans, bananas, cucumbers and oysters were reputed to be powerful love stimulants.

Even potatoes, when they were brought from South America to Europe by the Spanish in the 17th century, were thought to have aphrodisiac properties.

Erotic writers from Greece and Rome laid great store by love stimulants, especially a brew made with 'satyrion' – a substance derived from the wild woodland orchid. It is said that Hercules drank such a brew and then proceeded to deflower the 50 daughters of his hostess.

Arabs, Hindus and Chinese have always excelled in the art of love and their erotic manuals are rich in aphrodisiac recipes.

POWERFUL PROPERTIES?

Many people today reject the idea of aphrodisiacs altogether, saying either that they do not exist or else that there is no scientific proof that they work.

Such a view may very well be right in a great many cases. But, there is also evidence that certain substances, in particular some foods, are endowed with properties that give one a sense of well-being that may enhance sexual desire. Are these aphrodisiacs?

One thing is certain – aphrodisiacs are much more likely to work if you think they will. And, for those of us who are willing to keep an open mind as to their 'powers', there is nothing to stop any of us trying a few out.

Fortunately, foods that are claimed to be aphrodisiacs are not all rare delicacies imported at great expense from exotic eastern islands – or indeed, the sort of ingredients you would be more likely to find in a witch's cauldron. Often they are widely available everyday substances such as honey.

It should be noted, however, that the ingredients for the cookery of love are not designed to cure impotency or frigidity, but are for people who want to extend their sexual enjoyment – even if this is simply by a little light-hearted experimentation.

Love dishes – even their preparation and presentation – may serve to brighten any sex life, however full.

But aphrodisiacs are not medicines. Treatment for a sex life in disarray requires a different remedy, such as more sleep, less anxiety, vitamins or perhaps counselling.

FOUR FOODS OF LOVE

The tradition of the ages is that if you eat well you perform well – and choice of food may be all-important. It has been said that the four best aphrodisiac ingredients are garlic, honey, anchovies and wheatgerm – all quality stuff.

Giving strength and stamina, garlic is claimed to have antiseptic and antibiotic properties which clean the blood and tone up the body.

And American scientists recently made the curious discovery that the main constituent of garlic's odorous and volatile oil is the same as one of the chemicals secreted by a woman when she is sexually aroused.

An instant source of energy, honey is a good all-round food for everyone. In the illustrations of such erotic books as *The Perfumed Garden* and *The Kama Sutra*, there are always sweetmeats made from honey and spices – essential fare for lovers. Honey is still used today in the widely available love-boost pills.

The mandrake was reputed to kill any man who heard it scream when pulled from the ground, so dogs were used to uproot it.

DID YOU KNOW?

To the ancient Greeks Aphrodite was the goddess of love and beauty and fruitfulness. The love potions they concocted in her name were offerings to her divinity – they drank them hoping that she would increase their sexual fortunes. Because of such reverence, all substances – herbs, spices, potions, drugs – consumed to improve sexual activity have been called aphrodisiacs.

The Romans called her Venus and this is Botticelli's *Birth of Venus*, painted c.1485.

Like most other seafoods, anchovies are especially rich in phosphorus, salt and many of the trace elements and minerals which our bodies constantly need. Oysters are the best-known seafood aphrodisiac – because they resemble the open female sex organs – but anchovies surpass them in quality.

Wheatgerm, present in wholemeal bread, is the richest source of Vitamin E on this planet. Called the 'fertility vitamin', a deficiency of it leads to sterility, impotence or other sexual problems.

No-one disputes the vitamin's essential contribution to health and vitality, but its qualities as an aphrodisiac are still a matter of debate.

SPICE IT UP

The subtle effect of aphrodisiac ingredients should never be underestimated – each person has his or her own preferences. So if one food, herb or spice does not turn you or your partner on, then try another one – but do not expect instant wonders.

You may choose caraway, a widespread ingredient in love potions since the days of Ancient Egypt, or coriander.

But beware of chillies – the right amount may release more passion than you expect, while too much might roast your passion altogether.

Chilli pepper sauce is regularly used as a companion to oysters – it is also an ingredient in several erection creams for men.

Another excellent love stimulant is one of the most versatile of all hot spices – ginger. Eaten at the end of a meal in a crystallized or chocolate form, ginger has the reputation of stirring one up sexually.

CHANGE WITH THE SEASONS

Spices are at their best on cold, dark winter days, whereas the more subtle repertoire of aphrodisiac herbs are most efficient on warm, light summer days. And such herbs must be fresh. Dried herbs have little or no effect at all.

Sweet basil is one of the most seasonal of love's herbs – it must be extremely fresh, and if its taste or smell arouse no excitement in you, then it is not for you.

You may have, however, a particular liking for the French drink, pastis, or the Greek, ouzo, in which case you should try aniseed in your food.

And if you are partial to mint, you may find its coolness arouses the passions on a hot summer's day. Various other herbs, such as parsley, tarragon and lovage, and foods, such as celery, nuts, watercress and

LOVE POTIONS

Although thought of as an encyclopaedia of sexual techniques, the *Kama Sutra* is far broader in scope. The chapter on attracting others to oneself has a lot of practical advice mixed with liberal doses of medicine, magic and ritual.

The subjects treated range from how to restore hair to how to subjugate others to one's will, how to increase sexual vigour and how to thicken and enlarge the lingam (penis).

Here are two recipes: To provoke sexual vigour – mix equal quantities of ghee (clarified butter), honey, sugar and liquorice combined with milk and the juice of fennel. The nectar-like drink will do the rest.

To prevent the object of your desires from marrying another – cut the sprouts of the vajnasunhi plant into small pieces. Dip them in a mixture of red arsenic and sulphur. Dry them seven times and reduce the mixture to a powder. If this is then combined with the excrement from a monkey and thrown over a maiden you will ensure that she never marries another.

And for a more simple one, although tantalizingly elusive, to subject a woman to your will all you need do is anoint yourself with an ointment made from the plant *Emblica myrabolans*.

asparagus, all have reputations as effective love foods.

The only way to discover if any of them increase your sexual desires or improve your sex life is to try them out.

THE DANGERS OF SPANISH FLY

A 19-year-old university student was having trouble seducing the girl he was dating and so sought the advice of a friend. One day out of the blue, his older friend slipped him a package of white crystals saying it was a famous old love stimulant called Spanish Fly which was known to be particularly useful for stimulating the sexual appetite of both men and women.

Later that evening the student emptied the contents of the package into his girlfriend's coffee and waited to see how she would respond. She died an hour later from severe internal bleeding. He was sentenced to five years for manslaughter.

Such a tragedy highlights the ignorance many people have about aphrodisiac drugs and other love potions. Spanish Fly is the dried extract of the bodies of dead green blister beetles *(Lyatta vesicatoria)* which live in southern Europe. If smeared on to the testes of unwilling horses or bulls, it makes them so uncomfortable they have to mate.

Taken internally it irritates all the mucous membranes, especially the urethra. Whether a man has his thoughts on sex or not, he usually gets an erection, with an itch in his urethra that needs scratching. Women get the same urethral itch. But more than a minute amount of Spanish Fly is deadly.

One of the aphrodisiacs popular in Ancient China was 'the bald chicken drug'. Apparently a civil servant who used it regularly fathered three sons after the age of 70 and so exhausted his poor wife that she could neither sit nor lie down. Eventually he threw the concoction into the barnyard, only to have it eaten by a cock. The bird promptly mounted the nearest hen, pecked away at her head and pleasured and plucked her until she was completely bald.

In 19th century France, Spanish Fly was a love potion with powers to restore the husband's desire and leave the wife with child – but more than a minute amount could kill.

Take a piece of pizza loving – use wholemeal brea

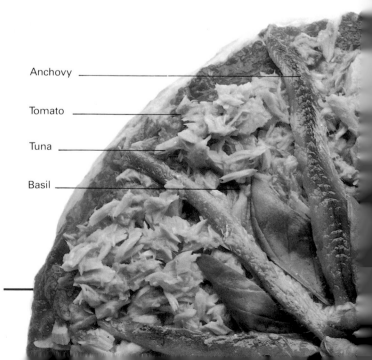

Anchovy _____

Tomato _____

Tuna _____

Basil _____

According to the classic Arabian manual on love-making, *The Perfumed Garden*, pounding the fruit of the mastic tree and mixing it with oil and honey provides a powerful elixir. Drunk first thing in the morning it was guaranteed to improve sexual performance.

In addition, Arab men had the alternative recourse of procuring the fat from a camel's hump, melting it down and then applying it liberally to the penis. This had a number of effects including 'making a previously small member quite splendid'.

SEXY DRINKS

Alcohol is a mild but much abused aphrodisiac. Small quantities have a subtle effect because they remove inhibitions and increase the flow of blood through the peripheral blood vessels such as those in the penis.

For most men, any more than a pint or so of beer – or a couple of glasses of wine – and the sedative effect of alcohol begins to dominate the stimulating effect. The optimum dose for a woman is thought to be less, probably because of her smaller body weight – about one and a half glasses of wine.

White wine is normally considered better than red, although the better the quality of either, the better the potential aphrodisiac effect.

As a general rule, the least acid wines such as claret make the best aphrodisiacs. Many people would say that champagne is probably the best drink to arouse the passions, and increase the sex drive. This may be true, but the effect will not last as long as a good claret.

Green Chartreuse and tequila are both high up on the alcoholic aphrodisiac list – green Chartreuse, for example, is said to contain essential oils that slightly irritate the bladder and pelvic region.

RHINO HORN

'Horny' is a word from the aphrodisiac language, derived from the use of the rhinoceros horn as a sex stimulant. Ground into a fine powder and drunk, rhino horn irritates the urethra, like Spanish Fly.

or the Vitamin E and choose the toppings you prefer.

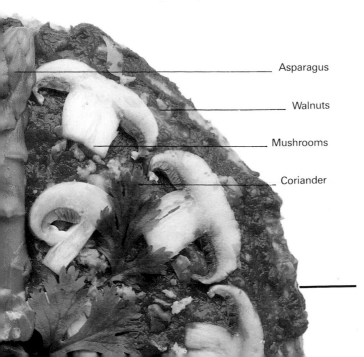

_____ Asparagus

_____ Walnuts

_____ Mushrooms

_____ Coriander

DID YOU KNOW?

The root of the ginseng plant *(Panax ginseng)* grows in China and has been revered as an aphrodisiac for a long time. It is said that the best roots are found on those plants growing on the fertile plains of Manchuria.

The chief attribute of ginseng is its ability to improve stamina, strength and power. As a result its aphrodisiac properties improve the quality and length of sexual intercourse, but, unlike most other aphrodisiacs, it does not provide the urge to have sex in the first place.

Ginseng can be smoked, chewed or made into a tea. It is claimed that it takes effect after 7 or 8 hours and may last as long as 10 days if only a single root is eaten.

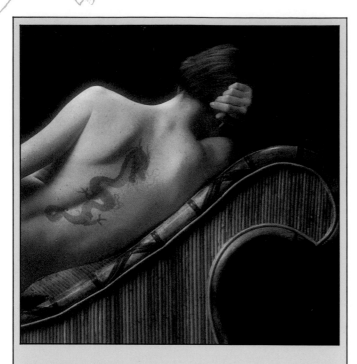

But its effect is only slight, while its cost is very high – not only to purchase, but also because several species of rhinoceros are threatened with extinction as a direct result of the aphrodisiac trade.

Cocaine is reputed to be a useful sex stimulant in that it prolongs intercourse, but the anaesthetic effects are said to reduce feeling and expressions of love. It is also very expensive, illegal and a slow poison that eats away at the nerves – far too high a price to pay for a temporary aphrodisiac.

Cannabis loosens inhibitions in a similar way to alcohol. A very popular aphrodisiac for centuries, the oil of cannabis is, by reputation, the source of the most exquisite sexual sensations. As well as altering perceptions, it enhances impulses and feelings. But cannabis is expensive and possession of it is against the law in certain countries.

ANAPHRODISIACS

The list of anaphrodisiacs – substances which lessen sexual urges and sexual activity – is long. Rather like the consequences of over-indulgence in alcohol, tran-

SEXUAL TURN-ONS

In some senses of the word, aphrodisiacs need not be substances which are eaten or drunk. To some, money and power are the most potent aphrodisiacs.

Clothes are an obvious sexual device which can be used to announce sexual availability. Some women are turned on by the sight of a man in tight trousers, or a chunky sweater, while the mere sight of a woman wearing black stockings, skin-tight sweaters and leather trousers will have aphrodisiac effects on some men.

Cosmetics, too, have stimulant qualities – lipstick, blusher, mascara, eye-shadow, bath oil and perfume all have alluring properties.

The whole range of sexual preferences have their own particular 'activators'. Some find tattoos exciting, while in certain cultures scarring of the skin is a turn-on. To others, the very thought of leather, whips and any of the other sado-masochism equipment is enough to stimulate them.

Then there are the visual foods for sexual stimulation – the hard and soft pornography books, films, magazines and videos.

Mechanical aids, such as 'french ticklers', which are used to stimulate the clitoris, penile rings to maintain erections and vibrators to augment the woman's arousal, all may achieve the desired result without the consumption of any substances.

According to a study reported in a journal of sexual medicine, self-hypnosis has an 86 per cent success rate in relieving impotence problems. The technique involves the separation of the conscious brain from the physical action by using mental images or a simple repetitive chore.

CAN THERE BE THE PERFECT APHRODISIAC?

The ultimate aphrodisiac would act on a person in three ways. It would stimulate the parts of the brain that control the sex drive, enhance the action of the peripheral nervous system that unconsciously regulates the way the sex organs work, and so alter the response of the blood vessels that supply the sex organs.

To affect the sex drive the aphrodisiac would have to work on part of the brain called the hypothalamus, as this controls the release of sex hormones into the blood-stream by the pituitary gland.

The hypothalamus is one of the oldest parts of the brain – it evolved very early on – and regulates instinctive 'animal' behaviour and vital biological functions.

The role of the hypothalamus is, however, also modified by other more 'civilized' parts of the brain which control our social behaviour and reasoning and can recall past events that modify behaviour.

In theory, by blocking these modifying influences it should be possible to release our 'animal' instincts.

The side-effects of this, however, would almost certainly be the release of other instincts of an anti-social nature and would quite likely turn the world into a collection of murderers and rapists.

Modifications of the connections between different parts of the brain by certain drugs have been shown to have an effect on the libido, but only when there has been a lower sex drive than is usually considered normal.

To increase the frequency and length of erection it would be necessary to alter the

quillizers and sedatives generally have a negative effect.

Opium in small doses produces erections in a man, although emission and orgasm are said to be retarded. Large doses, however, have the opposite effect and lead to impotence. Other anaphrodisiacs are coffee and tea when drunk in excess, vinegar, tobacco, lime juice, camphor, lemons, lemonade, valerian and bromide.

APHRODISIACS IN YOUR BODY

The libido or sexual drive depends upon the proper working of the sex glands. This in turn depends on the pituitary gland and the hypothalamus (both in the brain) and the relationship that exists between them.

There is no such thing as a universal aphrodisiac – a substance which, turned into a pill and then eaten, stimulates all aspects of a person's sex life. The nearest we might get to that is hormones – testosterone, for example.

But testosterone, the male sex hormone which is also present in women in small quantities, only seems to work for those people who have little or no testosterone in the first place.

Another problem is that women would suffer the development of secondary sexual male characteristics – such as facial hair and increased leg and body hair – if they took too much testosterone.

The production of testosterone is governed by a hormone with the cumbersome title of Luteinizing Hormone Releasing Hormone (LHRH). This chemical, released by the hypothalamus in the brain, causes the pituitary gland to secrete Luteinizing Hormone – this stimulates the testes to make testosterone.

It seems that small doses of LHRH can actually work as a sex stimulant, increasing sexual activity and stimulating both the male and female sex drive.

But before it could become commercially available, many more trials will have to be undertaken, and a

control of the nerve supply to the male sex organs which, in turn, would change the way that the blood vessels react. Certain nerves sustain the resting 'tone' of both veins and arteries. By inhibiting the nerve action the arteries that supply blood to the penis enlarge and the veins contract.

When erection occurs, due to erotic thoughts or physical stimulation of the genitals, the arteries in the penis increase their volume and it is filled with blood and swells. At the same time the veins which carry blood away from the penis, constrict and keep it erect by blocking the outflow of blood.

By stopping the controlling nerves it should be possible to keep an erection forever. Certain spinal injuries which damage these nerves have been known to pro-duce permanent, and painful, erections.

Unfortunately, all of the drugs known to medical science that do alter the volume of blood in the penis not only affect the blood supply to the genitals, but also the blood supply to other organs such as the heart, kidneys and liver. In addition, drugs avail-able induce feelings of tension, nausea and anxiety – producing a state in which even the biggest erection could never be enjoyed.

While science can work out ways that chemicals can induce what could be called aphrodisiac effects, the disturbance that they cause to the systems of the body as a whole means that there is little chance that a safe, proven, and acceptable aphrodisiac will ever be produced. Love is prob-ably the best alternative.

APHRODISIAC BATHS

A warm bath, scented with aromatic oils, may work wonders for your sex life. Remember to run the bath before adding the essential oils, as they should float on top of the water.

The bath should be reasonably hot, so that the steam rises. This allows you to inhale the fragrance captured in the moist air. When you emerge from the water, the oils will cling to your skin without leaving an oily residue.

Essential oils with aphro-disiac qualities include:
Black pepper
Cardamom

Clary sage
Jasmine
Juniper
Orange blossom
Patchouli
Rose
Sandalwood
Ylang ylang

For your man
2 drops of black pepper
5 drops of clary sage
2 drops of ylang ylang
5 drops of sandalwood

For your woman
3 drops of patchouli
2 drops of ylang ylang
2 drops of orange blossom
5 drops of sandalwood

For you together
3 drops of jasmine
3 drops of rose
7 drops of sandalwood

cheap supply will have to be found. This may be achieved by genetic engineering – it is already accepted in the biotechnology market that the first company to discover a safe, effective aphrodisiac will strike gold.

THE SCENT OF SEX

While extra hormones may work to improve your sex life, your body is already producing chemicals that act as sexual attractants. These substances, called pheromones, are made by glands in the sex organs and special sweat glands in the armpits.

Exactly how they work is unclear, as they are odourless and impossible to detect, but they seem to excite the sex centres in the brain.

They were first detected in animals and are known to work over remarkably long distances – a female gypsy moth can attract a male from more than 3 kilometres.

Humans will probably never be able to attract a mate from any greater distance than across a crowded room, but there is no doubt that both men and women are continually transmitting sexual signals to others.

Sniffing the chance of a profit, cosmetics companies are now marketing aftershaves and perfumes that contain human sex pheromones.

There is no reliable evidence to show if these 'natural aphrodisiacs' work in practice (perhaps because the users are sensibly keeping the secret to themselves), but laboratory tests have shown that they can affect the way someone perceives others as more or less attractive.

Both men and women were provided with surgeons' face-masks which had been impregnated with a pheromone, and asked to judge the attractiveness of photographs of people of the opposite sex. They consistently awarded more points than another group given face-masks impregnated with a neutral chemical.

Despite this sudden scientific interest in natural sex chemicals the idea is not new. The whores of Naples were reputed to dab the moisture from their vaginas behind their ears to attract custom. Villagers in Austria are reported to have gone to the local dance with hand-kerchieves that had been kept in their armpits for several days. Armpits may be sexier than you think — and certainly a lot cheaper to use than bottles of aftershave.

PERFUMES

It seems strange that if our natural body chemicals can act as sexual attractants that we should spend so much time and money washing them off and covering them up with cosmetics — especially as most perfumes contain extracts from the sex glands of animals such as the musk deer and the civet.

But there is no doubt that scent and perfume are a turn-on for many people. Perhaps it is because they suggest cleanliness, but most probably because we associate perfumes with our earliest sexual encounter. This is continually reinforced by advertising campaigns that suggest that cosmetics equal sexual success.

Yet the power of aromatic substances as seducers has long been recognized.

While Europe remained in the grip of the Middle Ages, the art of love blossomed in Arabia. Sheikh Nefzawi compiled his great erotic work *The Perfumed Garden* and gave specific instructions as to how a man can capture a woman by the use of various perfumes.

AROMATHERAPY

Roses, orange blossom, and jasmine are also used as aphrodisiac essential oils in aromatherapy. You either believe in aromatherapy or you do not – but a soothing bath with fragrant oils will almost certainly put you in a relaxed mood and ready for a sensuous lovemaking session.

The next time you smell the same aromatic oils, the association between them and the feelings of sexiness and well-being you experienced before should be enough to trigger those feelings again.

ALCOHOL AND SEX

Alcohol has long been considered an aphrodisiac by different cultures. In small amounts it can reduce anxiety and lessen inhibition. Consequently sexual overtures and encounters are easier. The quantity, however, is critical because in increasing doses alcohol has the opposite effect, causing a slowing down of all motor nerve responses and temporary sexual incapacity. One of the results of chronic alcohol use is that sexual performance can be permanently impaired.

The degree of concentration of alcohol in the blood depends on the interaction of a variety of factors, among which are: the amount and strength of the alcohol taken, the length of time spent drinking, the presence or absence of food in the stomach and the age, sex, weight and particular metabolism of the drinker.

2 measures Relaxation, decreased social inhibitions, mild arousal.
Sexual response Increased blood flow, which can facilitate erection

4 measures Speech slurred, some difficulty in co-ordinating movements, increased sexual aggression.
Sexual response Affects centres in brain that control orgasm, necessitating more stimulation for orgasm

6 measures Movements awkward, staggering, exaggerated emotions.
Sexual response Many women find orgasm more difficult. May be more difficult in men too

8 measures Thoughts incoherent, movements uncontrolled.
Sexual response Increasingly difficult to maintain erection, and orgasm often impossible

---

PROSTITUTION AND THE LAW

The oldest profession remains outside the law in some parts of the world, while in other countries it is legally sanctioned to varying degrees – in some cases operating under government licence

I t is not illegal to be a prostitute in England, Scotland and Wales. But the laws surrounding prostitution are so complex that they can greatly restrict a prostitute's activities.

The main areas in which prostitutes work are on the streets, either taking clients back to a room, or going with them in their car, in certain saunas and massage parlours, nightclubs and hotels, through escort agencies and from their own homes. A few also work for Madams who run their own establishments. All outlets for prostitution have their own legal complications and risks.

WORKING THE STREETS

Although in the United Kingdom prostitution is not in itself illegal, soliciting for clients is. This makes working the streets a particularly hazardous form of prostitution, especially if the police have decided to 'clean up' a certain area.

LOITERING WITH INTENT

The police can stop any woman suspected of loitering or soliciting in a public place. This can include doorways or entrances of buildings or virtually anywhere. If the police wish to, they can treat a hotel as a public place, and they can also charge a woman who attracts the attention of men in the street by gesturing to them from her window or balcony.

If the woman is charged and subsequently convicted by the courts, she is likely to be fined or put on probation. The only evidence needed to convict a prostitute is the word of a single police officer.

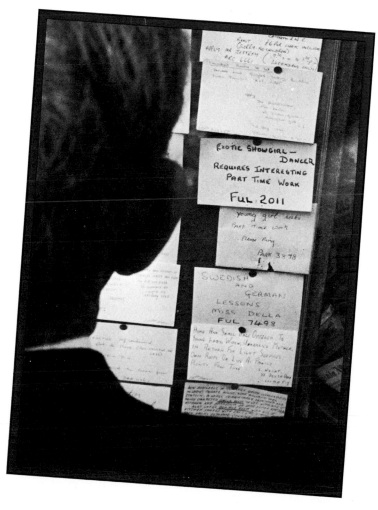

These women work in a brothel in Nevada, USA. Nevada is one of the few states in America that has legalized prostitution. Brothels, however, may not operate within 400 yards of a schoolhouse or church, and when one was found to be within the limit, the townspeople decided to rebuild the school.

Right In 1975, French prostitutes staged a number of sit-ins in churches to protect their rights. Ten years later they staged a hunger strike in a church to protest the planned closure of 350 flats where they used to work.

FINES – A VICIOUS CIRCLE

Since prison sentences for loitering and soliciting were abolished under the Criminal Justice Act of 1982, some courts are imposing far heavier fines than was previously the case.

The National Association of Probation Officers is concerned that many prostitutes are caught in a vicious circle. The fine for one offence can be so high that they resort to further prostitution to pay it off, only to be charged and fined again. Eventually they may end up in prison, not for soliciting, but for non-payment of fines.

The Association's research leads it to believe that a greater number of women are now ending up in jail for failure to pay fines than were imprisoned under the previous legislation for debt, loitering and soliciting combined. Since a large proportion of prostitutes are single parents, this creates further problems for the children concerned.

KERB CRAWLING

In Britain until 1985 only women could be charged with soliciting. But under the Sexual Offences Act passed that year it also became an offence for men to solicit women in a street or in a public place.

In 1986 the further restriction was added that men may not solicit women from a car. Men are now 'barred from kerb crawling persistently and in a manner which is likely to cause annoyance to the women solicited or nuisance to people in the neighbourhood'. It is also an offence for a man persistently to solicit women in the street for prostitution even without a car.

THE PROS AND CONS OF LEGISLATION

Although this legislation might appear to equalize the situation between prostitutes and clients, it has been vigorously opposed, and not just by prostitutes. It has been argued that not only do prostitutes lose clients, but such legislation can lead to even greater harassment for them, and furthermore, interferes with the basic freedom of ordinary citizens.

Another effect of the changes in the law according to prostitutes and their supporters, is that prostitutes are now even more isolated, and subject to higher risks, because they are no longer able to chat to and assess potential clients before going with them.

Alternatively, it is argued that the changes in the law have changed former 'red-light' areas making them more pleasant for ordinary residents.

THE 'COMMON PROSTITUTE' LABEL

In London and some other parts of England, a woman is cautioned on two separate occasions for soliciting before she can be charged for the first time.

After she has been cautioned twice, she is labelled a 'common prostitute' even before she has been tried and convicted – unless she can get the caution cancelled within 14 days.

A THREAT TO JUSTICE

The label is then used in court when a charge is brought. Understandably, this may prejudice her chances of a fair hearing. Standard practice in other offences is that a past criminal record is not revealed to the court unless the current charge is proven.

The term 'common prostitute' is applied even if the woman has only committed the offence once, but in the minds of the public – and in particular, the jury – 'common' is linked to frequency and/or vulgarity.

This label can also be brought up in other court cases in which a prostitute may be involved – such as rape or custody. This is a matter of great resentment among many prostitutes who feel that the way they earn their living should not prevent them being treated as other women are, or be seen as having any bearing on their ability to care for their children.

Many prostitutes are single parents and claim that they remain in prostitution specifically to have more money to spend on their children.

PREMISES AND ADVERTS

It is legal for a prostitute to work from her own home or rented premises on her own – although there may, of course, be objections from neighbours.

It is illegal for prostitutes to advertise their services directly in shop windows, newspapers or magazines.

DID YOU KNOW?

In 1979 Southampton Council in southern England debated a proposal to establish and run legalized brothels. State-run brothels exist in some countries such as West Germany and Peru, but most prostitutes' organizations are firmly against them. French prostitutes op- posed the reopening of state brothels in France in 1975, stating adamantly, 'We refuse to be civil servants of sex completely without freedom.'

Experience of state- run brothels suggests that those working in them become even more isolated from their families, the community and other women. They lose their freedom and independence and are unable to control either their workload or work- ing conditions. One pros- titute from a state-run brothel in Nevada, USA, reported that girls had to agree to work an average of a 12-hour-day, and sometimes much longer.

An argument put forward for state-run brothels is the certainty of regular medical checks. Prostitutes, how- ever, will assert that their customers always wear sheaths and that they themselves go volun- tarily and frequently for check-ups.

Most get around the problem by using a widely understood code in advertisements such as 'French lessons' or 'model'. To stay within the law, they may only quote a price when the client asks 'how much?'

Many prostitutes believe that if advertising laws were less restrictive, there would be less need for street soliciting or for 'red light' areas where prostitutes congregate and which provide one of the easiest ways for clients to meet them.

A further disadvantage of this law is that two or more prostitutes are not allowed to live together or share premises for work since this arrangement constitutes a 'brothel'. They and their landlord run the risk of being prosecuted.

This restriction of numbers makes both personal and professional life more difficult. Having someone else on the premises makes life less lonely, and offers greater protection. Prostitutes are at the mercy of the law, but more immediately they risk physical danger and abuse every time they go with a client.

They lay themselves bare in every sense of the word to unknown men, occasionally with quite horrifying results. And not only must a prostitute live alone, but girlfriends who drop in on her can come under suspicion of working with a prostitute and thus lay her open to a charge of keeping a brothel.

Strangely enough, as the law stands in Britain, it is quite legal for landlords knowingly to rent accommodation to single prostitutes. But if the landlord charges an extremely high rent or extorts favours from her, he runs the risk of being charged with living off immoral earnings.

Usually areas in cities where the lights are bright and stay on all night signify just one thing – that women are around and available, if the price is right.

HOTELS

Rather than work from their own premises, some prostitutes use a hotel or several hotels as their base – usually going back to the client's room but sometimes renting a room of their own. This may involve tipping hotel staff to indicate likely clients or to turn a blind eye to what they are doing.

It is always risky. If a prostitute is loitering in the lobby or bar of the hotel, for example, the management can call the police and she can be charged with soliciting in a public place. Most hoteliers try to act more discreetly, so as to avoid a scandal.

SAFETY IN NUMBERS?

Some prostitutes prefer to sacrifice some of their independence for the greater security and companionship of working in certain sex-linked enterprises, such as saunas and massage parlours.

Others act as nightclub hostesses where their main task, as far as the management is concerned, is to persuade the clients to buy large quantities of the very expensive drinks. Arrangements for sex are usually conducted separately.

Although blatant advertising is not allowed, prostitutes follow a well-known code to ply their trade. Offering 'shoes size 6' or lessons in a foreign language are just two examples.

But these areas are not necessarily any safer for prostitutes than working the streets. The police can prosecute the owners of an agency, club or sauna if they have evidence that prostitution is being practised on the premises – or even away from it – by at least two women, with the management's approval or even just their knowledge.

The charge may be running a brothel, causing women to become prostitutes, exercising control of prostitutes or living off immoral earnings. The woman working for the organization can also be charged with aiding and abetting in the running of a brothel.

Yet as the law stands it is perfectly legal to act as an escort, to have sex with a customer for personal reasons and to accept tips as long as these can be shown not to be in exchange for sexual services.

FRIENDS AND RELATIONS

One source of great discontent for prostitutes is that the law makes no distinction between a man who may be their boyfriend or husband and large-scale exploitative pimps who live and feed off a number of girls.

Any man who associates with or lives with a prostitute can be charged with living off immoral earnings and any woman living with one can be charged with controlling a prostitute.

These charges can apply not simply to husbands, boyfriends or girlfriends, but also to sons and daughters aged more than 18.

GUILTY UNTIL PROVEN INNOCENT

Significantly, in these cases the defendant is considered guilty until he proves his innocence – completely reversing the usual procedure in a criminal case where the defendant is considered innocent until proven guilty.

The best protection family and friends have against being charged is to have an independent source of income for which it can be shown that income tax is being paid.

The application of such laws increases the sense of social isolation that many prostitutes feel. They are unable to spend their money as they wish or to associate with whom they choose without the possibility of incriminating those people who are close to them.

CAMPAIGNING

Until the 1970s it seemed to many ordinary people that prostitutes inhabited a shady, alien world.

Around this time prostitutes started grouping together to insist on their rights as ordinary citizens, and to campaign against the laws that penalize them.

Following a spate of murders of prostitutes in Lyons, France, where police not only seemed to be offering little protection but actually to be increasing harassment, a group of local prostitutes went on strike.

They staged a sit-in in a church in Lyons in 1975.

One of the benefits of the profession is that transactions are conducted strictly on a cash basis, with flexi-hours.

In Amsterdam's red light district love is for sale and men can window-shop at their leisure before making a purchase. By putting sex out in the open, both customer and prostitute are protected.

Their action was followed by groups of prostitutes all over France. The extensive coverage in the news media of the issues behind these concerted actions did much to dispel the myths about prostitutes. People began to realize that, leaving aside their choice of profession, prostitutes were mainly ordinary women.

COLLECTIVE OF PROSTITUTES

1975 saw the formation of both the French and English Collective of Prostitutes. Similar organizations representing their interests have been set up in the United States, Canada, Australia and many other countries.

The English Collective of Prostitutes, or ECP, is opposed to any institutionalized form of prostitution such as state brothels or special red light areas, since these would remove a prostitute's independence.

WOMEN'S LEGAL AID

In 1982 the ECP started a legal service at King's Cross Women's Centre in London entitled LAW, or Legal Action for Women, to help women who needed advice or legal support.

Like other women's groups, prostitutes are gathering together, growing stronger and discovering how to help themselves.

HOW PROSTITUTES VIEW THEIR PROFESSION

Advantages
☐ A quick way of making a reasonable amount of money
☐ Payment on the spot
☐ Flexible hours which can fit in with children, housework or other commitments
☐ Independence
☐ More variety than most other work options
☐ Wider experience of life, possibility of meeting interesting clients
☐ Camaraderie and support among fellow workers

Disadvantages
☐ Leading a double life, fear of being found out by children, neighbours or boyfriends
☐ Not being able to count on the same police protection as other women
☐ Anxiety about reporting offences such as rape or assault to the police in case they themselves are arrested
☐ Worries over being arrested, appearing in court, paying fines or going to prison
☐ Fear of being accused of being an unfit mother and losing custody of the children
☐ Anxiety that those they live with or associate with may be arrested and charged
☐ Coping with difficult, perhaps violent clients
☐ Performing acts which may be distasteful to them
☐ Handling the social stigma attached to prostitution
☐ Working unsociable hours, often outdoors in bad weather

SEXUAL TABOOS

Few people still believe that masturbation results in blindness – and western women no longer have their noses cut off for adultery. But sexual taboos still play a significant role in society – sometimes for very sound reasons

Those who have witnessed, and particularly those who were closely involved in, the sexual revolution of the past two decades or so could be forgiven for thinking that the idea of sexual taboos is a little quaint or not part of our culture. For them, taboos are of another time, or another place, not here and now in our so-called permissive society, where – within reason – anything goes.

TABOO OR NOT TABOO?

The qualification 'within reason', however, is the clue to our understanding and acceptance of sexual taboos.

We deplore and punish rapists and paedophiles – adults who have sex with children. We recoil with disgust at the very thought of people fornicating with animals.

Such activities are absolutely taboo – that is, those who indulge in them are viewed with fear and revulsion. We do not think for a moment that they should be allowed to 'do their own thing'. We wheel out the entire apparatus of legal and social sanctions to combat them and their activities. That is the nature of a sexual taboo.

Some taboos are strong and others weak, with sanctions to match, but in all cases they relate to activities considered harmful – harmful to society as a whole or to the individuals involved.

The nature of tabooed activities themselves, however, can vary astonishingly between one culture and another, and one time and another.

ORIGINAL MEANING

The term 'taboo' itself is relatively modern. We owe it to Captain James Cook, who noted during his exploration of the South Pacific in the 1760s and '70s that the Polynesian islanders conducted relations between the sexes quites differently from the customs in Europe.

Above all, and highly noticeably, the women were quite uninhibited about displaying their bodies in public and before the hungry eyes of English sailors. Yet they recoiled from the prospect of eating together with men, even their own men.

Captain Cook reported that the Polynesians used the word 'tabu' to describe such forbidden activity – from 'ta' meaning 'marked' and 'bu', meaning 'completely'. Taken together, the meaning was something like 'completely marked off', 'out of bounds'.

So the word tabu, or taboo, entered the English language to describe the curious sexual restrictions of others.

It did not occur to 18th-century Europeans that their own rules, their own 'do's and don'ts' might strike others, including their 20th-century descendants, as highly curious ways of behaving too.

Anyone suggesting today that masturbation caused blindness or any such calamity would excite ridicule, not fear. Yet many a middle-aged – or even younger – man will have vivid memories of being frightened by such misguided notions.

Quite properly, therefore, we have come to use the term taboo to describe our own rules as well as those of our more mysterious fellow humans.

INCEST

It is doubtful if any known form of human activity has been universally tabooed, although some taboos are a great deal more general than others. Incest is one of the strongest taboos in the western tradition and far beyond it – but not everywhere.

Mother-son incest, a great rarity in the world at large, is actually a compulsory ritual among the Kubeo tribe of South America. At puberty, a boy must have sex with his mother as an initiation into adult life. Among the Tutsi tribes of East Africa, a bridegroom who finds himself embarrassed by impotence on his

wedding night may turn to his mother for the 'cure'.

Father-daughter incest is a more puzzling case. It is the most common form of incest in the modern western world, far more common than is generally supposed and cloaked in great secrecy and shame because it is so strongly tabooed. Yet, with the exception of the occasional Persian emperor or Egyptian pharoah of antiquity, it seems never to have enjoyed any respectability.

Brother-sister incest usually excites less revulsion, even though it is taboo in most societies, and it is the form of incest that is most famous for occasionally escaping the net of taboo altogether.

The royal families of Hawaii, the Inca of Peru and best-known of all, the Ancient Egyptians, promoted marriages between brother and sister. Cleopatra's

younger brother was both her husband and uncle, although the luckless 12-year-old was murdered when his sister developed a taste for non-incestuous sex, first with Julius Caesar and then with Mark Antony.

The most curious exceptions to the incest taboo occur with male-female twins in a few widely-scattered societies.

In Bali, where the usual taboo is observed, it is assumed that an embryonic brother and sister who have shared the same womb are bound to have indulged in sexual activity during the long unsupervised period together. Therefore, they may – if they wish – marry each other as adults, after a purification ceremony. The Aymará Indians of South America also confer a similar privilege on twins.

In the Marshall Islands of the Pacific this assumption of prenatal incest between boy-girl twins is also made, but with less happy consequences. For his assumed crime, the boy pays with his life.

Above *Not only did Jupiter escape the human incest taboo, he also took part in a bestial union with the beautiful mortal Leda, when he came to her in the form of a swan and made love to her. Helen of Troy was supposedly one of their children.*

Left *In myths and legend, the gods were considered exempt from the taboos affecting mere mortals. The Roman god Jupiter married his twin sister Juno.*

BESTIAL SEX

Bestiality, which means any sort of human sexual activity with animals, is another widespread taboo, although as with incest there have been exceptions.

In times long past the Yoruba of Nigeria had a custom whereby a young hunter copulated immediately with the first antelope he killed. And the Hopi Indians are reported to have encouraged adolescent boys to direct their sexual energies towards animals. This allowed the boys to gain sexual experience and also protected the girls.

Where bestiality occurs (whether taboo or not) the animals most commonly used are sheep, goats, cattle, dogs, pigs and horses, although occasional claims have been made for less likely 'partners' – even snakes and turtles.

The most bizarre claim of all was made by the 19th-century explorer Richard Burton, who reported that some Middle Eastern peoples copulated with female crocodiles, not for pleasure but because the act conferred magical properties.

MAN'S BEST FRIEND?

In western societies, occasional bestiality is probably more common than is generally supposed, although it is almost invariably confined to rural areas. Hence the many coarse jokes about shepherds and wellington boots.

In the more remote parts of Australia regular travellers – such as sales representatives – have a saying that 'when the sheep start looking good it's time to turn the car around and head for home'. A simple jest, of course, but in his exhaustive researches into sexual behaviour in post-war United States, Alfred Kinsey reported that 17 per cent of boys raised on farms had experienced at least one orgasm with an animal.

In the face of such a strong taboo, such activity would be extremely furtive and for obvious reasons easily concealed. The novelist Lawrence Durrell, however, observed an almost touching openness among certain shepherds in Cyprus. They would single out a particular sheep for their attention, groom it lovingly and even deck it out with fancy ribbons and colourful trinkets.

HOMOSEXUAL TABOOS

Regarding incest and bestiality as taboo usually raises little controversy. Homosexuality, by contrast, is highly controversial. It is also an area where definitions are important, at least as regards taboo.

Exclusive homosexuality has always been regarded as deviant, for an unarguable reason. If it became the norm, the human species would be threatened. Whatever else taboos may be about, they are certainly directed towards survival. Not even the most committed gay would welcome a world in which heterosexual behaviour went out of fashion.

Homosexuality with a bisexual context – whether within a particular individual who is bisexual or within a society that is overwhelmingly heterosexual – is a different matter. It is here that controversy exists and that taboos have fluctuated wildly.

The Ancient Greeks, to whom we owe so many of our ideas, thought it entirely natural that men enjoyed sex with attractive youths. The youths would in their turn behave the same way as adults – but all along the line, marriage and procreation formed the normal pattern for these men.

The Romans, who inherited Greek culture, had mixed feelings about the matter, but such behaviour figured largely in 'normal' life.

In sharp contrast, first the Jewish and then the Christian religions severely punished homosexual acts of any kind. They were utterly taboo.

Put simply, the Jewish-Christian view prevailed. This did not mean that homosexual activity was

In most societies, even those where male homosexuality is restricted, lesbianism has not been subject to taboo. It has simply been ignored.

stamped out, but it did mean that throughout western history it has attracted ridicule or worse and has therefore been a 'closed' activity – with the occasional exception.

CHANGING ATTITUDES

Less than a generation ago it could have been left at that. But the opportunity presented by the rapid loosening of sexual restrictions during the 1960s and '70s was eagerly grasped by large numbers of homosexuals, and with striking results.

To begin with, the laws aimed at preventing and punishing homosexual acts have been considerably eased in most western societies.

Equally important, opinion at large has shifted along with the law (or vice versa).

In other words, many people who once regarded, or would have regarded, homosexuality as taboo no longer do so.

BUT GIRLS CAN BE GIRLS

It may seem one-sided to consider homosexual taboos as if they only concerned male homosexuals, but the fact is that very few societies have ever concerned themselves sufficiently with lesbianism to formulate taboos about it.

This is not to say that lesbianism is a human rarity, merely that male-dominated societies, primitive or advanced, ancient or modern, have for the most part simply ignored it.

HETEROSEXUAL CONTROLS

It is with sexual behaviour between men and women who are not closely related that most taboos are concerned. In a sense that should cause no surprise. It is the most common form of sexuality, and therefore the one most likely to have profound social consequences. Yet, the keynote of taboos in western society has been on sexual repression.

Religious doctrine and moral instruction have laid the heaviest possible emphasis on what individuals should not do.

The list of 'don'ts' is exhaustive. It has included every form of sexual activity bar one – conventional love-making within marriage for the purpose of having children. Anything and everything that strayed from that purpose was immoral.

That plainly ruled out pre-marital sex, adultery and of course masturbation. It also ruled out, within marriage, oral sex, anal sex and contraception.

The emphasis on the missionary position as the only 'proper' one stemmed from it too, because that position was thought to be particularly likely to result in conception.

IMMORAL PLEASURE

With this rigid ban on sex for pleasure alone, it was not a very big step to the belief that ideally it should not be pleasurable at all.

DID YOU KNOW?

☐ The Ainu of northern Japan have a taboo against pregnant women twisting ropes, in case the baby also twists in the womb.

☐ The romantic – and often uncomfortable – ideal of sex in the open is very much a product of western civilization. The idea of making love under the stars would horrify many African peoples who consider such activity as showing disrespect for Nature.

☐ There is also a taboo followed by many Greek Orthodox Christian couples against holy pictures being displayed in bedrooms where sex is likely to take place. And many Spanish Roman Catholics, while having holy pictures in their bedrooms, will turn them to face the wall when they are making love.

☐ Within Russia, there is a widespread taboo against 'milk incest' – people may not marry the children of a woman who wet-nursed them.

☐ A classic example of how one culture could affect another occurs with the Puna indians of La Paz, who were converted to Christianity in the 18th century. Although they had many taboos, they believed that they could all be broken on Good Friday. Their excuse was that, since God was dead on that day, he would not remember any sins they had committed.

Taking the pleasure out of sex for men was difficult, but for women, unfortunately, the possibilities were greater. It is easy to laugh at the Victorian advice to well-brought up brides to 'lie back and think of England', or at the old saying that 'sex is the price women pay for marriage' (and 'marriage is the price men pay for sex'). The list is endless.

MASTURBATION

Male masturbation has variously been said to cause insanity, epileptic fits, rheumatism, impotence, acne, idiocy and asthma – not to forget the old favourites, blindness and hair sprouting on the palms of the hands.

Apart from unnecessary feelings of guilt, no-one ever came to harm by masturbating. And ridicule has usually been the only sanction applied, although some Victorians did go to elaborate lengths to prevent indulgence in 'the solitary vice'.

There still exist as museum pieces weird contraptions that would make anyone blanch. A particularly fiendish anti-erection device was a metal ring with four metal spikes pointing inwards. Presumably shackled to the suspected penis at night, it would certainly have encouraged erection-free slumber.

Less potentially painful, and more sophisticated, was an erection detector linked to a bell in an adjoining room, which would alert a parent.

SLIDING SCALE OF PUNISHMENT

The punishment, or lack of it, dealt out to offenders is the best indication of the seriousness of the taboo.

As a rule, premarital sex and sex between engaged couples has been treated more leniently than adultery. Divorce and disgrace (particularly for the woman adulterer) have been typical punishments for adultery, but it can be worse.

The Jévaro of South America allow the injured husband to kill his adulterous wife or to mutilate her genitals, while her lover gets off lightly with a slashed scalp.

Considering that rape and incest have almost always been taken even more seriously than adultery, the scope for punishment has been limitless. One example is quite enough. The Cayapa Indians of Ecuador apparently used to punish incest by stringing the guilty couple up above a table covered with lighted candles and roasting them to death.

SEX IN MARRIAGE

Sexual taboos within marriage fall into two categories – particular acts that should not be performed, and times (and occasionally places) to avoid sex altogether.

Because it is usually impossible for outsiders to know what couples who are quite legitimately in bed together actually do in the course of lovemaking, taboos in this area are weak. They really do no more than reflect the general climate of opinion about sex.

If sexuality is severely repressed and thought of as somehow dirty – a necessary evil – then people are not likely to be imaginative or experimental in their love-making techniques.

Even at the worst of times, however, there would have been fortunate couples who managed to shrug off their inhibitions and discover the pleasures of varied positions, oral sex or whatever 'turned them on'.

MENSTRUATION TABOOS

The principal taboo about the timing of sexual intercourse concerns menstruation. The superstition that a menstruating woman is 'unclean' runs deep in many cultures.

The Greeks and Romans believed variously that contact with women in this condition would blunt the blade of a knife, rust iron, or turn wine sour – while the blood itself, if lapped up by a dog, would turn the poor creature rabid.

Today, the taboo against having sex with a menstruating woman remains widespread – in Africa, Asia and among Orthodox Jews.

But in the long run, sexual taboos, like other firmly held beliefs, survive or fall by the wayside depending upon how their relevance is perceived.

A taboo that becomes widely seen as hurtful rather than helpful is a taboo on the way out. That is one of the clearest lessons to be learned from our recent experience.

Oral sex has been tabooed in some societies, but has long been a feature of Japanese erotic art.

SEX SPOTS OF THE WORLD

What makes a place qualify as a sex spot? Are some cities really more erotic than others? The answer may only be in your mind – but sex spots can renew the most jaded appetite

The idea that some places are sexier than others is a little curious. After all, sex only requires motive (desire), means and opportunity, so why should a couple spending a weekend together in Paris have a more rapturous time than, say, in Birmingham – at least in terms of their sexual pleasure?

Yet most of us imagine that there is a difference – that Paris, for example, is particularly, even uniquely, romantic, that Rio de Janeiro is raunchy, and that Bangkok is 'naughty', to put it mildly. Are these simply modern myths, or is there really a better time on offer in one place rather than another – and where exactly would one go to get it?

TWO'S COMPANY

The answer, of course, is that personal tastes and individual circumstances can be the only true guide.

A couple in the first flush of love would see little point in a holiday which caters for singles.

But a single woman who does not at the moment have a steady relationship might consider a singles holiday ideal. She is bound to meet plenty of new people and in a free and easy atmosphere she can behave exactly as she pleases as the night wears on. She might even embark on a relationship that will outlast the holiday itself.

To take another example, a couple who have a happy and perfectly stable relationship might decide to sample some of Amsterdam's notorious nightlife for the sheer novelty of it.

A man on his own might find a few days and nights in Bangkok a great tonic – most certainly, if he wished it, it would be an erotic experience not easily forgotten.

ONE NIGHT IN PARIS . . .

An American writer in the 1920s described Paris as the place 'all good Americans go to when they die'. This heavenly claim may be a little strong, but Paris is beautiful to a rare degree, sophisticated and stylish, and simply throbs with a picturesque variety of street life. It stands alone as the city of love, where to be unashamedly and openly in love is accepted, and even encouraged. It is the perfect spot to choose if you are planning a romantic honeymoon trip.

CABARET

Parisian nightlife is as rich and varied as you can find anywhere in the world. Cabaret is a French word, and Paris boasts hundreds including three of the best in the world.

The Lido, which features the famous Bluebell Girls, puts on a lavish show, which combines choreographic artistry with more than a touch of eroticism.

The Moulin Rouge is even more famous – the home of the Can Can, portrayed by Toulouse-Lautrec during the Gay Nineties.

And the Crazy Horse proves that striptease can be both erotic and skilful, and can excite men and women alike.

The new centre of Paris nightlife is Les Halles, which until the 1970s was the city's celebrated meat market. Like London's Covent Garden, Les Halles has become extremely fashionable, with cafés, bars, restaurants and nightclubs radiating outwards from the centre. Prostitutes are not difficult to spot, but commercial sex is not the lure that it is in some other

European cities. It is simply part of the vivid scene and is certainly not the focal point of the city.

AMSTERDAM

Amsterdam is a different proposition. Like Paris it is a beautiful city, although on a much smaller scale. The citizens are mainly affluent and middle-class, and the city houses some of the world's finest art treasures. Yet for the past decade, this city of gabled town houses and tranquil canals has 'enjoyed' a reputation for sex that is unrivalled in Europe.

SEX ON STAGE

The Dutch have a great reputation for tolerance and friendliness, and even the briefest excursion into Amsterdam's red-light district – on the other side of

Parisian cabarets are renowned for their erotic, sensuous and agile dancers. The shows are a feast for the eye, lavishly produced and enjoyed by both men and women.

the square fronting the railway station – confirms it.

The quality of live shows can vary as much as the quality of ordinary cabarets or striptease acts – and so can the price. The atmosphere can be almost genteel, the sets and lighting sophisticated and the performers beautiful and highly imaginative in their routines. Or it can be a sleazy dive with minimal comfort and staging, where heavy-breathing men with rapt expressions lick their lips at the sight of two bored people fornicating joylessly only a few feet away from them.

The better live shows attract a great many couples who are there out of curiosity and for harmless titillation. Some clubs even encourage audience participation – and it is quite astonishing how the mood of sexual abandon can melt normal inhibitions and create a relaxed atmosphere.

WINDOW SHOPPING

Live shows apart, there is a quite picturesque quality to prostitution in Amsterdam. In the jumble of tiny streets criss-crossing the red-light district, front rooms at pavement level are given over to prostitutes. The girls, many of them young and beautiful and often Indonesian, sit in chairs by the window or lounge provocatively across the single bed which, with the chair, is the sole furnishing of the minute room. The lighting is usually soft and alluring, and the girls, wearing sexy lingerie, are quick to smile and beckon in the idle 'window-shopper'.

As prostitution goes, it is an attractive system, and because the girls using the rooms are registered and regularly examined for veneral diseases it may be considered to be comparatively safe – sex with the street girls, however, is not.

The morality of prostitution can be argued, but not the medical facts of venereal disease. No man should ever fool himself into thinking that it is truly safe to use a prostitute – however tempting it may be.

HAMBURG

Amsterdam's closest rival in Europe as a centre of commercial sex is Hamburg. This prosperous north German seaport, middle-class and utterly respectable for the most part, boasts the most notorious street of shame in the world – the Reeperbahn.

Hamburg natives tend to give the Reeperbahn and the surrounding seedy district of St Pauli a wide berth, but it is undeniably their top tourist attraction.

While the Berlin of the 1920s and early '30s had a deserved reputation for decadence, today's Reeperbahn in Hamburg is better described as tawdry. Brothels, massage parlours, blue movie houses, peep shows and live shows abound – and so do clip artists who are expert at separating a fool from his money.

Live shows are the big trap. They advertise free entrance and cheap beer (about local pub prices or even less), and while a moment's thought would make any sensible person wary of such a 'bargain', smooth-talking touts are there to allay any suspicions.

So the 'customer' is drawn inside. He heads for the bar and orders a beer, for which the bartender refuses immediate payment – you pay at the end, which is normal procedure in German bars.

COSTLY COMPANY

The trouble is, one of a number of young ladies sitting around the club will soon join him, and however strong his determination not to get involved, there really is no way to avoid buying her a drink. And why not, when drinks are so obviously cheap?

Rather, beer is cheap. The girl will order white wine, but then white wine is as common as beer in Germany and not at all expensive – or so he thinks.

While constantly engaging the beer-sipping tourist in conversation (about his home, his business, his wife, his need to relax – all the usual clip-joint patter), she drinks her wine quite quickly, and tries to persuade him to help her finish the bottle and start on another.

The wine will be the most expensive he has ever bought in his life – perhaps 100 times the price of his glass of beer. He may be angry as well as embarrassed, but he will pay – credit cards are welcome, and probably necessary.

ROMAN HOLIDAY

It is almost unheard of for women to pay men for sex, for an obvious reason. A woman who desires casual sex, even sex with a stranger in a strange place, has little difficulty in getting it. She simply has to make herself available – the world is full of men eager to gratify her.

Perhaps nowhere is this so blatantly obvious as it is in Rome, the eternal city. Young and not-so-young Roman males wish to perpetuate the myth of the Latin

Whatever the city you happen to be in, the red-light zones are easy to spot. They are usually in areas where flashing neon lights beckon the visitor.

The quality of live shows in Hamburg and Amsterdam varies greatly, ranging from sleazy, straightforward sex on stage, to less blatant shows which simply aim to titillate.

lover, and female visitors can expect to receive their special attentions.

Bottom-pinching and whistling and the like may strike most women as a distinct turn off, but the truth is that the handsome Italians who cruise the Via Veneto are in the habit of succeeding with foreign women. They rate unaccompanied Swedish and Danish girls a near certainty – with the English not far behind.

NEW YORK

Where Paris is chic, subtle as well as worldly, New York is brazen – even strident.

Natives of 'the Big Apple' never doubt for a moment that theirs is the most exciting city in the world, and many visitors readily agree.

With the variety and pace of New York life, it is not surprising to find that the sense of urgency, the determination to 'get it now' has a powerful influence on the New York sex scene.

As a bustling, hustling metropolis and a seaport, New York has its fair share of prostitutes – and porn shops, blue movies, massage parlours and the rest. But the fear of herpes and terror of AIDS has spawned a new and highly curious form of commercial sex.

TELEPHONE SEX

Incredible though it may seem, there is an increasing trade in dirty telephone calls.

The client simply phones up a number, agrees a price, gives over a credit card number, and the woman on the other end of the phone then carries on whatever sort of obscene conversation he requires to achieve orgasm.

New York's best-known contribution to the sexual revolution, however, has been the singles bar.

These popular drinking and eating establishments, specifically catering for single men and women in search of a partner sprang up during the 1970s, and are now an established and accepted part of New York life.

The customers tend to be young, professional people who work hard, play hard and are impatient of traditional dating and mating patterns.

Prospective partners chat each other up and may well be in search of something more than a one-night stand, but the basic question of 'your place or mine?' is never far from the surface.

GROUP GROPE

Another New York innovation, although it is now widespread, was the establishment of clubs for group sex – the commercially run orgy.

The most celebrated of these was Plato's Retreat, a plush pleasure palace for swinging couples – and couples only, to exclude prostitutes and to keep the sexual balance right.

The scene is easy enough to imagine – bars, saunas, blue movies and rooms given over entirely to copulation. For some, this is a fantasy made flesh, and for women every bit as much as men. Perhaps more so, for women do not suffer from the severe restriction on sexual performance caused by orgasm that men do.

Under these circumstances a woman who really wants to let herself go can enjoy sex to the very limit of her physical endurance. There have been many reports of women claiming 30 or more lovers in a single session.

RIO DE JANEIRO

Several thousand miles south of New York lies Rio de Janeiro – fleshy, dangerous and every bit as highly sexed as the swaying rhythms of the all-pervasive samba music.

Every February, the city explodes in a riot of sensual self-indulgence during Carnival. But the Brazilians do not need that excuse to indulge in sexual mayhem. Unlike most 'sin cities', where tourism is the cornerstone of the sex industry, Rio's seems more an expression of the life-style of its inhabitants.

BANGKOK

The friendly face of commercial sex is even more remarkable in southeast Asia. Bangkok, in particular, can lay fair claim to being the sex capital of the world.

Carnival-time in Rio de Janeiro is recognized as a time when everyone 'lets their hair down'. Uninhibited, topless dancers are one of the attractions.

Prostitutes in Bangkok are well known for being relaxed and friendly, as well as being good lovers. Here, earning money as a prostitute does not carry the taboos and prejudices it does in the West.

The American involvement in Vietnam had a profound effect on the lovely old Thai capital. War-weary GIs flooded into Bangkok for what was officially called R&R (rest and recuperation). They found the Thais more than willing to provide for their needs – discos, clubs, saunas, everything a soldier on leave wants to find – particularly girls.

Thai women have long been noted for their delicate beauty, and they have earned a reputation for pleasing men.

It would seem that the willingness, the enthusiasm, the genuine charm displayed by the girls of Bangkok stems from the fact that they do not see themselves as despised outcasts from normal, respectable society.

Most of them are peasant girls from the impoverished northeast of the country, and by selling their favours in the bars, discos and massage parlours of Bangkok they are able to make a huge contribution to their families back home.

This sense of virtue weighs heavily against the dubious means of achieving it, and they are therefore free to ply their trade with pride and pleasure.

There are two centres of nightlife in Bangkok – Patpong and Soi Cowboy. In both, a typical bar will serve drinks at a reasonable price, while 20 or 30 bikini-clad girls mingle freely with the customers. They are all registered (and therefore receive regular medical check-ups), and they come across as seductively friendly rather than as pushy.

The famed massage parlours are staffed by similar smiling beauties, only too happy to transform a relaxing body massage into an erotic dream come true.

To come back to the original question, then, romance and sex are where you find them, whether 'playing' at home or abroad. For this most personal of pleasures, the rules are your own.

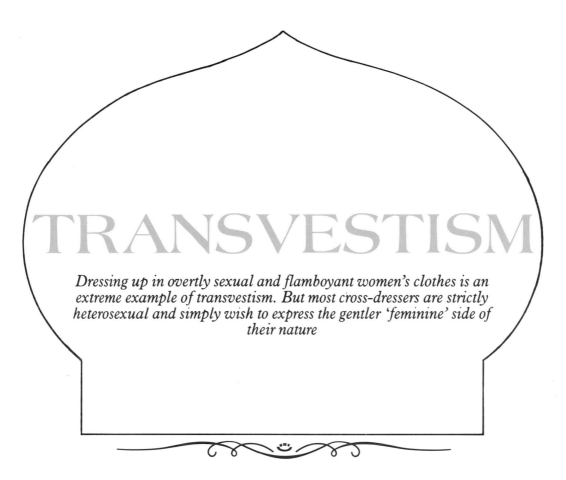

TRANSVESTISM

Dressing up in overtly sexual and flamboyant women's clothes is an extreme example of transvestism. But most cross-dressers are strictly heterosexual and simply wish to express the gentler 'feminine' side of their nature

Transvestism is not just the casual cross-dressing seen at a fancy dress party. It is felt as a deep need – offering some form of emotional or sexual satisfaction. Without being able to dress in the clothes of the opposite sex from time to time, a transvestite will feel that something very important is missing in his or her life.

AN ESCAPE TO FEMININITY

Although transvestism can in theory be found in both men and women, in western culture it is much more commonly found in men. This may be partly because women have a greater flexibility in what they can wear – jeans and trousers are today conventional attire for women. But there are still strong prohibitions against men wearing dresses. And it is likely that this very prohibition makes cross-dressing important to some men.

Men are often made to feel that they must live up to many expectations – of achievement, assertiveness, dominance, aggression, prowess – and for some men this is too much to bear. So transvestism becomes an 'escape to femininity'.

TYPES OF TRANSVESTISM

There are at least two distinctively different types of transvestism for a man – the fetishistic and the femiphilic. In the first case, the clothes become a desirable object – simply wearing a pair of panties or a bra can induce an orgasm.

But sometimes the man gains pleasure from being able to express a more gentle, sensuous or feminine side of himself. It is the love of the feminine – or femiphilia.

Transvestites are commonly men who, while happy to be masculine for part of their life, also want to express a more feminine side occasionally. They develop an alternative feminine personality. It has been said that tranvestites have two names, two personalities and two wardrobes.

BECOMING A TRANSVESTITE

What makes a person a transvestite? There is very little evidence for any genetic or hormonal abnormalities in transvestites, so most explanations stress significant family childhood experiences coupled with social learning later in life.

Some psychiatrists suggest that transvestism occurs as a result of a boy's experiences with his family – a dominating or hostile mother, an absent or weak father, or an older sister who forces him to wear her clothes.

A traumatic experience may set up lifelong – but unconscious – feelings in the little boy, by which dressing comes to symbolize either his hostility for his mother or his love for her – or even the masochistic feelings he felt when being forced by his sister to wear dresses. But these theories are often very complex, and there is little agreement on them – even among psychiatrists.

Much more simple (and probably more accurate) are those theories which suggest that a simple child-hood experimentation with dress – trying on your sister's panties, putting on some lipstick, masturbating with a smooth material, walking around in high heels –

is found to be enjoyable in itself. The desire to repeat the experience just flows from the amount of pleasure derived from 'dressing up'.

A DOMINANT PATTERN OF BEHAVIOUR

Many transvestites talk about how such experiences first happened in childhood, and how their desires were strong well before puberty. The desires become stronger and stronger as they go through life. Typically, the desire will raise a number of problems – which in turn tend to make their transvestism more and more important to them. It can easily become the dominant preoccupation of a person's life.

THE PROBLEMS

Being a transvestite can be emotionally exacting, as well as presenting more practical problems to be overcome. The type of problems with which transvestites are confronted include the following:

Secrecy From his earliest experiences, a transvestite will typically not tell anyone about his desires and will have to find furtive, solitary moments to practise his 'hobby'. Because it is usually such a secretive act, it is hard to estimate how prevalent transvestism is (although experts believe it is found in less than one per cent of the population).

In one study of 504 transvestites in the United States, some 50 per cent of the men said that they kept their transvestism entirely secret.

Other men may be 'caught out' by wives who have found their dresses crumpled and have become suspicious. And others may actually tell their wives in the hope that they may practise more openly in the house and, as happens in a few cases, have their full approval. But even in such instances, 'coming out' is usually preceded by a long period of secrecy.

Guilt Few transvestites actually want to put a stop to their transvestism, but most spend some time having to cope with feelings of guilt. They may, for example, spend years building up a 'secret wardrobe' – only to destroy it later in a fit of shame. Sixty seven per cent of men in the United States study had destroyed their wardrobe at some time.

Access to clothes In childhood the most common solution is to 'borrow' clothes from a sister or mother. By adulthood it is not uncommon for the transvestite to engage in clothes-line theft.

Frequently, a wife's wardrobe is the object of desire, but often he wants to obtain his own clothes – perhaps of a special material or design.

Some may, over time, develop the confidence to simply enter a retail store and act as if they are buying a gift for their wife.

Alternatively, it may be easier to purchase clothes by mail-order (some firms specialize in transvestite interests). But even here there may still be problems – for example, explaining to others what is in the parcel when it arrives in the post.

Carnival time in Rio is a time when people can dress in outrageous costumes and parade the streets. Men can dress in women's clothes and be accepted. For many transvestites, this is not possible.

THE TRANSVESTITE COMMUNITY

Although it is neither as large nor as well organized as the gay community, there does exist a transvestite community – which publishes magazines, arranges meetings and generally provides support and guidance.

In Los Angeles, a leading transvestite representative – Dr Virginia Prince – established the transvestite journal, *Tranvestia*, in January 1960.

Virginia Prince – born Charles Prince – is a research chemist and is unusual in that he spends all his time dressed as a woman, but has no desire for sex surgery. He has written a number of 'advice' books on transvestism, and has helped initiate transvestite groups across America and around the world.

THE BEAUMONT SOCIETY

In England, the Beaumont Society was formed in 1965 and is primarily aimed at non-fetishistic heterosexual cross-dressers. It is not opposed to fetishistic kinds of transvestite experience, but believes it is easier and clearer for the membership to cater for one specific group.

Since it was formed, it has attracted a membership of more than 2,000 people, and is organized on a regional basis. As well as holding local meetings (where members can cross-dress), it produces a regular magazine which contains fiction about transvestites,

Cross-dressing is found in most societies and cultures of the world. This transvestite comes from Bombay, India.

advice on cross-dressing and more general studies of the transvestite experience. It aims clearly to dissociate itself from pornographic intent.

TRANSVESTITE EROTICA

In contrast, there are also a number of magazines which specialize in transvestite erotica. Here, elements of fetishism and sado-masochism merge. The stories and photographs very frequently describe a man being forced to wear 'special' clothes (for example, a child's dress, a rubber dress, or a nurse's outfit) by a dominant woman.

RADICAL TRANSVESTISM

During the 1970s a number of new groups developed around both transvestism and trans-sexualism. Some of these were breakaway groups from the Gay Liberation Movement and others emerged in opposition to the more conformist Beaumont Society.

They argued that transvestism was a radical act which challenged society's conventions. They thought that when men opted to wear women's clothes, they were challenging the way society dictated male and female roles.

Many feminists disagreed with this opinion. Far from improving the woman's lot, they saw transvestites

DID YOU KNOW?
The term transvestism to describe the desire to wear the clothes of the opposite sex was coincd by the German sexologist Magnus Hirschfeld in 1910. Much less commonly, transvestism is also referred to by the term eonism, after an 18th-century Frenchman (right), the Chevalier d'Eon de Beaumont — who spent part of his life living as a woman and acting as a spy. Nowadays, scientists refer to it as 'gender dysphoria'.

as mocking the feminine – from the safety of really being men, transvestites were simply playing at stereotypical versions of being a woman.

There are many different ways in which a transvestite may dress up. With the exception of some of the fetishists who may seek special uniforms (such as nurses' uniforms), materials (such as rubber) or garments (such as corsets), the majority of transvestites seem to want to dress just like ordinary women.

DRESSING UP IN PUBLIC

Often, dressing in women's clothes may be linked to a desire to be able to go into public places – and pass as a woman. Obviously, outlandish garb would be too conspicuous. The study of 504 transvestites in the United States found that 34 per cent went out in public dressed as women – to restaurants, shops or meetings. The enjoyment for some transvestites does seem to be linked to passing as a woman in public.

For some, pleasure comes from being with other transvestites – there is a desire to see and be seen. 'Drag Balls' tend to be more common in the gay world – but for the heterosexual, transvestite meetings held by organizations such as the Beaumont Society provide situations where the transvestite can dress and relax in the company of like-minded people.

IN THE HOME

For most, transvestism is restricted to the privacy of their home. If the wife has come to an understanding of transvestism, she may be happy to sit with her 'dressed' husband just watching television or reading. In this situation, the transvestite's pleasure lies not simply in dressing up as a woman for a while, but also in being accepted by another woman.

Secrecy is a key issue for others. They may have to plan their lives very carefully – a separate 'study' where they can lock the door and dress for an hour on their own, a separate bed where they can furtively wear the chosen garments some nights, a stolen half-hour while their wife goes shopping. Sometimes pleasure can be enhanced in these circumstances by the danger of 'being discovered'.

ARE TRANSVESTITES ABNORMAL?

When the phenomenon of transvestism was first considered in modern society, it was seen by doctors as some sort of abnormality or perversion. But most of the more recent studies that have compared transvestites with a wider sample of men have found few differences – there are few signs of their being in any way abnormal.

One study conducted on 269 members of the Beaumont Society has suggested that transvestites may be more socially reserved and slightly more emotional than the general population. Another study suggested that they were above average in intelligence.

Above *'Drag artistes' are immensely popular entertainers. Their act is played 'tongue in cheek' – they are heavily made-up and wear flamboyant women's clothes.*

Top *For many transvestites, going out in public dressed as a woman is a necessary step to take, as well as an enjoyable one.*

There is little or no evidence of transvestism being an illness. Nevertheless, because people often have very little direct contact with transvestism, they may fear it and believe it to be a disorder.

Some people believe that transvestites are violent people, because of the way they have been portrayed in some fictional films such as *Psycho*. This image is far from realistic, and has nothing to do with true transvestism.

A HARMLESS HOBBY?

It may be best to view transvestism as a type of hobby – a special fascination with items of female dress. Like all hobbies it will require a degree of expertise (in dressing), regular contact with other hobbyists (through organizations) and a fair degree of free time to allocate to it. It can cause problems if carried to extremes, but in general, like most hobbies, it is a fairly harmless, specialized form of pleasure.

CROSS-DRESSING

The act of wearing the clothes of the opposite sex embraces a wide range of experiences. Although they often overlap, there are three main motivations – theatrical, erotic and gender-linked.

THEATRICAL CROSS-DRESSING

It is only since the 17th century that women have been allowed on stage. Prior to that, men would usually play any female roles.

This tradition lives on today in a few boys' schools – where the boys play all the roles – and in the famous 'panto dames'. Cross-dressing is also a popular form of entertainment, and many pubs and clubs employ 'Drag Artistes' who attract large crowds.

EROTIC CROSS-DRESSING

Clothing is worn close to the body and often becomes highly erotic in itself. Many men (it is much less common with women) are 'turned on' by women's clothes – both individual items (such as shoes, skirts, stockings, panties) and whole outfits. Usually, the enjoyment in wearing such clothes causes an erection, and masturbation is very common. For some men the act of intercourse is greatly enhanced if their partner will allow them to wear women's clothes during it. Since the clothes become a sexual fetish, this is often called fetishistic cross-dressing.

Erotic cross-dressing can be linked to many other sexual practices. For some men, there is a desire to be forced to dress in women's clothes and to experience some humiliation – often at the hands of a strong woman (sado-masochistic cross-dressing).

For others, sexual gratification is only possible if they are observed by others when cross-dressed.

MYTHS OF TRANSVESTISM

Transvestism is known to assume many different forms. And this complexity has given rise to a wealth of myths and misconceptions. The truth is, transvestism . . .

☐ has no particular connection with homosexuality – most transvestites are heterosexual, and most marry and have children. In one study of 262 transvestites, 74 per cent were married and 69 per cent had fathered children. In this same study, the rate of homosexuality was less than that for the population as a whole

☐ does not at all imply effeminacy – most transvestites are fairly masculine in their manners until they 'dress'

☐ is not the same as trans-sexualism. The typical transvestite has no desire to change sex physically – and only wants to feel like the opposite gender for specific periods. Trans-sexuals, in contrast, feel they have been born with the wrong body and that they really are the opposite sex. Unlike transvestites, they will actively seek sex-change surgery. Being dressed as the opposite sex is only a small (social) part of being the opposite sex

☐ is not connected to hermaphroditism. The hermaphrodite possesses the gonads of both sexes – ovaries and womb, testicles and sperm – and hermaphroditism is an extremely rare condition

☐ may be linked to other sexual variations, but it may also exist on its own. In some transvestism, masochism may play a role – a desire, for example, to be bullied into a female role or dressed as a maid. In some transvestism, exhibitionism may play a role – there is a desire to dress up and pass as a woman in public.

GENDER-LINKED CROSS-DRESSING

The motive behind much cross-dressing is the desire to experience the world of the opposite sex. Once more it is usually a male experience. A typical case is one in which the cross-dresser is fully aware that he is a man and wants to remain a man, yet loves the feminine and at times wants to dress up and feel like a woman. He feels more at peace, and more comfortable in the clothes of a woman. For periods he can leave behind the stresses and strains of his usual male role and enter a feminine one which he regards as being more relaxed. This type of cross-dressing is the most usual form of transvestism.

A SPECTRUM OF TASTES

This type of cross-dressing also comes in many forms, ranging from those men who may just want to 'dress' on special occasions, to the man who wants to wear women's clothes all of the time but who nevertheless is not interested in changing sex.

SEX
AND MAGIC

To practising witches, the ultimate act of worship is the sexual union between man and woman, and although driven underground by Church and State, sexual magic has survived to the present day

Completely naked, blindfold and loosely bound hand and foot, the potential candidate wishing to be initiated into a witch coven enters a traditional ceremony of purification and acceptance into the cult.

The initiator will bestow upon him or her the fivefold kiss – beginning with the feet and working up the body, kissing the knees, the genitals, the breasts and the lips. Then, kneeling at the altar – still unable to see or move freely – the candidate may be ritually flagellated.

Solemn vows are then taken and an oath of allegiance sworn before all the members of the group, or coven. Feet and eyes finally unbound, the new initiate is anointed with oil and wine and kissed again as a mark of his or her new-found faith.

THE ORIGINS OF WITCHCRAFT

Witches worship twin deities, the god and goddess who are known by many names, but basically represent the potent forces of the male and female, and the union of opposites.

In prehistoric times, the earth as provider of crops and animals, and therefore of continuing life, became gradually worshipped as the great and fertile earth mother. She was always depicted as a pregnant woman, her breasts huge and heavy and her stomach full and swelling.

Her consort, sometimes known as The Horned One, as he often wore a headdress made of antlers, was equally vital in appearance, and usually had an erect penis.

THE SEARCH FOR FERTILITY

One concern of early societies was the encouragement of fertility, and to this end various rituals and sacrifices were performed. A form of sympathetic magic developed where men and women would go out into the fields to have intercourse, believing their union would encourage the union of the earth mother with her lover. Their offspring would be the crops to be harvested the following season.

SEX AS WORSHIP

Sex magic cults have always regarded the act of sexual intercourse as an act of worship celebrating both human and divine creativity and this belief is still held nowadays by witches throughout the world.

Britain and northern Europe are dotted with numerous ancient sites and places formerly sacred to the old nature religions. Centuries ago, when the countryside was less populated than it is now, it was far easier for a group of like-minded people to meet in such a place. Many accounts exist of these gatherings in honour of the old gods, and it is possible to form a clear picture of what actually took place at a sabbat, or witches' meeting.

The popular image of witches flying on broomsticks is derived from the witches' use of ointments containing narcotics. These created the impression of flying, and the broomsticks symbolize a penis.

THE SABBAT

A large bonfire would be lit in some lonely and secluded place. There would be cakes and wine and dancing. Witches were usually naked, or 'sky clad', as they danced around the leaping flames in a circle. Sometimes they would anoint themselves with special ointments containing hallucinogenic substances which gave them the sensation of flying freely through the night air.

The culmination of the dance was 'the Marriage of Heaven and Earth' – the ceremonial lovemaking of the high priest and priestess. The men and women of the coven would then follow, their sexual relationship being an outward sign of veneration to the gods of life.

In some covens, possibly those without a sufficient number of men, the high priest was expected to couple with all the women present. He usually had to resort to some kind of dildo, or false penis, to achieve this feat of sexual prowess, as there might be as many as twenty women present. This probably accounts for the old stories, mostly acquired under torture, of the devil's penis being cold and extremely hard.

AMULETS AND TALISMANS

Sex in a magical context is believed to release a special power which may be put to use in creating a talisman, or fuelling a ritual with enough strength to achieve the desired result.

One such ritual, designed to create a powerful amulet, involved a mock chase between a couple. They would dance seven times around the base of a large tree by the light of the full moon. The woman pretended to be trying to escape, but on the seventh round of the dance, she would allow him to catch her. They would then make love beneath the tree. At the climax of this rite, a leaf was picked from the tree and moistened with the mingled sexual fluids inside the woman's vagina.

OLD LEGENDS – MODERN MYTHS

Some of the old beliefs connected with ancient sites survive to the present day. The Rollright Stones near Long Compton, Oxfordshire were believed to be able to cure barrenness in a woman. She must go on the night of the full moon to the stone circle and take off her clothes, dance three times around the stones and then embrace the King Stone in such a way that its shadow covered her naked body.

This stone stands outside the circle and is approximately nine feet high. The symbolism of the circle and upright stone is clearly sexual – the stone an erect penis and the circle the vagina.

The great pre-historic giant carved into the chalk hillside at Cerne Abbas, Dorset is far more obviously sexual – his penis is visible for miles. He too has a reputation for curing barrenness. A childless couple wishing to conceive should spend the night lying together between the giant's legs. It was believed that conception was then certain to take place. This practice has continued well into recent years, even at the risk of pneumonia.

WITCHCRAFT AND CHRISTIANITY

As the Christian Church became more firmly established during the Middle Ages, it absorbed many of the old pagan festivals into its own calendar, and even built churches on the sites of ancient temples. When the altar in Notre Dame Cathedral, Paris, was repaired at the end of the 18th century, an altar dedicated to the Horned God was discovered beneath the Christian structure. The original workmen had obviously not dared to destroy it.

Throughout Europe from the 14th century until well into the 18th century, witches were hunted down, tortured and often burned to death by zealots.

The 42-metre-tall, 2,000-year-old Cerne Abbas giant carved into a chalk hill in Dorset, Southern England still carries the reputation of curing infertility.

Madame de Montespan was the mistress of King Louis XIV of France. She is known to have taken part in a black magic ceremony, that included a human sacrifice, to retain the favour of the king. She was later arrested, but released, for her part in the ceremony.

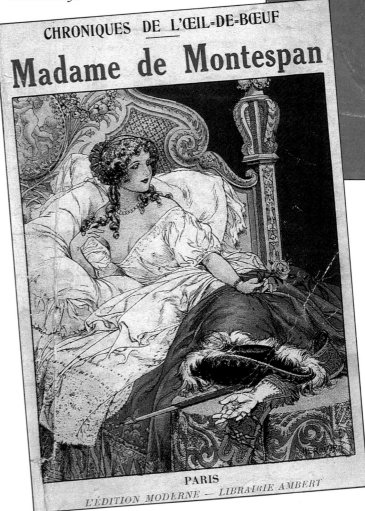

CHRONIQUES DE L'ŒIL-DE-BŒUF

Madame de Montespan

PARIS
L'ÉDITION MODERNE – LIBRAIRIE AMBERT

This history of persecution began seriously in 1484, when two Dominican monks were appointed official inquisitors for Germany by the Pope. Father Jacob Sprenger and Father Heinrich Kramer had written what has come to be one of the most famous manuals for witch hunters, the *Malleus Maleficarum* or 'the hammer of the evil-doers'.

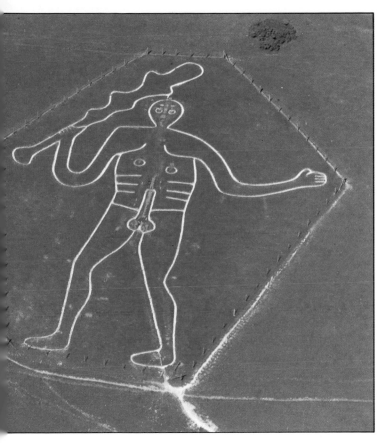

large amounts of money and ambitious desires, she offered initiation into her coven.

In the garden of her large house in a Paris suburb, she had a temple dedicated to Ashtaroth, the goddess, and Asmodeus, the horned god. Black drapes shrouded the walls and the altar, which had a mattress beneath the cloth. Black candles provided the final touch. Assisted by a Catholic priest, La Voisine appealed to the old gods on behalf of her well-to-do clients.

Athenais, the Marquise de Montespan, sought her help when she desired to become the mistress of King Louis XIV. And later, as her physical beauty faded, she underwent an expensive, horrific, and desperate ceremony in the hope that it would revive the king's flagging sexual interest in her.

Arriving late on a cold January night, Madame de Montespan made her way to the private temple in the grounds. Stripped naked, she lay upon the black altar with her legs hanging over the edge so that her vagina was completely exposed. Arms outstretched, she held a lighted black candle in each hand.

The priest took his place at the altar, standing between her parted knees. His robe was embroidered with pine cones – a fertility symbol representing the tip of a penis, and sacred to the horned god. Consecrating the host in the name of Asmodeus, god of sexual potency, he inserted the wafer between the lips of Madame de Montespan's vagina.

HUMAN SACRIFICE

On this occasion a human sacrifice took place, although usually it was a pair of white doves. Standing on the woman's stomach was a chalice which was filled with the sacrificial blood. The priest removed the wafer and the chalice which he handed to his assistant, before lifting his skirts and penetrating the Marquise. He prayed until he reached orgasm, then annointed both of them with the blood. After the ceremony Madame de Montespan left with the consecrated wafer, and some of the blood to mix into the king's food.

Her position at court as official mistress remained secure, and she and the king continued to occupy adjoining suites at Versailles. But the following year La Voisine, and others, were arrested and tortured.

Eventually, the involvement of the king's mistress was discovered, along with the names of many other aristocrats. Louis personally destroyed all documents mentioning Madame de Montespan, unaware that the Paris police had kept file copies. She was not prosecuted, but not surprisingly, the king completely avoided her company and replaced her with a woman known to be a devout Christian.

RASPUTIN – THE MAD MONK

Both male and female witches are reputed to have been able to make themselves sexually irresistible, and to have wielded considerable power of fascination over the opposite sex. Russian mystic and visionary Grigori

In this book they set out questions to be asked and degrees of torture to be applied to those suspected of practising witchcraft. Thousands of men and women were to suffer horribly as a result, but the Inquisition succeeded only in driving witchcraft underground. The two priests, who were presumably celibate, concluded that 'all witchcraft comes from carnal lust which is in women insatiable'.

THE BLACK MASS

The Black Mass, a favourite theme of occult novels and horror films, bears little or no relation to true witchcraft, but is an altered form of the Catholic Mass and must be performed by a priest if it is to be considered effective. It is a grotesque mixture of conventional Christian ceremony with sexual elements borrowed from earlier religions.

A number of accounts exist, one of the best-known being that of the activities of a 17th-century coven in Paris, presided over by Catherine Deshayes, or La Voisine as she was known.

A young widow with one daughter, La Voisin had built up a reputation among the wealthy aristocratic ladies of Paris. She sold beauty preparations, and was considered to be a reliable fortune-teller. Her knowledge of herbs also meant that she could supply aphrodisiacs, and concoctions to procure abortions. She was even rumoured to be able to rid wives of unwanted husbands, including her own. For those with

Rasputin had extraordinary charisma, despite his rather alarming and unattractive appearance.

A wandering life as a holy man and healer had led him to the Russian capital of St Petersburg, where he was presented to Tsar Nicholas. The Tsar's two-year-old son suffered from haemophilia – a condition in which even the slightest injury causes unstoppable bleeding. Somehow Rasputin was able to stop the bleeding, where all the Tsar's doctors had failed.

Secure in the protection of the court, Rasputin took an apartment in St Petersburg, where he received an endless stream of people who sought his help.

Many of his visitors were women, who found themselves mysteriously unable to resist his hypnotic gaze or his sexual advances. Rumour had it that even the Tsarina had submitted, and her closest friend undoubtedly had an affair with him. Various accounts of his murder in 1917 all indicate that more than one method was needed to kill him – his remarkable vitality seems to have been with him until the bitter end.

ALEISTER CROWLEY

Another notorious figure in the history of sex and magic is 'The Great Beast' – flamboyant magician Aleister Crowley. Nicknamed 'The Wickedest Man in the World' by the popular press of the day, his experiments with ritual sex involved a bizarre selection of partners of both sexes.

Drug-taking was often part of the proceedings. With his strange sense of humour, and philosophy of 'Do What Thou Wilt', he revelled in the adverse publicity, and did nothing to discourage wild tales of human sacrifice and other unimaginable depravities.

Many of these lurid events were supposed to have taken place at the Abbey of Thelema, his rented villa in Sicily where Crowley had decorated the walls with explicit erotic murals.

Magica Sexualis – the branch of magic which uses sex as a part of the ceremony – has always taught that sex has three functions: reproduction, enjoyment and the exchange of some kind of vital energy usually, but not always, at the point of orgasm. For this to take place both partners must be in tune with each other so that the exchange becomes both harmonious and powerful.

According to his writings, Crowley used most sexual variations as part of his magical rituals, but often hired prostitutes for the purpose and so did not strictly adhere to the old teachings.

He seems to have been especially fond of anal sex with either male or female assistants, and also masturbated frequently. Despite his addiction to heroin in later years, he lived to be 72. He died in relative obscurity in 1947.

THE CHURCH OF SATAN

In 1966, almost 20 years after Crowley's death, The Church of Satan was officially incorporated in San Francisco, California. Its leader is former police

Grigori Rasputin enjoyed a considerable reputation as healer, mystic and visionary in 19th-century St Petersburg. His magical qualities and hypnotic gaze also seem to have made him irresistible to women. His reputation was enhanced by his survival of several attempts on his life, until his murder in 1917.

photographer Anton La Vey. Believed to be based on, and inspired by, Crowley's philosophy, the gratification of the senses and the exaltation of sexuality and carnal pleasure are central to the beliefs and teachings of this group.

Hollywood film star Jayne Mansfield was attracted by their ideas, which closely mirrored her own. At this point in her life she was with her third husband, drinking heavily and taking drugs in a vain attempt to relieve the inevitable pressures of a star's life-style. Her initial success, which owed a good deal to her voluptuous figure, was over, and she was earning her living by public appearances and as a nightclub cabaret act.

The secret Friday meetings of the Church of Satan provided her with another outlet for her frustrations. At the centre of these rituals the body of a naked woman provided the altar. Possibly she sometimes took this role as a member of the favoured inner circle of weekly worshippers.

TRAGIC END

The following year Jayne was killed when her head was completely sliced off in a tragic road accident. At

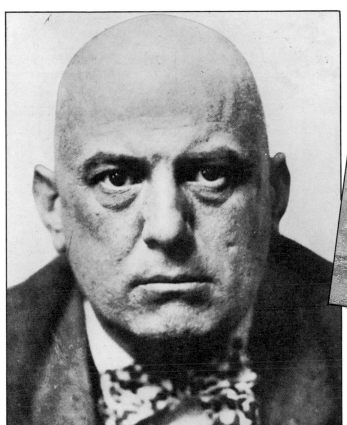

Aleister Crowley (left), enjoyed notoriety as the high priest of sexual magic during the 20th century. He performed some ceremonies at his rented villa in Sicily and painted the walls with symbolic erotic murals (below).

Crowley channelled his artistic talent into the black magic field. This is his design for the devil card in the Tarot pack.

about the same time, Anton La Vey appeared as the Devil in Roman Polanski's film *Rosemary's Baby*, a story of a devil-worshipping cult in modern Manhattan.

Widespread changes in public opinion towards the occult, and the repeal in 1951 of the last of the British Witchcraft Acts, has meant that after centuries of secrecy witchcraft has at last begun to emerge into the open. Practising witches have openly acknowledged their faith on television and radio, risking only ridicule, not death or imprisonment.

LOVE SPELLS

Magical help in matters of love and sex has long been sought by both men and women. Many old love philtres and potions which were intended to inflame the object of affections consisted of unpleasant, if not even dangerous, ingredients.

☐ A modern West Indian love spell involves boiling a pair of knickers which you have worn. Some of this water is then used to make a drink for the man you wish to become your lover. Apparently he will be powerless to resist you after he has consumed it.

☐ A very old belief still existing in parts of Greece states that if you can manage to spit into the mouth of the one you wish to enslave, they will be yours forever.

☐ To discover the face of their future husband, Greek girls take a square of blue silk and, on the night of the full moon, float the square on a still pool of water where the moon is reflected. A man's face is supposed to appear upon the fabric.

☐ A comparable English practice suggests taking a candle, and sitting alone in front of a mirror eating an apple. The face of your future husband will then appear peeping over your shoulder.

☐ Ancient advice on the Art of Fascination, or seduction, is extremely practical. The three basic steps to follow are:
1 Fix the object of your lust intently with your gaze.
2 Touch him, or her, with your hands.
3 Breathe on him.

☐ An ancient witchcraft manuscript gives the following description of how to use your eyes:

'For when your eyes be reciprocally bent one upon the other and are joined beams to beams, the lights to lights, then the spirit of one is joined to the spirit of the other and strong ligations made and most violent love is only stirred up with a sudden looking on, as it were, with a Darting Look, or piercing into the very inmost of the heart . . .'

☐ The idea of giving some form of gift to the prospective lover is also very common. This ritual was used by a male witch, or warlock. He would obtain a pretty hand-mirror, and then somehow contrive to catch a reflection in it of two dogs copulating. An added difficulty was that this had to be on a Thursday at 8 am, 3 pm or 10 pm, while forcefully uttering this charm:

'I the dog and she the bitch,
I the helve and she the axe,
I the cock, and she the hen.
As my will, so mote it be!'

The looking glass was then presented as a gift to the object of his lust. Once she had looked into it she would be consumed with desire.

☐ A much simpler spell employed an apple:

'Write on an apple before it fall from the tree, Aleo, Deleo, Delato, and say, I conjure thee, that what woman or virgin toucheth and tasteth thee may love me and burn in my love as fire melteth wax.'

☐ One of the strangest of all love charms for men comes from the 16th century.

'Take the tongue of a sparrow and close it in virgin wax under thy clothes for the space of four days, then take it and keep it in thy mouth under the tongue and kiss the woman thou lovest.'

There is no advice as to what to do should she discover this curious object.

A sex magician conjures up his dream woman.

SEX AND THE CINEMA

Explicit scenes of sex such as those in Last Tango in Paris *hit the big screen in the 1970s. But what is the true story of sex and the cinema?*

'Kiss me, my fool' commands Theda Bara menacingly in *A Fool There Was* (1916). Her victim – a married man with a child – virtually disintegrates before our eyes, and the most famous screen 'vamp' of them all has succeeded in destroying yet another man with the power of sex.

Vamps, so called because of their vampire-like behaviour towards men, were extremely popular fantasy figures in the early days of silent cinema. Downtrodden waifs and chaste virginal heroines provided the backdrop for these macabre females.

Theda Bara, born in Cincinnati, was shown in one studio still glowering over a skeleton – presumably that of one of her lovers. And the publicity men invented a suitably mysterious background for her, as the daughter of an Eastern potentate, or of French-Arab descent.

Her name was supposed to be an anagram of 'arab death' – she was man-hungry, world-weary and specialized in the seductive destruction of any man unwise enough to become her lover. She was also safely non-American – implying that only foreigners had what it takes to be truly depraved.

EXCITING TITLES

The titles of some of Theda Bara's films hint at the kind of forbidden thrills in store for the audience – *Sin, Her Double Life, When a Woman Sins, When Men Desire*. Not much beyond kissing was ever seen – merely implied in the lurid advertising. She also played a succession of famous 'femmes fatales' including Cleopatra, Salome, and Carmen.

But erotic exotica was not only for male audiences. Some years later Italian heart-throb Rudolph Valentino's sudden death in 1926 inspired several female fans to commit suicide, and there was mass hysteria at his funeral.

Ironically, off-screen he was a man whose sexual problems and probable homosexuality were kept secret at the time. Yet his smouldering gaze and apparent virility in films such as *Blood and Sand*, or as a passionate Arab in *The Sheik and Son of the Sheik*, made him one of the major romantic idols of the 1920s.

However, the promise of nudity and abandoned behaviour was no guarantee of a big box-office hit. The great director, D W Griffiths, whose melodramatic film of the American Civil War, *Birth of a Nation* (1915), had earned millions of dollars, followed it with *Intolerance* (1916). Subtitled 'Love's Struggle Through The Ages', the film explores the idea of intolerance through four periods of history. But despite a lavish Babylonian orgy scene featuring specially employed nude prostitutes, the film was a commercial failure.

THE HAYS CODE

In response to fears of federal intervention in their affairs, and the growing concern of such bodies as the Legion of Decency, in the 1920s movie moguls invited Republican politician Will Hays to help clean up the industry's tainted image.

Hays, who was president of the Motion Picture Producers and Distributors Association of America, had a spotless personal reputation. He initially drew up a list of guidelines which were to become the Production Code that would be fully implemented by 1934.

MORALITY CLAUSES

At his suggestion, morality clauses were inserted into artists' contracts – attempting through threatened sackings to control or modify their behaviour off screen.

A number of scandals had already rocked Hollywood. Stories abounded of wild parties, orgies and cocaine-inspired excesses. Silent comedian Fatty Arbuckle, for example, had been charged with murder in a sensational case in 1921 involving an actress, possible rape and gallons of bootleg liquor. Prohibition

CINEMA RATINGS

From 1913 all films released in Britain and passed by the British Board of Film Censors carried either a 'U' or 'A' Certificate.

'U' (universal) indicated recommendation for children's performances. 'A' (public) was a guide for parents, but came to mean anyone under 16 had to be accompanied by an adult.

In 1932, 'H' was introduced for horror films, again, as a warning. It was absorbed into 'X' in 1951, limiting audiences to over-16s.

In 1970, British ratings

America was horrified by the salacious details, and although Arbuckle was acquitted his career was in ruins.

But until 1934 there still existed a reasonable amount of freedom in films – especially comedies and musicals. Although intercourse was never depicted, explicitly – it could only be hinted at – semi-nudity and verbal innuendo were standard ingredients of many of the best-known films of the era.

Sexy dress and dialogue were features of 1930s musicals. This dancer from Busby Berkeley's Gold Diggers of 1933 *wears a daring see-through costume.*

In the 1940s, risqué sexual themes such as extra-marital affairs required subtle treatment. Nothing overt is shown in Casablanca, *but the sexual tension between Bergman and Bogart carries the unmistakable message.*

were: 'X' – 18 and over, 'AA' – 14 and over, 'A' – Advisory, and 'U' – universal. Current British ratings are '18', '15', 'PG' (parental guidance), and 'U' (universal).

In the United States, ratings did not appear until 1968, when 'U', 'A' and 'X' were introduced.

American censors cannot ban a film.

Categories in use in the 1980s are: 'G' – general audience, 'PG' – parental guidance advised, 'R' – restricted (under-17s need an accompanying adult), and 'X' – no one under 17 to be admitted.

MUSICAL FANTASY

The first 'talkie' was released in 1927. And sound made the film musical possible. With an economic depression gripping the United States, audiences wanted an escape from harsh reality – glamorous Hollywood musicals provided an ideal and entertaining fantasy world.

Extravagant and revealing costumes, risqué dialogue and exuberant dance routines were director Busby Berkeley's speciality.

For 'Pettin' in the Park', a number in *Gold Diggers of 1933*, the girls are wearing see-through dresses, with their underwear clearly visible beneath. As the couples lie down to kiss and cuddle on the grass their skirts fall back revealing innumerable thighs and stocking-tops.

The following piece of dialogue is from Berkeley's most successful movie, *42nd Street* (1933): 'Where are you sitting, dearie?' asks a chorus boy. 'On a flagpole,' answers the chorus girl as she sits on his lap.

COME UP AND SEE ME . . .

But some of the most legendary lines of sexual innuendo belong to Mae West, who was to fall foul of critical pressure from the Legion of Decency, as they tried to 'protect' the public from moral corruption in movies.

In 1933, *She Done Him Wrong* was the film of the year. A low-budget production, it was completed in only 18 days, and starred Mae and her protégé, the young Cary Grant, in a story set in the more carefree days of the Wild West. The perennially misquoted 'Come up and see me sometime' originates from this film: what she really said was, 'Anytime you got nothin' to do – and lots of time to do it – come on up.'

With her generous figure encased in tight-fitting dresses, masses of jewellery and a slow lecherous wink, she was almost a parody of femininity. Some unkind critics even suggested that she was a man in drag. But in complete contrast to the somewhat sinister sexuality of the silent era, she implied that sex could be both frivolous and funny.

Sex with a sense of humour was also the province of the screen's first 'dumb blonde' – Jean Harlow. Rumoured to ice her nipples before each take, she was photographed in languorous poses wearing loose-fitting satin and no underwear. Her hair dyed a startling platinum blonde, Harlow was promoted as a tough little gold-digger who knew how to use sex to get what she wanted.

Marlene Dietrich and Greta Garbo also personified sex in their films, although in very different ways. Dietrich often dressed in men's clothing, and her androgynous appeal to both sexes was daringly exploited – 'The woman even women can adore' ran one publicity picture caption.

Garbo, even when she took the role of a courtesan in *Camille*, had the precious gift of a mysterious and fascinating allure, and this was a quality which she carried through obsessively into her private life.

Seen here with a young Cary Grant, Marlene Dietrich's smouldering eyes, husky 'foreign' voice and androgynous sexuality made her one of the all-time sex idols.

By 1939, the Hollywood Production Code (Hays Code) was being strictly adhered to by all the studios, and the permissive pre-code days were a thing of the past. Much controversy surrounded Clark Gable's famous throw-away line in *Gone With The Wind* (1939), 'Frankly, my dear, I don't give a damn,' containing as it did a forbidden profanity.

Yet it was sanctioned by the censor, as was the scene where Rhett Butler forcefully carries Scarlett up the stairs to the marriage bed. Although she wakes up alone the following morning, her secret smile leaves no doubt about what has taken place between them the night before.

SEX IN THE FORTIES

During the 1940s, sex did not disappear from the screen, but it had to be presented carefully in order to get by the Hays Office.

Illicit sex, like crime, must be seen not to pay. Married couples had twin beds, homosexuality and lesbianism were never mentioned – and nobody ever undressed.

Sexual symbolism was often used to suggest activities the camera could not show, including fountains, trains entering tunnels and sunsets. Perhaps one of the most amusingly blatant examples of this is a number called 'The Lady in the Tutti-Frutti Hat' from a musical entitled *The Gang's All Here* (1943).

The singer Carmen Miranda dances between rows of show-girls who are all waving giant-sized replicas of bananas slowly up and down.

ADULTERY

The romantic love triangle in *Casablanca* (1942), starring Ingrid Bergman and Humphrey Bogart, ends with the heroine making the 'right decision' to leave her rediscovered former lover and stay with her idealistic husband.

But although nothing is seen in the flashback sequence of their brief affair in wartime Paris, emotions are so highly charged between Bogart and Bergman that something clearly did happen.

Brief Encounter, made in Britain in 1946, is another

ECSTASY

In 1933 there appeared a film which was to become famous for its nude scenes, its sexual details, and the fact that its unknown lead went on to become the famous star, Hedy Lamarr.

In *Ecstasy*, which was made in Czechoslovakia, Hedy Lamarr played a young bride married to an old and impotent man. Frustrated, she seeks divorce after a year.

In a film with very few words in it, she expresses her sexual frustrations through riding her horse through the woods, and swimming nude.

When the horse bolts, she chases it, still nude, through the trees, eventu-

TALL.... TERRIFIC.... and TROUBLE!

HOWARD HUGHES'
Daring
PRODUCTION

The Outlaw

INTRODUCING
JANE RUSSELL

JACK BUETEL
THOMAS MITCHELL
WALTER HUSTON

UNITED ARTISTS

Jane Russell's ample assets are clearly displayed in this publicity poster for The Outlaw. *The 1950s was the era of the cinema sex-goddess in the US and Europe.*

film dealing with a sensitive subject while avoiding any direct sexual references. The story of two middle-class, middle-aged, married people who meet by chance, it follows the progress of their platonic but nevertheless intensely romantic friendship.

When they do manage to borrow a flat – perhaps with the intention of consummating their relationship – they are unexpectedly interrupted. And respectability triumphs in the end as they both return to their respective spouses.

Uncontrollable desires, and the darker corner of human nature were cleverly portrayed in the many

'black thrillers' of the period. The veiled eroticism of *Cat People* (1942) has a lovely young woman believing she is descended from a race of cat women who turn into ferocious panthers when sexually aroused.

Biblical fantasies, the series of Tarzan adventures featuring a barely clad hero, and musicals with lots of leg all provided excuses for showing far more flesh than would otherwise have been considered suitable.

PIN-UPS

Throughout the war years, the pin-up girl was considered essential to the morale of the troops. Betty Grable, a typically wholesome example, was pictured in a swimsuit to show off her famous legs – which were insured for thousands of dollars.

Other major female stars, such as Bette Davis and Joan Crawford, were glamorous and sophisticated. They were often shown in dominant roles, such as successful career women, or super-bitches who sublimated their sexuality. Their men were frequently weaker, and the women usually got the upper hand.

FATAL ATTRACTION

Yet fully clothed erotic tension was successfully depicted in some films. In *The Postman Always Rings Twice* (1946) a bored young wife of a much older man falls for a younger man – but their powerful physical attraction proves to be fatal. And in *Gilda* (1946) Rita Hayworth's striptease only involves her long black gloves, but is still very arousing to her audience.

ally meeting a handsome young man who hands her her clothes, and performs a little first aid on a bruised foot. That night she seeks out his cabin, and the camera relays to astounded audiences the sexual ecstasy on her face as they make love.

The United States authorities destroyed *Ecstasy* for obscenity, although copies got through the net. Lamarr's rich husband later attempted, unsuccessfully, to buy up all prints of the film. The British censor did not pass *Ecstasy* until 1950, and then it was deemed suitable for viewing by adult audiences only.

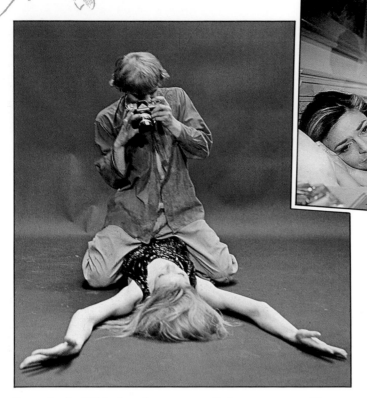

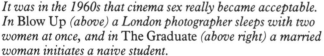

It was in the 1960s that cinema sex really became acceptable. In Blow Up *(above) a London photographer sleeps with two women at once, and in* The Graduate *(above right) a married woman initiates a naive student.*

'Sex-kitten' Brigitte Bardot (right) played an important role in popularizing French cinema in the 1950s. She has since withdrawn from public view, but her natural beauty and sensuality remain legendary.

SEX COMEDIES

Sex comedies made their appearance in the 1950s. Containing no sex whatsoever, plots centred around an untouchable virgin taming a lustful male whose intentions are finally manipulated into being honourable. Rock Hudson and Doris Day starred in a number of these, causing one Hollywood wit to remark, 'I knew Doris Day before she was a virgin.'

But not all sex comedies were quite so bland. *The Seven Year Itch* (1955) deals with the possibility of marital infidelity. The affair never happens – but Marilyn Monroe's mixture of innocence and irrepressible sexuality makes it seem as if it might at any moment.

Passions ran dangerously high in *From Here to Eternity* (1953), when the adulterous lovers, played by Burt Lancaster and Deborah Kerr, were seen embracing, wearing as little as possible on the beach.

BREAKING THE BARRIERS

It took a serious work of literature by a famous writer, Tennessee Williams, to break the barriers in Holly-

wood. *A Streetcar Named Desire* (1951) was one of the first films in English to be granted a British 'X' certificate, and depicts both nymphomania and rape.

Baby Doll (1955), also written by Tennessee Williams, deals with the darker side of sexuality again. The 'baby doll' of the title is a young woman whose husband has promised to leave her intact until her 20th birthday. Until then, he is reduced to voyeurism, spying on her in her 'nursery'. The film contains suggestions of fellatio – and gave its name to baby-doll pyjamas.

THE SEX GODDESSES

This was the golden age of the sex goddess, personified by Marilyn Monroe, whose vulnerability combined with sexual promise continues to fascinate.

These symbols of female allure were all noticeably well-endowed, and films were advertised with posters showing generous amounts of cleavage. Despite her small role in *The Outlaw*, the 'mean, moody and magnificent' Jane Russell was featured on the publicity posters lying provocatively on a pile of straw, as she displayed both legs and breasts.

Hollywood stars remained essentially untouchable fantasy women, but European actresses seemed far more sensual and available. From Italy came Gina Lollobrigida and Sophia Loren – both sultry and voluptuous. And in 1956, French 'sex kitten' Brigitte Bardot was launched as an international star in *And God Created Woman* directed by her then husband, Roger Vadim.

Bardot pouted, undressed and made love with evident guiltless enjoyment in all her films – which went a long way towards popularizing French cinema. But American movies were still noticeably restrained in their treatment of sex, and it was not until the early 1960s when restrictions lifted that it could be portrayed with any realism.

THE SIXTIES

Three comedies directed by Billy Wilder were to push back the frontiers a little further. *The Apartment* (1960) deals with the story of a young and ambitious office-worker played by Jack Lemmon. Promises of promotion lead him into a double life as his superiors use his home for their adulterous rendezvous.

Irma La Douce (1963) was the first American film to openly use a brothel for a background. Perhaps the Parisian setting and poignant humour of a love affair between a prostitute and a policeman helped.

Of the three, *Kiss Me, Stupid* (1964) caused the most controversy and public moral outrage. A provincial song-writer decides to offer his wife to a television star – her favours in exchange for a chance at success.

BREASTS IN HOLLYWOOD

The following year, 1965, breasts made a breakthrough as a black woman tore open her blouse to reveal all in *The Pawnbroker*. Finally, bowing to the inevitable, censorship was virtually abolished in the United States in 1966. Turbulent social change and financial setbacks had all but destroyed the major Hollywood studios – they had to move with the times or go under.

Meanwhile in Britain, mainstream cinema was becoming increasingly daring. The first James Bond movie, *Dr No*, was released in 1962, heralding the start of a hugely successful and long-running series. Actor Sean Connery was James Bond – a sophisticated amoral adventurer whose casual approach to sexual encounters only made him more attractive.

Tom Jones (1963), based on an 18th-century novel by Henry Fielding, followed the adventures of a cheerfully promiscuous young man played by Albert Finney. Possibly the most suggestive scene in the film is where Tom and his latest conquest are eating together – sucking and licking their food very erotically.

Tastes and times were changing rapidly. The demands of younger audiences were having their effect on the film industry worldwide. However, in the 1960s, it was only Scandinavian film-makers who showed explicit scenes containing full-frontal nudity, intercourse, oral sex, anal sex and masturbation.

BRITISH REALISM

The new upswing in the British film industry also produced a number of starkly realistic dramas exploring the problems of sex and relationships among ordinary people.

It was now possible to be open about lesbians and homosexuals – *The Killing of Sister George* (1968) shocked many people by depicting a lesbian household. Central to the plot was physical love and painful jealousy, previously only considered a heterosexual concern.

Avant-garde American artist and 'personality' Andy Warhol took advantage of the times to make a number of films featuring trans-sexuals, male prostitution, lesbians, and relentless male and female nudity. Titles like *Blow Job* (1964), *Harlot* (1965), *Fuck* (1969) and *Flesh* (1970) sounded exciting, but their length and lack of plot make them boring rather than titillating.

Towards the end of the 1960s, commercially successful films, such as box-office smash *The Graduate* (1967), were constantly breaking new ground. Set in and around the comfortable and affluent suburbs of Los Angeles, *The Graduate* shows a young inexperienced student's initiation into manhood by an older, wiser, married woman.

Ken Russell's *Women in Love* (1969) based on D H Lawrence's novel, contained a controversial nude wrestling sequence between the two leading men, who, although heterosexual, had professed love for each other. *Blow Up* (1967) had David Hemmings as an

In the 1970s, sex scenes became even more explicit. Shots of the varied sexual adventures of a beautiful young woman are the focus of Emmanuelle. *But in the 1980s, sex seems to have taken a back seat in the cinema*

Although their historical settings differ by more than a century, The French Lieutenant's Woman *(far left) and* Blue Lagoon *(left) both have a romantic view of sex at odds with many films of the '80s.*

THE HAYS CODE

The Hollywood moguls brought in Will H Hays to clean up the image of the movies, which was under fire from press and pulpit. Hired in 1922, Hays attacked the private lives of film people at first, and helped draw up a Doom Book containing 117 'unsafe' names. Films themselves did not come under official strictures until 1934. After that date they had to follow the Hays Code, which stipulated:

☐ No scenes of passion allowed unless essential to the plot.
☐ No showing of excessive and lustful (open mouthed) kissing, embraces or postures.
☐ The sanctity of marriage and home to be upheld.
☐ No explicit treatment of adultery and illicit sex, which, if necessary to plot, should not be justified or presented attractively.
☐ Rape and seduction only to be hinted at where essential to plot.
☐ Rape and seduction are never the proper subject of comedy.

☐ All reference to sexual perversion is forbidden.
☐ White slavery is a forbidden subject.
☐ Mixed white and black sexual relations are forbidden.
☐ Children's sex organs should never be shown.
☐ There should be no screen treatment of childbirth.
☐ Sexual hygiene and diseases are unfit subjects for screening.
☐ Complete nudity is banned altogether.
☐ Indecent or 'undue' exposure is forbidden.
☐ Scenes including undressing should be avoided.

Suggestive dialogue was also censored by the Hays Office, to which the Hollywood studio chiefs submitted all scripts before shooting began, so as to avoid wasting money on cuts and re-shooting. The Code was not reviewed until 1956, when the only specific bans were on the screening of venereal disease, sexual perversion, and foul language. After 1966 the Code contained no specific prohibitions.

amoral London photographer tumbling into bed with two models at once.

THE SEVENTIES

By the early 1970s such pornographic films as *Deep Throat* were being shown in specialist cinemas, attracting huge audiences. *Deep Throat* remains one porno movie which is famous even among people who have never seen it.

Films revolving almost entirely around sexual frankness were now on release in ordinary cinemas. An anonymous liaison between Marlon Brando and Maria Schneider in *Last Tango in Paris* contained the now notorious anal sex scene, complete with discussion about butter as a potential lubricant.

Meanwhile, in *Emmanuelle*, Sylvia Kristel fulfils one erotic fantasy after another – from sex in an aeroplane to a passionate lesbian encounter.

Even major stars were to be seen having simulated sexual intercourse, as in *Don't Look Now* (1973), with Julie Christie and Donald Sutherland.

SEX AND VIOLENCE

Sex and violence were increasingly linked in the mid to late 1970s. Such films as *Looking for Mr Goodbar* (1977) preached that the wages of sin, in this case a series of casual partners, are death – managing to include a good quantity of sex and nudity before the final denouement, where Diane Keaton is killed.

Public outcry against *Dressed to Kill*, with its disturbing sadistic fantasy sequence and violence towards women indicated that perhaps the trend had gone too far.

Two of the most successful movies of the 1980s have skirted round the subject of sex in a way which would have probably delighted the censors of earlier days.

Although doubtful rape is central to the plot of *Passage to India* (1984), nothing sexual beyond some erotic Indian temple statues is ever shown. And in the same year, Academy award-winning *Amadeus* proved that a film with no major stars, nudity or explicit scenes could be a runaway success.

With the growth of the video market, people are able to view potentially arousing material in the privacy of their own homes. Although club cinemas still show soft-porn films, it can be much more pleasant to watch sexy stories in comfort.

But as D W Griffiths discovered more than 50 years ago, sex and nudity are not the only ingredients for success. Perhaps cinema has come full circle.

WHAT IS BEAUTIFUL?

*Beauty comes in all shapes and sizes. Everyone forms their own ideal,
whether influenced by culture, or simply by individual preferences*

Throughout the world, there is so much variation in taste that it is impossible to decide on absolute and universal standards of beauty.

One male American anthropologist, who had lived with a group of Amazonian Indians in Brazil, reports that the Indian women he thought were spectacular beauties were ignored by the native men, who instead went into raptures about women that the anthropologist himself did not even find attractive.

Women regarded as beautiful from earlier periods in western history very frequently strike most modern westerners as decidedly too chubby to be really beautiful. And even people living at the same time in the same culture disagree about what is beautiful.

UNUSUAL PENCHANTS

Some traits are considered beautiful in one culture and unattractive, even grotesque, in another. For example, on the Japanese Okinawa Islands in the 1950s, women were thought to be beautiful if they had gold teeth. Sometimes even healthy teeth were fitted with removable gold caps. Among some Vietnamese, however, teeth were lacquered black. In yet other societies, teeth are filed to points or else a certain number are removed.

Aztec mothers used to dangle objects close to their infants' eyes to bring out a mild cross-eyed condition, considered beautiful, and Kwakiútl Indians would flatten their children's heads with boards to create a desirable profile.

Long and pendulous breasts are ideal among the traditional Zande and Ganda of Africa and heavy, firm calves and thighs are prized by the Mehinaku of Brazil.

Easter Islanders of the Pacific like women with a large clitoris and the Tsawana of Botswana, southern Africa, require women to elongate their labia.

Darwin noted that early travellers among the Hóttentot of South Africa found women with enormous buttocks regarded as great beauties, whereas a few generations later this taste had changed.

NO PREFERENCES

In some societies, for example the Lepcha of Sikkim and Nepal, an absence of any criteria for attractiveness except availability and the right sex organs has been reported. And, according to traditional Confucian Chinese canons of morality, for a woman to try to be attractive was thought to be unnatural and even a crime. It was even shameful for a woman to be sexually attractive to her own husband.

Hasidic Jews prohibit talking about physical attractiveness, as it is not considered to be a subject serious adults should concern themselves with.

LOOKING HEALTHY

As far as is known, all people throughout time have found a healthy appearance, if not precisely beautiful, then at least attractive. People whose bodies are not

what is seen as 'normal' – for example, those who have had a limb removed or who have six fingers – are usually at a disadvantage.

However, a very small minority of people are turned on by amputees – a fetish known as apotemnophilia.

Skin afflictions such as ringworm or yaws, bad breath and decaying teeth are invariably drawbacks, although baldness in a man can be an asset.

Only one exception to such general reports about the attractiveness of a healthy appearance comes from an account by an early 20th century traveller in Africa. Among the Fang, in what is now Gabon and Cameroon, women sought out men who had leprosy – at least for adulterous affairs. This rings so untrue that in the absence of a good deal more evidence it should, perhaps, be discounted.

HAIR FASHIONS

A good head of hair has sometimes been regarded as a sign of health and sexual attractiveness. However, there are societies in which, by contrast, both men and women shave their heads, as baldness –

Japanese women, with their jet-black hair and porcelain-white skin, are considered beautiful by many. Following the old custom of painting their skin white, just like the Geisha girls, accentuates their fragile, exquisite beauty.

This Eritrean refugee in the Sudan shows how facial scarring can add to, rather than detract from, an already beautiful face. Few people in the western world, however, would go to such lengths for the sake of beauty.

at least induced baldness – is a social requirement.

In some societies, women and men pluck away their eyebrows and eyelashes entirely, as well as all, or most of, their body hair.

Nilotic groups in East Africa, such as the Nuer and the Luo, traditionally shave their entire bodies every few days.

For either sex to have body or pubic hair is considered to be disgusting in these cultures, as it is considered that it makes people seem too much like animals.

In the western world, there are different traditions involving body hair, but with rare exceptions only women have removed some or all of it.

In the *Shulhan 'Arukh*, the handbook of religious rules used by orthodox Jews, it is taken as a matter of course that women will remove the hair from their underarms as well as their pubic hair. This is an ancient fashion still sometimes found in the Middle East. In Iran, for example, a woman is expected to shave off her pubic hair when she becomes a bride. However, the *Shulhan 'Arukh* specifically prohibits men from removing their pubic hair.

REMOVING HAIR

The Ancient Greeks and Romans continued the Near Eastern tradition of depilation, which also included removing men's underarm hair. In Turkish baths throughout the world, such depilatory services are still available to both women and men.

It has been primarily the English-speaking world of Britain and the United States where women remove body hair and where its presence is regarded as unattractive by the great majority of people, both male and female.

On the continent of Europe, this has not been the case, although recently such tastes for being smooth-skinned have apparently increased.

It is interesting that being smooth-skinned has not caught on among men, even though in certain situations some men by tradition shave their bodies.

Swimmers shave to cut down on friction in swimming competitions, and so do body builders when trying to show off their muscular development as clearly as possible.

To some people, wearing a can of pineapple juice in a hole made in their earlobe is a way of appearing more attractive. To others, it seems simply interesting or even funny. But their choice of ear adornment is obviously taken very seriously by some people.

Since, in western art, body hair is almost never shown, it might be argued that even on men a hairless body is considered more beautiful. But the striking thing is that almost nowhere is it appropriate for men to want to, or to try to be 'beautiful'. It is infinitely more important to a man to be 'masculine'.

WHAT WOMEN WANT

When men from different societies are asked what they find attractive in women, they frequently produce lists of physical characteristics. But women seldom do the same for men. Generally, men in all societies are more interested than women in the physical appearance of their partners.

What a woman looks for in a man – or so the evidence suggests so far – is high status: power, riches and a reputation for 'manly' virtues such as bravery.

Critics of this view suggest that women have traditionally been economically dependent on men and that it is for this reason that they look for these qualities. Once women are genuinely free of that dependency they will be able to concentrate more on the physical attributes of sex appeal.

GENTLEMEN PREFER BLONDES

When movie stars become famous for being particularly good-looking, the criteria for attractiveness in men as opposed to women would seem to differ in unexpected and trivial ways.

In Europe and America, the actresses who are known for their looks have very frequently been blondes – Catherine Deneuve, Marilyn Monroe, Jean Harlow and Lana Turner. However, there is a great variety of types thought to be beautiful. The dark-haired Elizabeth Taylor, Gina Lollobrigida, Vivien Leigh and Ava Gardner, or the redhead Maureen O'Hara are all examples.

Curiously, a great many of the actors who have become 'heart-throbs' have been dark-haired or at least not blonde – Gregory Peck, Paul Newman, Alain Delon, Mel Gibson and, going back a while, Valentino. Robert Redford is perhaps the most famous blond actor known for his good looks.

THE MAGIC OF YOUTH

Another nearly universal dimension to the notion of beauty is a general male preoccupation with youth. Practically everywhere, both heterosexual and homosexual males regard youth as one of the main requirements in a lover.

In the heterosexual context, this could easily be related to the facts of reproduction. Men can sire children up until their 90s, if not beyond, whereas women can seldom bear children beyond 50 and usually stop much earlier.

If sex appeal has anything to do with a sort of biological 'wiring' for efficient reproduction, as biologists tend to maintain, then for males to be interested in older women would not make much sense.

This is, however, just a tendency. There are women who seek out men for their looks and not their status, and there are men who seek out older or even elderly women.

'LOVE OF THE OLD'

When a significant age difference occurs between partners and the younger person actually prefers older people, possibly of his or her parents' generation, one speaks of this interest as *gerontophilia* ('love of the old').

In present western society, a certain ambivalence exists about relationships between older women and younger men, although such affairs seem to be treated with increasing tolerance.

In earlier times in western society, particularly during the 18th century, and associated with the royal courts of Catherine the Great of Russia and of the Napoleons, it is said that high-status older women were sought after by younger men and that almost a cult of older women set in. But generally, men everywhere have preferred youth in their partners, whether male or female.

Societies where it is reported that men prefer older women or at least seek them out as lovers can be found in parts of Asia, South America, North America and Africa.

BODY FAT

In some societies body fat is highly prized, but in others it is despised. Generally, women who have broad hips and tend to be chubby are more commonly thought to be beautiful in most cultures.

Western fashion models with protruding high cheek bones and who border on anorexia would strike most men in the world as far from appealing.

FAT IS BEAUTIFUL

One man, originally from Iraq, related the story of when he first went to the United States as a student. He carried with him his traditional bias of preferring fat women. One day he met a full-figured female student, approached her, and said 'Congratulations on your fat'. She almost attacked him physically. He, in turn, was bewildered by her response.

In several societies, before marriage, girls are even fattened up to be particularly appealing to their husbands.

WHAT IS HEALTHY?

Why should there be such extreme differences of taste on such a basic physical trait? No doubt many factors come into play. Experts tend to link the question to what comes across as being healthy.

In many situations where food shortages exist, an ample body suggests that the person will have a greater chance of survival. Where there is no shortage, then finer distinctions such as causes of heart attacks and comparable disorders may be taken into consideration.

Experts speculate that somehow, unconsciously, people make decisions about what body shape looks healthy. They then link this to their own biological programming in deciding what they are to find as sexually attractive.

WHAT COLOUR SKIN?

In many instances, there is a probable social reason for a taste, rather than the prompting of some biological

In cultures where food shortages exist, having an ample body signals that the person has the means to eat in excess, and therefore stands a greater chance of survival. But in other cultures, where food is abundant, people strive to be slim so that they have long, healthy lives.

BEAUTY CONTESTS

Apart from the beauty contests which are all spin-offs from commercial contests first held in the United States in the early 20th century, there are practically no records of beauty contests of any sort from any other society.

The Ancient Greeks held beauty contests for both women and men which usually had a religious significance. For example, in one contest held where the Olympic Games took place, there was also a male beauty contest where all the winners were dedicated to the goddess Athena. Apparently, male beauty contests were more common than female ones.

The establishment of Christianity, which was against playing up the body in such a positive way, brought about the end of the beauty contests that still existed.

When such contests were revived in the 20th century, the emphasis switched to female contests. Male contests tended to play down the idea of beauty and play up body building as a sport. The early female beauty contests were sometimes thought to be indecent.

Only one other society has developed any kind of beauty contest – and it is for men only. This group is the Bororó Fulani of western Africa who include the contest as a part of yearly ritual dances. Facial beauty is judged as well as the attractiveness of the make-up and the general appearance.

universal. Skin colour is an example. Some white people have fantasized that dark-skinned men instinctively prefer white women. The irresistible white woman was thought therefore to be in constant danger of rape because of the uncontrollable lust she aroused. All of this is myth.

The anthropologist Ian Hogbin writing about the dark-skinned Wógeo of Papua New Guinea said that they found Europeans too much like albinos, whom they thought repulsive. One Wógeo man said he could understand why Europeans wore so many clothes.

PREFERRING LIGHT SKINS

But some exceptions do occur. In several dark-skinned societies, girls have their skins bleached or otherwise whitened. This is true of the daughters of nobles among the Lau of the Pacific, and of Dogon girls in general in West Africa. Garo boys of Assam admire girls with light skins, but not light-coloured eyes like those of northern Europeans. They think such eyes look like a goat's.

The Chaga of East Africa have changed their taste. Since the coming of Europeans (who have held power), light-skinned people are no longer disliked for their colouring.

Similarly, in West Africa, in many groups such as the Hausa and Nupe, men tend to marry light-skinned women. Probably this preference has something to do with contacts with light-skinned Arab and Fulani groups who have held political power or wielded enormous prestige for a long time in the area.

SUNTANNED SKIN

Among white westerners an almost opposite development has taken place, presumably also influenced by ideas of status and prestige. Traditionally, the whiteness of a woman's skin has been a mark of beauty, which is why women of quality always used parasols.

But then parasols were forgotten and suntan lotions that would help deepen a tan appeared. This occurred only in the 20th century. In the 1920s, fashionable women started to sport suntans rather than keeping their skin ivory-pale.

The explanation for this about-turn has to do with economics and new signs of status. Up until the 20th century, working class people were largely farm workers who would inevitably become dark by working long hours in the sun.

But then they began working in factories, and light-coloured skin has taken on the connotation of lowly status. Now, only the rich can afford to sunbathe on beaches at any time of year and sport year-long tans.

The peculiar thing is that the older fashion, which shunned tanning, was the healthier. Although sunlight is a source of vitamin D, it also causes skin cancer and other disorders, as well as bringing about a premature ageing of the skin. So trying to look beautiful can be detrimental to people's health.

The athletic beauty of Jamaican singer Grace Jones stands in sharp contrast to the more commonplace blonde-haired, blue-eyed beauty of the West. However, some cultures would ignore such women in favour of those with large, pendulous breasts or heavy calves and thighs.

White skin used to be the mark of high class, as only labourers had brown skin. Now, year-long tans are only sported by those who can afford to travel to the sunspots.

NUDITY

Nudity – and attitudes to it – varies all over the world. Yet almost every culture continues to find ingenious ways of exaggerating the naked body and making it look more erotic

The 20th century has seen a strange pattern concerning sex and clothes and nudity. For while the 'civilized' countries have continued to encourage the 'primitive' peoples of the Tropics to cover up their breasts and buttocks, and to adopt dresses and trousers, there has been a marked trend in those same countries to shed clothes as often and as much as possible, in public as well as in private.

The more daring female swimwear of the 1980s, for example, shows not only a reasonable portion of breast and buttock, but also reveals a part of the genital area. This is shaved – and would no doubt be considered indecent or at least in poor taste if it were not.

COVERING THE GENITALS

For the most part, societies of all descriptions appear to agree that it is both logical and proper to cover the sexual organs in public – at least as adults.

The exceptions are becoming rarer by the decade as the Third World becomes rapidly 'westernized', and are now primarily restricted to the desert regions of Africa, with nomadic tribes such as the Nuer of the Sudan. Interestingly, although the men of that tribe normally go naked, high-ranking chiefs wear leopard-skins as a mark of their status – but draped over their shoulder.

In those societies where people still go about naked, training in modesty nevertheless occurs from early childhood. Boys may be beaten if they have erections in public, and girls are trained not to expose their labia.

To western eyes, jewelry, paint and exotic headware serve only to accentuate nudity. Yet in Papua New Guinea, this girl's breasts would probably go virtually unnoticed.

Girls may be prohibited from sitting with their legs apart, for example, or from climbing trees in the presence of men.

BARE BREASTS

The exposure of breasts, however, is far more widespread, and is still the accepted norm in many rural areas of the developing world. In such societies, breasts tend not to be thought of as erotically interesting to men – they are regarded primarily, and sometimes exclusively, as the source of nourishment for babies and young infants.

In the West, though, breasts are almost always seen in an erotic context, and fashions have developed to emphasize size and shape without actually revealing them – plunging necklines, padded bras, lifting cups and so on. This trend has reached its zenith in a treatment where silicone is inserted to increase firmness and improve shape.

Actually exposing nipples, however, would generally be decried as immodest. And such niceties are not confined to women. It is not so long ago that in the United States it was the custom that photographs of male models in beachwear or underwear ads were actually printed with the nipples 'airbrushed' away – if the model did not have a convenient towel slung around his neck with the ends covering the relevant points.

EXPOSED MIDRIFFS

Each society can have its own particular cultural taboos about the exposure of certain parts of the body. In some parts of Indonesia, for example, women go topless but must not expose their ankles.

Among Samoans the navel must not be revealed – whereas among Hindu women in India the bare midriff is the norm, even in very formal situations. A bare stomach, by contrast, is uncommon for females in the western world, except in the case of swimwear – although much of the back might be revealed.

For males, an innocuous bare middle is almost unheard of in a normal 'indoor' setting – the exception is the very informal style associated with young men with flat stomachs who cut off the bottoms of T-shirts to emphasize their physical condition.

PENIS DECORATION

In some traditional societies, the men actually try to accentuate their sexual organs, by using a penis sheath (or 'phallocrypt'). Here, the shaft and head of the penis is covered, but the scrotum is still exposed.

Certain New Guinea tribesmen have sometimes made use of long gourds decorated with fur, held upright by strings and suggesting a huge erection. Shells, horns, basketry, bark cloth and bamboo are all employed traditionally in the making of such phallocrypts, while modern materials have included toothpaste tubes and opened sardine cans.

In a wet T-shirt contest, one contestant knows the tricks of the trade. Interestingly, the vital statistics of the competitors were almost exactly the same.

In 1973 at Treehouse Fun Ranch near Los Angeles, the queen of a nude rodeo beat 30 contestants. 7000 dollars was shared among the winners.

Men who have adopted western clothing sometimes wear phallocrypts under their trousers – and at least one Ancient Egyptian fashion evolved as a combination of a kilt and a penis sheath (the *shendjut* kilt).

EXAGGERATION

An adornment that resembled the phallocrypt in European fashion was the extraordinary codpiece, which first appeared in the 14th century but by the end of the 16th century was generally regarded as indecent – or quite simply as rather silly.

Paintings from that 200-year period show some very

Research shows that male nudity does little to sell to men or women – a point not lost to advertisers. At worst it can look ludicrous, at best it can have a boyish charm.

newspapers feature every day an attractive, well-proportioned girl, with the accent more on the 'best girl on the beach' than 'sexy starlet'.

In the lower levels of advertising, however, the use of nude or topless girls can be far more provocative, and is often accompanied by explicit sexual innuendo.

Pouting females are shown draped over the unlikeliest of machines and tools. This technique is called 'borrowed interest', where the focal attraction of the advertisement has no direct relevance to the nature of the product being advertised. Babies and animals feature too, but for male products the scantily clad or nude female figure is the more logical alternative.

She is not just there to catch the male eye, of course – in a more subtle sense she is (or will be) the man's 'reward' for purchasing the product.

Surveys shows that the majority of women do not object to the use of naked females in advertising in principle – they are more concerned with whether it is distasteful or degrading. More important, in a commercial sense, are a series of survey findings in both the United States and Britain, which maintain that 'brand recall' in men – the ability to remember the actual name of the product – is significantly worse when there is a nude or near-nude girl in the advertisement.

PART NUDITY

'It is part of the recovery from Puritanism that most people now make love naked and most lovers sleep naked,' wrote Alex Comfort in the *Joy of Sex*. 'Nakedness is the normal state for lovers who take their work at all seriously, at least as a basic requisite . . . Clothes, when they are worn, are there to be taken off.'

Even so, clothing can be an integral part of sex. Indeed, some people find the opposite sex more attractive in a certain garment than when naked – in wet T-shirts and suspender belts, for example.

The modern one-piece swimsuit, now making a comeback against the bikini, is now designed not just to uncover as much as possible, but positively to accentuate the sexual attractiveness of the wearer.

NATURISM

The permissive age heralded something of a boom in organized naturism, but the trend was soon halted by the arrival of topless and then openly nude beaches, especially in Europe.

Institutional nudism has taken a knock since the late 1960s when for a brief period it became fashionable for a number of 'committed' naturists. The widespread and informal acceptance of nudity as a real option – both at home and, more important, in various public resorts – has undermined its formerly unique status. Now, it seems, no one really looks twice.

famous and respectable men wearing codpieces, and they have survived on many suits of armour. In some instances, they became so large that they were used as pockets.

The only modern equivalent may be the kind of crotch padding allegedly concealed by rock bands and some film stars.

EXPLOITING NUDITY

The exposure of skin – if not of pubic hair – has moved a long way from its coy corner in the West in recent years. In Britain, for example, several national

EXHIBITIONISM

Explicit self display can be natural or offensive, whether it is practised by the professional stripper or the amateur flasher. Yet, everyone has a touch of the exhibitionist in them

I f someone were to be described to you as an exhibitionist, how would you imagine them? As a show-off? A sexy dresser? Or a 'flasher'?

Indeed, all these sorts of people could be described as exhibitionists, for exhibitionism describes a wide range of human behaviour. At one end is harmless showing off, at the other is indecent exposure.

SELF-DISPLAY

The mildest, most common and almost necessary form of exhibitionism reflects the concern we have for how others see us. The way we dress, the way we walk, and what we say all display signals which help us to become known as a particular kind of person.

Sociologists have argued that social life would be impossible without this 'impression management'. We all have to present ourselves in particular ways – or others would simply not know how to respond to us.

Many of us – especially when we are young – take this 'impression management' into a more distinctly sexual area. Clothing can be deliberately designed to present the body as a sexual object.

In the 15th and 16th centuries, young European men wore cod-pieces over the penis which were designed to attract female eyes and to reveal their

masculinity. And today, certain clothes – from tight jeans and unbuttoned shirts, to skimpy skirts and padded bras – accentuate the sexuality of the wearer.

Fashions may change dramatically according to culture and time, but one of the constant reasons we dress up in attractive colours and exotic materials is to have ourselves seen as an erotic object by others.

STAGE SHOWS

This sort of exhibitionist dressing is carried further in the more self-conscious posings of a model or a pop star. Many pop stars, for example, dress themselves up in costumes aimed to eroticize their bodies and excite their audiences.

From Madonna to Prince, much of the pop world has a strong exhibitionistic streak. In some instances, it is taken even further – as in the simulated intercourse in the performance of stars like Rod Stewart or the late Jimi Hendrix.

STRIPPING AND EROTIC DANCING

There is nothing new about erotic dancing – Salome danced for King Herod nearly 2000 years ago. But in modern times, striptease has become an occupational skill. And today, it is more fashionable for men to be strippers.

In recent years, male strip shows for female audiences have become increasingly popular – from the local 'hen nights' to the well-known Bloomingdale's in New York.

Male strippers usually strip down to G-strings and may exchange caresses or gropings with customers – in return for money being tucked into their scanty attire.

A research study of one such night spot in the United States found that it attracted a wide range of women – housewives, secretaries, students and professional women, aged from 18 to their 60s.

The results of this study are fascinating, because of what they suggest about changes in sexual behaviour of men and women when usual roles are reversed. While the man is in the role of displaying himself and being watched as a sex object, the women in the audience often become very aggressive – shouting at him, trying to get his G-string off, and demanding and offering sexual experiences.

Some of the male dancers in the study claimed that they often felt exploited and degraded. One man said, 'Who would think that women could be so aggressive? I come away with scratch marks, bites and lipstick on my butt.'

TOPLESS BARS

The 'topless bar' emerged in the early 1960s in the North Beach area of San Francisco. Although there was initially a legal struggle over these bare-breasted female dancers and waitresses, they were soon tolerated and 'topless bars' spread rapidly.

Topless bars first appeared in the 1960s in some of the more 'permissive' areas of the United States. As such bars – and even shops – became profitable, the topless waitress has almost become a profession in its own right.

Within a few years, the 'bottomless bar' appeared – although it was generally less well received.

MOONING

'Mooning' – baring your buttocks and prominently displaying them, usually out of a car or house window – has been very popular among the college youth of the United States since World War II.

It is not usually an erotic act, but one of defiance and bravado. In 1986, when Queen Elizabeth visited New Zealand, a Maori bared his backside to her, in an act that was clearly political rather than sexual.

STREAKING

Streaking – sprinting naked past a startled group of people and then disappearing – is a similar form of exhibitionist behaviour. It is more likely to be a youthful protest against adult values rather than a sexually provocative act.

Streaking became especially popular on university campuses in the United States and Britain in the 1970s. In one famous case at Memphis State University, 200 streakers unleashed themselves on some 5000 spectators. The students involved said that it was a way of attracting attention, but also a rejection of authority.

Probably the most famous 'streaker' was the man who sprinted across the pitch at half time in the 1974 Rugby Union international between England and France. The 50,000 spectators were obviously delighted at this original exhibitionist's action. A handy policeman's helmet provided a 'modesty shield' in case anyone was offended by his nudity.

Madonna, a classic example of exhibitionism on stage, is well known for her raunchy performances at concerts. Her movements – like her lyrics – are both suggestive and teasing.

this 'damnable evil of nudism' throughout the 1930s in the United States, and managed to pass much anti-nudist legislation. Many nudists were sent to prison.

SOCIAL NUDISM

Nakedness is not always intended to shock. For some, it can be a way of life – although outsiders might interpret it is as exhibitionism. In popular opinion, nudism is often linked both to exhibitionism and voyeurism. But to practising nudists, this is not the case. Indeed, they take great steps to screen so-called 'deviants' from their midst. Single men may have a difficult time if they try to join.

From the nudists' viewpoint, nudism is to do with health – not sex. One American national nudist association says: 'Our goal is the healthy mind in the healthy body. This is not only a creed but a way of life. Sun, light and air are vital conditions of human well-being. We believe these elements are insufficiently used in present day life, to the detriment of physical and mental health.'

The first nudist camps were established in Germany in the early 1900s. Initially, they were considered immoral, lewd and centres of promiscuity. A Baptist minister, Braxton Sawyer, crusaded furiously against

PRUDISH NUDES

Nevertheless, nudism did become very popular in Europe and the United Staes during the 1950s and 1960s. Almost prudish and puritanical in their attitudes, many of the earlier camps stressed vegetarian diets, non-smoking and non-drinking, as well as much exercise.

A study of nudist camps in the United States in the early 1960s found that nudists were typically married and often brought their children to the camps. They were slightly less religious than the average population – as well as being more educated. Teenagers were relatively rare in the camps.

Although nudist camps still exist, the relaxation in standards of dress and the growth of 'nude beaches', has meant naturism has been somewhat in decline in recent years.

Yet, despite this trend, completely nude beaches are still far from being the norm. Although many European countries allow topless bathing, Denmark is the only country in Europe to allow unrestricted nudism along its entire coastline.

FETISHISM

What kind of person is sexually turned on by a pair of shoes, a woman's glove or even rubber underwear? These fetishes are surprisingly common and belong predominantly to the world of men

Most people have heard of a foot-fetish, and more and more there is talk of people who are 'into leather' or 'into kinky sex'. Sex boutiques throughout the world display clothing and other items that are supposed to be sexual turn-ons. All these, and many more, are what we think of as fetishes.

The term 'fetish' was originally used for religious or magic objects found in certain African and other non-western cultures. The meaning was apparently extended in 1888 by Dr Alfred Binet to refer to objects which could arouse intense sexual interest.

Various sexologists use the term with slightly different gradations of meaning, but traditionally it has included articles of clothing, certain parts of the body and sometimes even noises or odours. For example, some theorists explain the appeal of a singer's voice as a kind of sex fetish.

UNUSUAL PREOCCUPATIONS

The term fetish is applied when members of a society consider a particular sexual interest as unusual. No-one in Europe or the United States would regard a man who was sexually turned on by a woman's breasts as having a fetish. But in many societies in the world, breasts are not considered as erotic at all – only infants who gain nourishment from them are thought to have any special interest in them. In such societies, a grown man who was 'into breasts' would probably be considered unusual and expressions like fetishism would be completely appropriate to describe his interest.

More recently, a distinction has been made between a sexual interest in inanimate objects and one focused on body parts. Interest in the first is still referred to as

fetishism, but interest in the second is often labelled as 'partialism'.

Making such a distinction has certain advantages for sexologists because partialisms are sometimes reported not only from advanced societies but also from very simple, more primitive ones. Fetishisms, instead, seem to be almost entirely restricted to advanced societies.

Writers on the subject do not necessarily make the distinction. Practically everyone talks about a foot-fetish but only the specialist speaks of a foot-partialism. And very frequently the two interests go together, as is suggested by the title of William Rossi's book, *The Sex Life of the Foot and the Shoe*.

Fetishisms and partialisms are almost always male interests and are practically never found in women. The few women who go in for such things seem to do so to please their husbands or boyfriends, or else they are prostitutes who offer specialized services for male clients. Genuine female fetishists or partialists are extremely rare in all societies.

COMMON FETISHES

Practically any item could become a sexual fetish, although some, like long black opera gloves, are familiar and others, like women's hats, are rare.

A classic literary fetish is a fur coat, made famous by the German writer Leopold von Sacher-Masoch (from whose name comes the word 'masochism') in his book *Venus in Furs*. Here he writes about his fantasy of being dominated and whipped by a woman completely naked except for a fur coat. Interestingly enough, very few other people are reported as having similar fantasies.

Some fetishists are more concerned with the material their fetish is made from rather than its form. There are two main subdivisions of such 'media' fetishisms, as they are called – materials that are hard and/or shiny such as rubber or leather, and those that are soft and often frilly, such as lingerie.

LEATHER

Perhaps the most significant fetish material in modern times is leather clothing, usually black. At present this is most often associated with a subgroup of male homo-sexuals who tend to congregate in so-called 'leather bars'.

All the clothing such a fetishist might wear could well be made of black leather, right down to his under-wear. The clothes tend to be custom-made and quite expensive. The general style approaches a motor-cycle uniform. Quite possibly this fashion was started by Marlon Brando in the 1953 film *The Wild Ones*.

Several leather fetishists – gay or straight – find themselves in a moral quandary because they are phil-osophically opposed to the killing of animals. Some try to assuage their feelings of guilt by substituting vinyl. However, this is almost universally rejected because of its texture, and, more importantly, its smell.

One leather fetishist who was also a vegetarian for

moral reasons decided that for him to buy one leather outfit would constitute killing only one cow, which was less contemptible than eating beef for the rest of his life, which would involve the slaughter of innumer-able cattle.

RUBBER

According to the British sociologist Maurice North, who examined fetishes in his book *The Other Fringe of Sex*, the most common material that constitutes a

DID YOU KNOW?

There is an unusual fetish called pygmalionism which involves sexual attraction to statues. In Ancient Greece a man desecrated a shrine to the goddess Aphrodite by trying to have sex with the goddess's statue.

More recently pyg-malionism of a kind has been reported from the Koryak of Siberia. Ap-parently some men sleep with stones they call their 'wives'.

Since fetishes of any kind are rare outside advanced societies, and pygmalionism itself is apparently exceedingly rare, this is extraordinary.

fetishistic interest is rubber. But this is difficult to gauge since rubber clothing generally has to be bought through firms that cater specifically for fetishists, whereas other types of clothing can be picked up in ordinary shops.

The range of rubber items available is quite considerable, reflecting the fantasies of the consumers. One British firm offers, among other things, a nun's habit in black and white rubber, a French maid's costume with all the possible accessories in rubber – a rubberized black satin mini-dress, long frilly white rubber bloomers, white rubber underskirt and white polished cap and bibbed apron.

SADO-MASOCHISM

Rubber fetishists in the English-speaking world tend to prefer black, but this is not necessarily true of fetishists from other countries. In West Germany, for example, the most popular items are rubberized versions of skirts and underwear in pastel shades.

Rubber and leather fetishisms are frequently accompanied by an interest in sado-masochism in various forms. Many rubber fetishists are devotees of what is called 'water sports' (or technically, urolagnia). That is, they are turned on by urine – either seeing someone

Above *Leather fetishism has a cult following among certain homosexual groups who adopt a way of dressing that has aggressively erotic overtones.*

Left *A classic literary fetish is for fur and involves the fantasy of domination by a naked woman wearing a fur coat. But research has shown that fur fetishists are not 'into' masochism, but the feel of fur itself.*

urinate or urinating on someone or being urinated on.

The frequent interest in raincoats of various sorts would seem to be particularly appropriate for such concerns. But unlike the classic exhibitionist who flashes while wearing nothing but a trench coat, the rubber fetishist requires other types of gear. Ordinary raincoats or nylon raincoats, or garments made of transparent plastic or crude imitation leather are definitely out.

Socially, clubs based on an interest in leather seem to be more common than those organized around rubber. In northern Europe and the United States, homosexual leather bars are a well-known phenomenon. There are no comparable 'rubber bars'. The sociologist Maurice North was unable to discover a single rubber fetishist club in all of England. But at least one such club existed in New York during the 1970s – The Five Senses.

For the most part, heterosexual fetishists would seem to have more difficulties finding partners and making contacts with like-minded people than homosexual fetishists. Heterosexual fetishists might have to settle for fantasies and masturbation, although some do resort to working out their fantasies with other males in spite of the fact that they are not genuinely homosexual.

SATIN AND VELVET

The soft, frilly media fetishists have very different preoccupations. They are generally into lingerie or clothing made of velvet or fur and are rarely interested in sado-masochism despite von Sacher-Masoch's fantasy. Women's underpants are a common fetishistic object but surprisingly enough, bras seldom are.

Men who are into underpants fetishistically frequently want them to be soiled or stained with menstrual blood. Used sanitary napkins are also known to be fetishistic objects.

Sometimes one can find advertisements for used underwear in personal columns of sex magazines. And in magazines directed at male homosexuals one occasionally finds ads for dirty, smelly jock straps reeking of urine or stained with semen.

BOOTS AND HIGH-HEELED SHOES

Form fetishists are not so much concerned with texture as with the object itself. And while leather or rubber in almost any shape might turn on a media fetishist, the form fetishist requires a particular item.

One of the most famous form fetishes is the shoe. The classic woman's shoe with stiletto heel is one such example. Whenever stilettoes are in fashion, male shoe fetishists are known to walk around all day with an erection.

Boots are another classic fetishistic item both for heterosexuals and homosexuals. Very frequently shoe fetishists are also sado-masochists. Prostitutes who cater to sado-masochists often wear boots to indicate their willingness in this field.

Why shoes should be of particular interest and have strong sado-masochistic overtones has occasioned much speculation. Freud suggested that shoes were in the first place vagina symbols. As for sado-masochistic interest, several aspects are relevant. Masochists might want to be trampled on by booted feet or to be stomped on with a sharp pointed heel.

Alternatively, the high arch of a shoe with such a heel suggests that the foot has been crippled and that the woman wearing them cannot easily run away – a fantasy that appeals particularly to people into bondage.

Other kinds of shoe rarely have much fetishistic appeal – for example no-one is excited by trainers, or gym shoes. And although pornographic photographs and films often present the models naked except for hats and shoes, hats are seldom considered turn-ons in themselves.

A QUESTION OF FASHION

The same is true of stockings, although black mesh hose has traditionally been a fetishistic item. Corsets, garters and gloves used to be staples in the fetishist's wardrobe, but because of changes in fashion, these items are losing their historic place of importance.

Some glove or garter fetishists can still be found, though. One case has been reported of a man who would steal women's gloves which he would slip over his penis and then masturbate.

It has been alleged that the composer Peter Ilich Tchaikowsky was a glove fetishist. He reportedly always carried with him the glove of a woman he loved but who did not love him. The rumour has it that he too used this glove while masturbating.

Fetishes can be quite idiosyncratic and any perusal of sex magazine 'want ads' will probably turn up interests that have not been mentioned here. And then there are still other fetishes which will not even appear in such advertisements: for example, pillows.

PARTS OF THE BODY

The classic partialisms usually involve breasts, feet and buttocks. In some African and Pacific island societies the labia minora have become a matter of intense sexual interest and they are stretched from childhood to be as long as possible.

Among the Tswana of southern Africa, an interest in elongated labia is so important in heterosexual relations that a woman might be abandoned by her husband if they are not long enough – after all, if they are too short what would he have to play with?

Hair fetishists are sometimes reported. They may become a public nuisance because they are known to cut a lock off an unwitting person's head. There are even men who are tooth fetishists.

The most famous of nationwide partialisms must be the former Chinese passion for bound feet. In traditional Chinese erotic paintings and drawings,

The long, pointed stiletto heel – a symbol of sexiness for many men. But for the shoe fetishist, who often has sado-masochistic tendencies, it conjures up more exciting thoughts.

women are usually shown naked except that they wear socks over tiny deformed feet.

The impression for people who have not got a sensibility for bound feet, is that far from being erotic, the pictures are almost comical. But bound feet were not a comic matter since the process of foot binding was very painful and practically crippled the women involved.

The earliest reference to the practice of foot binding dates back to the 12th century, where it is said that an emperor two centuries before had his dancing girls bind their feet. From the court, the custom spread to the nobility and through the centuries even further down the social ladder until it became a general fashion for girls from respectable families that could afford to do so.

The most desirable feet were called 'Golden Lotus'. These were the smallest, no more than 7.5 cm (3 in) long. The 'Silver Lotus' was about 10 cm (4 in). Feet longer than this tended to be considered ridiculous and invited nicknames such as 'goose foot'.

So important were tiny feet in China that a girl whose feet had not been bound would have difficulty in finding a husband. And a prostitute whose feet had not been bound would be denied wealthy clients.

The fashion of foot binding ended at the turn of the century, but many Chinese people still remember female relatives whose feet had been bound.

UNUSUAL INTERESTS

Fetishisms and partialisms are actually subdivisions of a large group of sexual interests now usually called 'paraphilias'. The term paraphilia itself was created to replace another expression, perversion, which seemed to some sexologists as a put-down or to suggest unnecessarily that such sexual interests were pathological.

Essentially, paraphilias are unusual sexual interests. Within Freudian psychoanalytic circles they are still called perversions, however. Fetishisms and partialisms are the most common paraphilias.

Some people, for example, enjoy enemas – both the getting and giving of (a paraphilia called *klismaphilia*). For them the enema itself and not the sex of the partner may be the essential erotic element.

When people who identify themselves as heterosexual, homosexual or bisexual have paraphilias, however, they usually want to experience their paraphilias with a partner of the appropriate sex.

DRESSING UP

Transvestism, the interest in dressing in clothing defined as appropriate only for members of the opposite sex, is a common paraphilia and sometimes, but not always, involves real fetishism as well.

Another clothing paraphilia is 'cisvestism', the desire to dress up in uniforms or other costumes that are appropriate to the wearer's sex, but not to his age or occupation.

Some cisvestites want to be dressed like little children, even as infants with nappies. More commonly, inappropriate adult styles are worn, including such things as Nazi uniforms, cowboy outfits and in the male homosexual world of northern Europe and America, motorcyclist garb.

WHY MEN?

Just why fetishes seem to be a male preserve is unclear. It may be that men from an early age are socialized to derive pleasure from sex and are allowed, if not actively encouraged, to experiment, so that their associations with sex are far broader than a woman's.

Another possibility is that since boys are much more familiar with pornography, they are used to thinking about sex without a woman being present. They may masturbate while looking at images and so later

in life are more easily aroused by inanimate objects.

With women it is very different. Until recently they were not expected to enjoy sex – lovemaking was essentially to make children or to satisfy their husband's needs. They would not have experimented, and any pleasure that they did feel would have been directly linked to a particular person within a loving relationship.

These are just speculations, however, and there may be other factors involved. It does seem, though, that as women's attitudes to sex broaden, a degree of fetishism is creeping into their lives. But for the moment, fetishisms, partialisms and paraphilias belong almost exclusively to the world of men.

The Chinese obsession with tiny feet lasted from the 10th century until the early 1900s. By the time girls were adults, they were virtually crippled and their feet looked more like pigs' trotters than anything human. Comments about large feet were the worst types of insult. Fortunately, although the memory lingers on, the cultural fetish which inspired the binding of feet has finally died.

BODY DECORATION

From make-up to tattooing, body decoration is one of the ways in which people 'talk' to each other the world over

In current Western society, make-up on the faces of women is the only form of body decoration that does not incur almost universal disapproval. The scarred face of an African or the tattooed arms of a teenage renegade are looked down on. And in all societies, forms of body decoration that are not currently in vogue are thought of as primitive.

There is some validity to this. In primitive societies where people do not cover their bodies with clothes, body decoration has been practised since very early times and can still be seen today.

Many primitive tribes paint their bodies and faces and the use of red ochre and carmine to add a healthy flush to the cheeks and lips has been around for well over 5000 years.

WHY DECORATE YOUR BODY?

In tribes where people cannot express their social status through clothes, as we tend to do in the developed countries, body decoration often fulfils that role. The first marks of social rank are usually added at puberty and more designs are added during the individual's lifetime as they climb the social scale. The chief, naturally, exhibits the most exotic body decoration.

Much body decoration and facial painting have a superstitious value and are thought to protect the wearer from evil spirits. Also, the use of a common pattern gives the tribe a heightened sense of group identity.

The people of Tierra del Fuego, for example, paint their bodies red, white and black. Some tribes in central Africa dye their skin red while Aborigines paint themselves white with mud.

Red lips contrasting with a pale skin are considered perfect make-up for a Japanese geisha hostess.

A PRACTICAL PURPOSE

In the past, body decoration also had other practical purposes. Beauty spots came into vogue to cover the pock marks left by smallpox, but in the 17th century they developed their own language.

In the court of Louix XV of France, what had been simple round patches became crescents and stars. If positioned at the centre of the cheek they indicated gaiety, at the corner of the eye, passion, on the nose, sauciness and on the forehead, majesty. In England, their position denoted political allegiance. The Whigs wore their beauty spots on the right cheek, the Tories on the left.

MAKE-UP

The Egyptians first developed make-up to protect their skin from the harsh rays of the sun. As well as applying a primitive suntan lotion to their faces, they used a hydrosilicate of copper on their eyelids whose immediate effect was to bring down the swelling caused by the intense glare.

But the use of make-up soon grew beyond the purely protective. Cleopatra, like most upper class Egyptian ladies, spent much of her time applying purely decorative make-up. She used black galena on her eyebrows and painted her lower eyelids green and upper lids blue.

FALL AND RISE

The use of make-up has fluctuated throughout history. During the austere days of the Greek culture and Roman republics, its use was restricted to whores and the wives of the rich. But by the time Nero came to power, Rome had fallen into decadence and the use of make-up was widespread.

Indian nobles' penchant for make-up is recorded in

Quite open about what they do, these Japanese gangsters using a public bath wear their tattoos as badges of allegiance.

the *Kama Sutra*. But while the Indians were painting their faces and dyeing their feet, in sixth-century Europe the Christian Church frowned on all cosmetics as a manifestation of the deadly sin of pride.

The return of the Crusaders brought cosmetics back to Europe – for the rich at least. Aristocratic men also started to use make-up to flaunt their social status.

TODAY'S LOOK

The use of make-up for heterosexual men ended with the Regency period when only elderly dandies still painted their faces. And with the beginning of the Victorian era, women became more modest and it was only prostitutes and actresses that wore make-up.

Since then make-up has made a slow comeback. In the sixties, when people had more money and more leisure, it was loud and garish. These days the use of cosmetics is more subtle. A natural look is in. But the use of cosmetics for most men nowadays is still out.

WHY MAKE-UP?

Apart from the role in protecting the skin from the sun, make-up is obviously used to make the wearer appear younger, more beautiful and, therefore, more sexually attractive. However, certain elements in facial make-up have remained constant.

A SHORT-LIVED FAD

In the late 1960s, when nudity became a shocking new fashion again, body painting had a brief heyday. It was an age of leisure when people could afford the time to have their bodies covered with elaborate designs.

This was the height of the so-called 'permissive society' and it was obviously very sensual both to paint someone's naked body and to have your own naked body painted.

Many of the designs were 'psychedelic' or drug inspired. It was considered even more sensual to have your body painted if you were taking drugs that heightened your awareness of the brush strokes.

The hippy movement which started at that time put great emphasis on rediscovering this sort of spurious primitive folk culture. The fad was short-lived.

Much attention has been paid to the eyes. They are outlined in black to improve the contrast of the white of the eye and make the eye itself look wider. Widened eyes usually accompany sexual arousal.

The lids are painted which again increases the contrast of the white. Blue is most common and has always been the most favoured eye colour.

The red applied to lips and cheeks apes the sexual flush. According to Desmond Morris, the human lips themselves ape the appearance of the vulva. So reddening them has a double sexual significance.

TATTOOS

Many people find tattooing – especially facial tattooing – frightening. And that is certainly one reason why some primitive tribes and teenage rebels in Western societies have them done.

People with tattoos share a certain comradeship. They have chosen to be set apart from those who do not have tattoos. They also share a bond of pain. Although effective painkillers are widely available, most tattooists refuse to use them. The pain they say, is part of it. And their clients agree.

There is a certain machismo to be gained from standing the pain – and a certain masochistic pleasure to be derived from it. Many tattoo fanatics are homosexuals.

SEX AND TATTOOING

There is certainly a highly sexual element in tattooing. In a recent survey, most people much preferred having their tattoos done by someone of the opposite sex. Naturally, for any extensive work to be done – or shown off – a certain amount of nudity is required.

Oddly, fewer than ten per cent of people have sexually explicit material as part of their tattoo design. But more than half had tattoos on, or near, erogenous zones.

For women, the buttocks, the breasts and the inner thighs remain favourite areas for tattooing. But there are quite a few who have their nipples, or vaginal lips tattooed or even the hood of the clitoris. Snakes and other phallic symbols remain favourite emblems, along with an arrow pointing to the vagina saying: 'This way in'.

IMAGINATIVE TATTOOS

The doyen of American tattooists, Spider Webb, says that men can be equally imaginative. One of his clients had a vagina tattooed on his belly to make a statement about his bisexuality. Another had his wife's name tattooed along his perineum, the narrow strip of flesh that joins the scrotum to the anus.

The penis is also a favourite area. One of Webb's clients had his penis tattooed as the handle of a whip, with the lash running up over his chest. Another had a demon tattooed on his belly with the penis as his forked tongue. The demon had to be placed so that it would

EARLY MAKE-UP

Much of the early make-up used was dangerous. Ceruse, a foundation originally developed by the Egyptians, was based on highly poisonous white lead. And kohl, used as an eyeliner, was made from antimony and probably blinded many, who considered it the price of beauty.

be eyeball to eyeball with anyone performing fellatio on him.

Most tattooing, however, although of a sexual nature, is not so exotic. Usually, lovers have each other's names tattooed on them to lend a permanence to their relationship.

MUTILATION

Another way of making a permanent body decoration is by scarring. In primitive tribes the skin is cut and ash is rubbed into the wound to prevent it from healing properly. Geometric patterns are favoured.

Apart from this, deliberate mutilation and the pain involved being part of the pubescent's rite of passage, it also says to enemies: 'If we can do this to one another, think what we can do to you.'

Scarring has also been taken up by some Western

Above *Piercing parts of the body such as the nipples often says, 'Look at me, I'm tough because I can stand pain'.*

Left *With their black uniforms, aggressive tribal hairdoes and liberally pierced bodies, the anarchistic punks expressed forcefully their rejection of society in the 1970s.*

Below *As she grew up this Ethiopian Mursi girl inserted larger and larger lip plates. On reaching womanhood, the full-sized wooden plate is used to attract a husband.*

sado-masochists. The deliberate scarring of the buttocks, breasts and other areas turns some people on.

Various concepts of beauty also demand mutilation of the body. The Mursi of Ethiopia, for example, put ever-larger plates in their lower lips to expand them to grotesque sizes. Ears, noses and necks are similarly enlarged and deformed.

CIRCUMCISION

But the most common form of mutilation is circumcision. This is not just confined to the Jewish religion but is practised widely in Africa. At puberty the foreskin of an adolescent boy is ritually hacked off, often by his father or a tribal elder. This denotes the transition into manhood. He now has to bear the pain on his own and can no longer turn to his father or his tribe for protection. In some cases, the adolescent girls dance naked in front of the recently circumcised boys in an attempt to arouse them and prolong their suffering.

In East Africa women are also circumcised. The lips of their vaginas are removed – sometimes the clitoris is cut off as well. This usually happens in particularly strict patriarchal societies where women are not supposed to derive any enjoyment from sex.

PIERCING

The discreetly pierced ear has been a common method for women to attach their earrings for many centuries. For men it came into vogue in the 1960s – until then, the practice had been largely confined to seamen and gypsies.

The punk rocker in the late 1970s added a new variation with safety pins being stuck through ears, lips, cheeks and nostrils. For the rest of society, this is plainly intimidating. It proclaims that the wearer is not afraid of pain.

Piercing is often taken to grotesque degrees, probably for sado-masochistic reasons. Nipples of both sexes are pierced, which helps keep them permanently aroused. Many women have a ring put through the lip of their vagina. Some have both lips pierced, a small padlock inserted and give the key to their lover to ensure their fidelity. In puritanical societies, the labia – or the edges of the foreskin – were sometimes kept permanently clipped together.

Men take the genital piercing even further, though. Some have small metal posts with balls that screw on the end inserted through the edge of the glans or an ampallang, a longer post, inserted through the tip.

Others have a ring inserted under the back of the glans which emerges through the urethra itself. This is called a Prince Albert and, according to tradition, was popular during Victorian times to secure the penis to the trouser legs.

After piercing, some men remove the sleeper before the wound is healed so that they can suffer the exquisite pain again. Others report that the ring increases their pleasure during intercourse.

SEX CULTS

It makes headlines every time, yet the power of the sex cult is as old as religion itself – shocking for some and spiritually awakening for others

Throughout history, human beings have given their sexuality an importance greater than that of simple reproduction or personal pleasure. The sex act itself and the sex organs – especially the penis – have had a mystical and religious significance in thousands of different cultures worldwide. In the widest sense, sex cults are as old as religion itself.

The temple prostitutes of Ancient Babylon, Greece and Rome practised ritual sex, sometimes as a fertility rite. The followers of the Greek god Dionysus held wild drunken orgies in his honour. In medieval Europe, fanatical Christian sects such as the Bogomils and Fraticelli of Italy scandalized the church by practising promiscuity and group sex for the greater glory of God. Sex cults today have many ancestors on which to look back.

WHAT ARE SEX CULTS?

While there are some sex cults which openly admit that their main aim and purpose is to enable their members to explore a wide variety of sexual activity, others would object vehemently to being called sex cults at all.

The 'orange people' who follow the guru Rajneesh, for example, would say that they are interested primarily in spiritual matters, and that the media coverage of their sexual activities is sensationalistic.

Similarly, some of the alternative idealistic communities which were set up in the 1960s and '70s in North America and Europe were not created simply to

The communes of the 1960s and '70s believed in free sexual expression and held group therapy sessions to help cast inhibitions aside.

afford their members free sex whenever they wanted it.

However, many of these groups place an important emphasis on sex or specific sexual activities, either as an end in itself, or as a means to achieve a higher goal. At one end of the scale are the religious, idealistic and psychosexual therapy groups who stress the importance

of free sexual expression – at the other are the clubs and sometimes fairly gruesome cults specializing in ritualistic group sex or sado-masochistic sex.

UTOPIAN SEX

Sexual jealousy and possessiveness have long been seen as stumbling blocks by those wishing to form idealistic, socialist communities. It was considered unnatural for human beings to have one exclusive sexual partner. And, if property was to be shared, so too was sexual contact. Such communities were proposed in Ancient Greece, and free sex was an integral part of a utopian community proposed by the poet Shelley in the early 1800s. Interestingly, stories of extravagant sexual promiscuity were reported in the Soviet Union after the 1918 Revolution.

In more recent times, hundreds of small communities were established in the '60s and '70s in which group sex, or at least sex in full view of other members of the group, was encouraged as a way of overcoming sexual inhibition and possessiveness. In the early months of the community or 'commune', many people undoubtedly found such a way of life stimulating and enjoyable. After a few months, however, people began to drift to more stable partnerships, finding the traditional sexual bond (or something very like it) if anything more sustaining than confining.

Under the guidance of their guru, the 'orange people' sought spiritual awareness through sex. But, when news of their group gropes hit the headlines, the public were outraged.

PROLONGED INTERCOURSE

One utopian group of particular interest is the Oneida Colony, founded in New York State in 1848, and which is now based on the West Coast. From the beginning, it believed in free sexual expression as an important element in establishing a harmonious community. The men of Oneida practise what their founder called 'male continence' – the male has full sexual intercourse without ejaculation. Sexual intercourse within the colony commonly lasted for periods of an hour or more, with the woman having several orgasms. The men experienced 'dry' orgasms, experiencing all the physical sensations of orgasm, but without actually coming or losing their erections.

A certain amount of training is required to achieve this. Oneida men would masturbate themselves to the point of ejaculation and then stop. By concentrating on the sensations in the penis and scrotum, they could learn to recognize those that were present just before the point of ejaculation. They also used the 'squeeze' technique, applying firm pressure just beneath the head of the penis to prevent ejaculation. By repeating these techniques over a period of months, the ejaculatory mechanism became effectively 'switched off'. Only after this point was reached did they experience the 'dry' orgasm, in some cases as often as three or four times during a lovemaking session.

The thinking behind such a technique must surely have been that sexually satisfied women would contribute more fully to working in the colony.

TANTRIC TECHNIQUES

The techniques of male continence have long been known in Eastern cultures – in Hindu literature, the method is called *karezza*, and is a feature of Tantric sexual practices in India and China. The sexual rituals of the Tantric cults are not primarily to increase sexual pleasure, but are used to balance the *yin* (female energy) and *yang* (masculine quality). In order to advance along the path of spiritual enlightenment, the follower of the Tantra must have large reserves of psychic energy, correctly balanced in its qualities of yin and yang. Prolonged intercourse, often lasting many hours, enables the male to draw yin energy from the woman. By not ejaculating, he also retains the yang energy of the sperm created by prolonged sexual contact.

Outside of Tantric practice, prolonged intercourse techniques were taught and recommended for the additional pleasure they brought the woman. Female sexual needs have traditionally been more widely understood in Eastern cultures than in the West, and mutual sexual satisfaction was understood to be important in maintaining a stable family bond. The performance of the typical selfish Western male is not highly regarded in many parts of the world.

Another feature of the 1960s and '70s in the West was the rise of religious cults. Some of these, such as the Divine Light Mission headed by the adolescent guru,

Maharaj Ji, preached sexual abstinence as a means to perfection. Others took a more popular line – the Children of God, for example, earned the nickname 'hookers for Jesus' because female members were encouraged to offer sex to potential recruits.

Perhaps the most famous of these cults is the 'orange people', the followers of the guru Rajneesh. Thousands of young people from Europe and the United States made the pilgrimage to Poona in India in the late 1970s to sit at the guru's feet. Some, no doubt, were attracted by the widely publicized complete freedom from sexual taboo that was part of the cult's philosophy.

Rajneesh, too, recommended techniques of prolonged intercourse, both to prolong enjoyment and to control sexual desires. (A disillusioned follower has since reported that Rajneesh did not practise what he preached – when the guru occasionally bestowed his favours on a privileged follower, he usually ejaculated on penetration.)

The freedom of sexual expression, and the resulting scenes at the ashram in Poona, attracted international attention and strong local disapproval that eventually forced Rajneesh to move to America. Group 'gropes' with as many as thirty or forty women participants were common. Women, in particular, seemed to discover the aggressive side to their sexuality and to lose their inhibitions, perhaps because their sexuality is particularly repressed in Western culture. Some male followers of Rajneesh felt intimidated as women went from man to man in extended sex sessions, or masturbated openly to achieve sexual satisfaction. The atmosphere was one of release tinged with hysteria.

SEX AND SPIRITUALITY

In reply to those who accused Rajneesh of simply selling sex (many followers donated large sums of money), Rajneesh argued that before they could achieve full spiritual awareness and personal growth, people had to explore and overcome their sexual obsessions and feelings of guilt. The quickest way to achieve this was to allow them to act out their desires – after a few weeks of sexual freedom, people would begin to look elsewhere for fulfilment. Given a free run of a sweet-shop, people soon get tired of sweets.

Today, the Rajneesh movement has been discredited in many ways. While many of Rajneesh's followers claim to have benefited psychologically and spiritually from their involvement with the cult, others suffered mental breakdown of varying degrees of severity, precipitated, they say, by their experiences. For these people, the sexual and spiritual enlightenment promised by Rajneesh was not forthcoming.

SEX AND WITCHCRAFT CULTS

Witchcraft, or 'natural religion' as witches themselves prefer to term their beliefs and practices, has long been popularly associated with sex rituals. Stories of covens in respectable suburbs are usually accompanied by a

Reaching out to people through sex, earned the idealistic Children of God the nickname 'hookers for Jesus'. The female members of the cult, which has now disappeared, offered sex to would-be recruits.

Although religious cults and commune-living no longer hold the same sway, isolated hippy and 'druid' groups still gather together every year to celebrate mid-summer solstice and be at one with nature.

blurred photograph of naked people dancing and chanting, or of an attractive witch obviously naked under her dark cloak.

True witches deny that sex plays such an important role in their religion. They often celebrate naked, but sex rarely takes place. The popular image owes more to fiction and to those cults that use witchcraft as a guide for group sexual activity.

These pseudo-witchcraft groups have often taken their inspiration from Aleister Crowley, the self-proclaimed satanist, drug addict and writer who was at the height of his fame in the 1920s.

Crowley undoubtedly had a forceful and magnetic sexual presence, and was able to attract willing young disciples of both sexes. Many of Crowley's rituals involved anal and oral sex, with Crowley usually taking the active role. Preparations of blood and semen (usually Crowley's) were consumed in rites intended to raise supernatural deities to do Crowley's will.

The publicity that Crowley attracted (and relished), and the stories of his sexual excesses attracted many imitators. After all, the ritualized sex, with its overtones of sadism and its use of masks and sometimes whips, perfectly matched some people's hitherto secret sexual fantasies of either wielding or yielding to power and dominance.

CEREMONIAL SEX

A typical modern satanist evening would begin with a ceremony loosely based on the Christian mass. The water and wine were symbolically desecrated and the

Clubs for 'swingers', as devotees of group sex called themselves, could be found in all the major cities of Europe and America. Usually the clubs were strictly for couples only, although some also allowed single women to join. Some clubs used fixed premises, although in some cases members' homes would be used.

The club would provide a relaxing atmosphere, a bar (soft drinks were encouraged) and snacks, with blue movies and sex aids for its customers. As many as two hundred people could be present on any evening. Group scenes involving five or sex men and women having sexual intercourse were popular.

Exclusively homosexual acts between men were rarely seen although women often paired up during an evening session. The only sexual bar was on the more extreme forms of sado-masochistic behaviour. As elementary codes of conduct, members were expected to observe basic hygiene and freshen up in the showers regularly, not to stay with one partner all evening or to make derogatory comments about others' personal appearance or sexual performance. And, to prevent possibly unpleasant scenes, couples who arrived together were expected to leave together.

SADO-MASOCHISM

For most men and women, a little playful bondage, with either partner occasionally taking the helpless role, may add excitement to their sex lives. The prostitutes who specialize in more excessive S and M routines, offering the services of a fully-appointed 'torture' chamber, tend to do so more for commercial rather than sexual or psychological reasons. However, there are devotees of S and M who claim that its emphasis on domination and submission offers a truer expression of human sexuality than conventional sex.

While in theory this may sound reasonable, in practice it has its dangers. People have suffocated after being left bound and gagged, and the borderline between some sado-masochistic acts and sheer psychopathic cruelty is perilously thin.

THE NEW CHASTITY

The sexual experiments and excesses of the recent past have declined almost as rapidly as they rose. Group sex and casual sex has always carried with them the risk of contracting a sexually transmitted disease, but these for the most part could be seen as inconveniences, something that responded to treatment after a few weeks. For heterosexuals and homosexuals alike, the rise of AIDS has changed all that.

Similarly, the interest in religious and spiritual exploration seems to have waned. The western world has entered a new era of comparative chastity and conservatism. Perhaps in twenty years' time the sex cults will again be fashionable. But perhaps there has been a more important change. Could people now be relaxed and open enough about their sexuality to find their fulfilment in their everyday relationships?

high priest bared his rump to receive the kiss of peace. Various deities may have been conjured by ritualized chanting. Afterwards, often aided by the use of drugs, the members of the cult pursued their own pleasures.

Satanists claim that their practices do indeed put them in touch with elements of the supernatural. And in the experience of many churchmen and psychologists, satanism is one of the most dangerous of the sex cults. Followers often find it impossible to disassociate themselves from the cult and often live in terror of reprisal if they attempt to do so. Perhaps because such cults tend to attract weaker, neurotic personalities who come to be dominated by the cult leader, instances of madness and suicide are not uncommon among those who have dabbled in satanism.

'SWINGING' CLUBS

In the 1970s, there was a huge growth in clubs and other organizations to cater for those who wanted group sex but did not want to join a religious cult to get it.

SEX SERVICES

Phone-call fantasies, 'dial-a-girl' for the night, torrid tours to Bangkok – the range of sex services is ever increasing. But who uses them and why?

Prostitution, it is said, is the oldest profession in the world. But it is only the tip of the iceberg of a massive industry that provides sexual services for lonely and desperate people who cannot find the satisfaction they crave from a normal, stable relationship.

Despite several puritanical attempts to clean up the business, the numbers and types of sexual services on offer are now greater than ever. They have even embraced technical advances. The development of the credit card has helped a whole series of telephone services flourish which would have been difficult to organize before. And some entrepreneurs have even investigated the possibilities of producing titillating computer games.

ESCORT AGENCIES

Men like to be seen out with women – especially good-looking women. Businessmen particularly like a pretty woman on their arm to impress colleagues, clients and commercial competitors. But in foreign cities or any place distant from home it can be difficult to rustle up the right sort of company on demand. So escort agencies – who are usually located in the hotel areas of cities and near the airports – cater for this need.

The agencies advertise in men's magazines and in the city listings magazines that cater for visitors, rather than residents. The service they offer is simple. Clients either phone the agency and are assigned a girl, or they visit the office and have the pick of the girls available. Payment is in advance and by credit card for phone bookings. Some agencies say that if you do not like the girl they send, they will send another.

Many of these agencies are legitimate in that they do not encourage or condone prostitution. But in some cases the girls may be available for extra-curricular activities, if the price is right. This will, of course, be negotiated with the girl herself.

Some agencies are a little more blatant though. Instead of offering presentable escorts for respectable men, they offer 'models' and 'hostesses', which have other connotations. Some even ask you to specify the type of model you want: 'Swedish au pair', 'Latin beach girl', 'French student', 'Alpine milk maid', 'Oriental dancer'. But even for an imaginative mind, it is fairly difficult to envisage a lonely businessman spending a quiet evening in an expensive restaurant with an Alpine milk maid.

Advertising pays, especially when it is carefully worded. After all, how can selling a 'Spanish chest', giving 'French lessons' or a 'continental' massage be against the law?

In the hotel areas of most cities, a lonely businessman can ask an escort agency to provide him with a companion for the evening. The service may be quite legitimate, or it may be thinly disguised prostitution

There are also agencies that supply a choice of handsome young men for women on their own in town. The men are well dressed and presentable at any social function. However, again, prostitution does go on under the guise of the legitimate escort business and it is difficult to draw the line between where one ends and the other begins. If one of the escorts fancies one of the clients, for example, goes to bed with them, then receives an expensive parting gift, is that prostitution?

Naturally, not all encounters between escort and client are as innocent as that. Some of the agencies insist that the escort beds the client if humanly possible and demand a proportion of any payment. This is blatant prostitution, but it too is couched in the cosy terms of the escort business to get round the law.

While there is nothing illegal about prostitution in many countries – anyone is at liberty to take money for their sexual favours and the law recognizes that this would be hard to prevent – soliciting, running a brothel and thereby living off the immoral earnings of others is against the law.

So the escort is breaking the law if he or she suggests going to bed with the client for money – that is soliciting – and the agency would be breaking the law if it took a kickback – that would be living off immoral earnings.

The loophole used is to get the client to suggest to the escort that they go to bed and that the two of them fix the price between them. The agency does not receive any part of the money the client hands over for these sexual services, although they do get a cut – usually the major cut – of the money the client pays simply for the 'company' of the escort.

MASSAGE PARLOURS

The health-giving properties of massage have been known for thousands of years – and these days there are many qualified masseurs and masseuses who abhor the seamy connections some people attach to the trade.

Yet, while these qualified masseurs and masseuses maintain the highest standards of their profession, there is another side to the business: an aspect that has brought massage parlours to the streets of every major city – masturbation for money.

To all intents and purposes, red-light district massage parlours work as if they were a regular part of the health services. You go in, pay your money, take your clothes off and have a masseur – or much more probably a masseuse – massage your aching limbs. The only difference is that you usually get to pick the girl you want to massage you – the massage parlour business has an almost exclusively male clientele.

As the law in this area is much stricter, the girls are careful not to suggest that they are going to do anything immoral. This would, of course, leave the owners of the parlour wide open to the charge of running a brothel.

In this type of parlour, however, the masseuse will usually do her best to arouse the client. But often a large tip will have to be negotiated before the masseuse will masturbate the client. And a larger tip still is required if the client wants to be fellated.

Intercourse rarely takes place and the masseuses seldom remove any of their clothing – this would leave them vulnerable if the place were raided. But loose clothing and short white coats that give the impression that nothing is being worn beneath them are enough of a turn-on for most customers.

The situation is much more lax for erotic masseuses, who visit their clients. They advertise in men's magazines, city listings magazines and some local papers. As they are not working on their own premises, the charge of running a brothel cannot be applied. So they are relatively free to do what they like, provided the client makes the initial suggestion.

Of course, there are qualified masseurs and masseuses who visit patients in their homes. But their services would not be advertised in men's magazines.

Visiting 'erotic' massage services are thinly veiled prostitution – the massage cover is used simply because advertising as a prostitute would, again, be soliciting and therefore illegal.

However, some do come close to the mark by advertising 'French' massage – a euphemism for oral sex. Others are 'gentle but firm', especially those with names like 'Miss Domina', and 'Miss Guidance'. The age and race of the masseuse is often mentioned too. There are 'baby-faced 18-year-olds', 'Caribbean girls' and 'experts from Denmark'. Then there are the blondes, redheads and brunettes – another give-away that a sexual service is being offered, for if you actually needed a massage for your aching limbs, it is doubtful that the masseuse's hair colouring would matter much to you.

PHOTOGRAPHIC MODELS

For many men, photographic magazines, photography itself and photographic models in particular are a source of intense erotic interest. The idea that simply by owning a camera you can get beautiful women to take their clothes off is perpetuated by even the most august camera journals – and by some of the seamier studios.

Along with props, lighting and photographic equipment these studios offer the services of models. They may specify their models as glamour, topless, nude, continental or exotic.

'Glamour' models will pose in underwear or a scanty swimsuit or maybe less. 'Continental' means that they will expose their genitals or adopt provocative poses. And 'exotic' suggests that the models may be persuaded to go even further.

These are only broad guidelines. The exact nature of what a model will and will not do has to be discussed with the girl herself. For the serious photography enthusiast, however, a visit to some red light district studios may prove a disappointment as there may not be any film in the cameras they hire out!

SPECIALIST TASTES

Those with specialist tastes are well catered for by the sexual service industry. Small ads in men's magazines offer nude photosets of 'big fat mamas – 45 to 63 years, 18 stone and over', 'big boobs – pictures of truly massive mammaries up to 84 inches' and 'forbidden fruit' – school girls, lesbian love, bondage, corporal punishment and nude mud wrestling.

These various tastes are catered for in magazines and videos as well. Other video companies just claim to cater for the connoisseur. Dominant themes are sex slaves, nude housewives, girls training as nude models and striptease artists, 'home-made' videos and imports from the US and Scandinavia.

Many of these items can be ordered by phone – with payment being made by credit card. And some com-

Some video companies cater for specialist tastes, such as lesbian love. Films can be ordered and paid for over the telephone. And there is often a phone-in service, giving information on new titles

panies run a phone-in information service on the latest videos available. Videos purchased can also be exchanged for an additional fee.

Some models promise 'horny' audio tapes to accompany their pictures and offer a customized service – they will make a tape to order.

KNICKERS

There is a brisk trade in worn panties. These are usually accompanied by a photo of a girl claiming to be the former owner of the undergarments, a sexy letter or tape from her or a video showing her wearing the knickers or taking them off. Those offering letters sometimes ask the client to specify their own fantasy which the letter writer will then address.

Foot fetishists are offered stockings and stilettos, and there are jockstraps for the homosexual market.

MAIL ORDER

Mail order services supply sexy and fetishistic clothing – erotic frillies, gymslips, directoire and school knickers, French maids' uniforms, leather wear, lingerie. As with regular mail order clothing services the client makes a selection by leafing through the company's catalogue. But in this case the catalogue itself is pornographic, and therefore expensive.

Sex aids companies also offer erotic catalogues featuring pictures of their products in use.

The clothing catalogues often specialize in areas of specific fetishistic interest – leather or rubber wear. And they offer free gifts – leather chokers, free basques or, from the sex aid catalogues, free vibrators.

Remember that any company that supplies goods by mail order is bound by the same rules of trading as a shop. If the goods are faulty, not fitted to their purpose or not as described in the advertisements you should demand your money back.

Some of these companies supply substandard products in the hope that the client will be too embarrassed to make a complaint through the normal channels. If you are embarrassed, write to the publisher of the magazine in which you saw the advertisement. They should help you.

PHONE CALLS

It is even possible to have an erotic experience by phone these days. Companies providing these services claim that there are beautiful girls just waiting for your call. All you have to do is dial their number and 'before you know it they will talk you to relief and ecstasy'.

The addresses only of these phone services appear in men's magazines as you have to write to them to arrange payment first. This is done by a running account or by using the ever-flexible credit card.

Chat-up lines can also be rung up. Though slightly titillating for some, the messages are not personalized and a great deal less raunchy. The numbers to call are advertised in local papers and in many magazines.

The ultimate sexual service for men is an 'adult sex tour'. Weekend tours of Amsterdam and Copenhagen are on offer and there are longer tours to the Far East – Bangkok is the favourite destination.

The organizers lay on travel and hotel facilities as well as tours of the red light district and visits to live shows, massage parlours and brothels.

SAFE CONTACT

In the wake of the AIDS and herpes scares, the latest service to be offered is 'safe sex'. For a small fee, connect services say that they will put you in contact with people with the same social or sexual interests without the risk of contacting these diseases.

However, as no foolproof method of detecting AIDS has yet been developed, it is unlikely that these companies can live up to their claims and quite likely that other companies in the realm of sexual services will see a decline in their custom.

Japan's 'telephone girls' take the phone-call fantasy one step further. Instead of being aroused by a faceless voice, men can focus their wildest fantasies on a 'real' woman

SEX AND HEALTH

Although the intensity of our sex drive waxes and wanes, it is nevertheless constantly with us, often well into old age. In the vast majority of people it seeks continuity of expression. Sexual diseases, apart from the physical suffering they cause, frustrate this continuity and so affect our state of mind too. An unwanted pregnancy can also interrupt an otherwise happy sex life, bringing with it stress that makes sex the last thing the pregnant woman is interested in. Both these situations can be avoided — or at least the risk of their occurring can be minimized — if we are well informed about the fine balance that must be struck between sexual expression and preserving health.

With the threat of Aids facing heterosexuals and homosexuals alike, careless sexual contact is more than ever a danger. An understanding of how this and other sexual diseases are transmitted goes a long way to helping us avoid risking our own health and that of our partners. Contraception is also, by definition, a matter of prevention and every sexually active person with a sense of responsibility gains a proper understanding of it.

This chapter discusses in detail the range of contraceptive methods available, many of them so efficient that there is very little need for an unwanted pregnancy to occur. It also looks at the main sexual diseases, including Aids.

CONTRACEPTION

Despite the availability of family planning and an increasing range of contraceptives, millions of women throughout the world still risk unplanned pregnancy because they and their partners do not use regular or reliable contraception

Every year two million American women have abortions, and the number of unintended pregnancies remains stubbornly high.

One reason is that information about contraception is often not reaching the people that most need it. As a result, couples and individuals often make the wrong decisions about the methods they choose, use them badly, or abandon them altogether. Others are not using contraception at all and simply taking a chance that they do not get pregnant.

It is not really surprising that this happens, since information about contraceptive methods is changing all the time. As methods are tested and researched, more risks and side-effects come to light and the more confusing it all becomes – for doctors as well as the consumers.

Choice becomes even more complicated as scientific research points to limiting medical methods of contraception to particular ages and groups of women.

At the same time women have learned to understand and appreciate their bodies far more and are less inclined simply to accept what they are prescribed. Increasingly, they are attracted by methods which they see as more natural, in keeping with the general trend towards a more natural lifestyle.

SHARING THE CHOICE

With the arrival of the Pill and IUD (Intra-Uterine Device) in the 1960s, women took responsibility for contraception and were relieved to have the means of preventing pregnancy under their own control. But many women now feel resentful that they shoulder all the risks and problems, while more men feel unhappy that they have no role to play.

Time and time again, studies show that men's intentions in terms of sharing responsibility for contraception are often very positive. Unfortunately, these same studies show that for most men there is a wide gap between intention and practice.

There is no ideal contraceptive, nor is there likely to be for decades. But good methods do exist. They all have advantages and disadvantages, and the way individuals or couples assess these very much depend on their lifestyle and attitudes to sex.

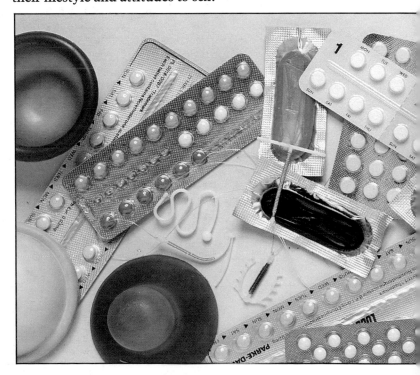

For many people there will be a different 'best method' at different times of their life. For couples the solution to sharing the responsibility may be to alternate between male and female methods.

Doctors and nurses can help you make a choice, and counselling services are gradually becoming more accessible to men as well as women, but in the end the decision has to be yours. A good choice of contraceptive can help you enjoy a relaxed sex life as well as protecting against unintended pregnancy.

THE PILL

When most people refer to the Pill, they mean the oral contraceptive which contains two hormones, oestrogen and progestogen, that stop women ovulating.

The Pill became available in the early 1960s and it gained popularity, after initial problems, to become the most used method of birth control and almost synonymous with contraception. But in the last 20 or so years a great deal of information has been collected on the effects of the Pill on women's health.

Some of this information is inconclusive and confusing, but it has resulted in more thought being given to minimizing side-effects and the production of a second generation of contraceptive Pills which contained much lower doses of hormones.

THE PILL AND THE RISKS

To some extent it has also become possible to identify those women who might run risks from taking the Pill, such as smokers, those who are overweight or those with high blood pressure.

Since the publication of reports in October 1983, suggesting possible, but unconfirmed links between taking the Pill and breast and cervical cancer, women are increasingly questioning that crucial balance between reliability and safety.

The great attraction of the Pill has always been its reliability together with its convenience. For many couples the Pill is the only method which allows them to be completely spontaneous in their lovemaking.

A chat with a counsellor to discuss the various methods may make the final decision easier.

Many women are trying to weigh up the plusses and minuses of taking the Pill. The most serious condition linked with the Pill is thrombosis, although the risk is very small unless you smoke or are overweight. Other side-effects include depression, weight gain, loss of sex drive and headaches, although these can often be stopped by changing to a different Pill. It is worth remembering, however, that the Pill may protect against some diseases such as cancer of the ovaries and rheumatoid arthritis. And it is certainly the most convenient form of contraception at present.

THE MINI-PILL

For some women looking to minimize the health risks of Pill-taking, a move to the mini-Pill will provide a good solution. Mini-Pills contain only one hormone,

MALE PILLS AND OTHER MALE METHODS

Probably the most intriguing possibilities for contraception lie in the development of a male Pill

Magazine surveys shows that men have a variety of reactions to the idea of shouldering the responsibility of contraception by taking a pill every day.

Women, too, while wanting to shift the responsibility, question how dedicated men would be in taking it regularly. After all, it is not the man who gets pregnant if he forgets to take it.

A male Pill is actually more difficult to 'design' than the female Pill because there is no single event — like the release of the female egg

— on which to work.

The most promising male Pill so far has come from China and was discovered by accident when it was noticed that in rural areas, where cotton-seed oil was used for cooking, the men had become infertile.

The first clinical trials on the plant extract gossypol, responsible for

the infertility, started in China in 1972 and were reported six years later. The results were very encouraging, the effectiveness was nearly 100 per cent and there were few side-effects.

Further research carried out by the World Health Organization (but which has been abandoned) showed that side-

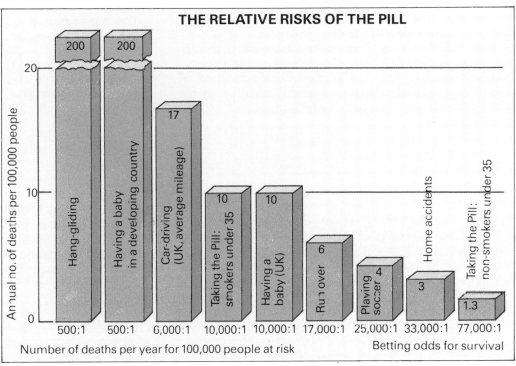

THE RELATIVE RISKS OF THE PILL

Annual no. of deaths per 100,000 people

- 200 Hang-gliding — 500:1
- 200 Having a baby in a developing country — 500:1
- 17 Car-driving (UK, average mileage) — 6,000:1
- 10 Taking the Pill: smokers under 35 — 10,000:1
- 10 Having a baby (UK) — 10,000:1
- 6 Run over — 17,000:1
- 4 Playing soccer — 25,000:1
- 3 Home accidents — 33,000:1
- 1.3 Taking the Pill: non-smokers under 35 — 77,000:1

Number of deaths per year for 100,000 people at risk   Betting odds for survival

progestogen, and the dose is lower than the progestogen dose in the combined Pill. They do not stop ovulation but prevent pregnancy in other ways, such as thickening the mucus at the entrance to the cervix to make it difficult for the sperm to penetrate.

As it does not contain oestrogen the mini-Pill is not thought to contribute to the risks of thrombosis, nor have mini-Pills been implicated in the recent cancer scares. On the other hand, they are less effective, and if a pregnancy does happen there is some risk of it being outside the womb – most probably in the Fallopian tubes. Women taking the mini-Pill also tend to suffer from irregular, or break-through, bleeding.

Mini-Pills must be taken every day at exactly the same time each day to be effective. They are usually considered most suitable for older women and breast-feeding mothers, but are not yet widely prescribed.

LONGER-ACTING METHODS

Depo-provera is a synthetic progestogen which is given by injection, usually into the muscle of the buttock. It is absorbed over a period of three months and stops ovulation.

Use of Depo-provera as a contraceptive has been controversial, and for many years it was only licensed in Britain for short-term use in special circumstances. In 1984, however, it was granted a licence for long-term use and is gradually becoming more readily available.

The controversy has arisen partly because of unpleasant side-effects such as irregular and frequent bleeding, weight gain and delays in return of fertility, and partly because of unsubstantiated fears of breast cancer and cancer of the lining of the womb.

There is concern that Depo-provera is sometimes

effects were more common than originally thought, and included a feeling of weakness, digestive problems and loss of sex drive.

The conclusion seems to be that gossypol itself will not be the male Pill of the future, but something similar may be developed instead.

Other male Pills could be developed from existing drugs, such as one used for hypertension and at present on trial in Israel. This particular drug acts as an 'ejaculation inhibitor'.

Alternative possibilities being researched include the injection of the synthetic hormone – 19-nortestosterone – which is used by some athletes to build up their muscles. Unfortunately, however, the drug has the strange side-effect of reducing the testicles to half their normal size.

A mixture of the hormones oestradiol and testosterone rubbed into the abdomen has also been unsuccessful as in trials it caused the men's partners to grow moustaches.

A male version of the 'releasing' hormone nasal spray and a mix of hormones introduced by a tiny pump have had no success so far.

given without proper explanation, so that women are misled about possible side-effects and sometimes suffer badly until the effect of the drug wears off.

The advantages of Depo-provera are its high reliability and ease of use. Most family planning experts, however, do not see it as a first-choice method of contraception, but rather as a useful addition to the range of contraceptives suitable for those unable to use other methods.

There is another injectable hormone called Noristerat now available, which lasts for two months and is used as an extra precaution after a vasectomy operation.

IUD, OR COIL

An Intra-Uterine Device (IUD) is a small 2.5cm (1in)-long flexible plastic device, now usually wound with copper, which is inserted into the womb by a doctor.

Coils come in a variety of different shapes and are normally replaced every two to five years, depending on

the type. Although no-one knows exactly how an IUD works, it prevents an egg from implanting in the womb lining.

Like the Pill, the coil was introduced in the 1960s, but has never achieved the same popularity. One reason for this was that early coils were not usually a first choice for women who had not had a child, for they were rather large in relation to the size of the womb.

More recently, copper-wound coils are smaller, but now there are different reasons why these are not recommended to women who have not had children. The problem is that the presence of a coil makes a woman more susceptible to pelvic infection which can be difficult to deal with and which could affect her ability to conceive later on.

The failure rate of the coil is about the same as the mini-Pill and, like the mini-Pill, pregnancies that do occur could be ectopic (occurring outside the womb).

One of the main disadvantages of the coil is that it often causes heavier periods. There may also be bleed-

INTRA-UTERINE DEVICES (IUDs) AND BARRIER METHODS

THE CHOICE:
IUDs (and applicator), the sponge, diaphragm, vault cap and cervical cap

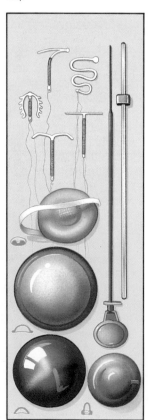

FITTING AN IUD (COIL)

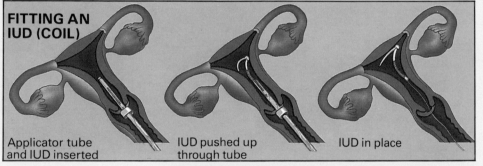

Applicator tube and IUD inserted

IUD pushed up through tube

IUD in place

The IUD is fitted by a doctor. It is threaded into an applicator, which is inserted into the vagina and through the cervical opening. The IUD is passed through the applicator tube into the womb Diaphragms and caps must be used with a spermicide, and initially fitted by a doctor or nurse, who gives instructions on how to use them The contraceptive sponge works on similar principles.

APPROXIMATE POSITION OF DIAPHRAGM OR CAP

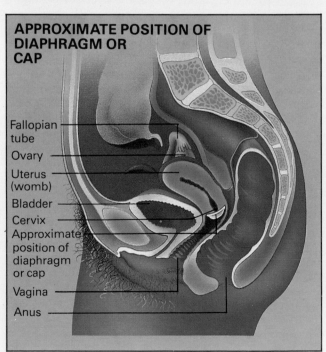

Fallopian tube
Ovary
Uterus (womb)
Bladder
Cervix
Approximate position of diaphragm or cap
Vagina
Anus

CONTRACEPTIVE METHODS AND EFFECTIVENESS

Information from leaflets and Fact Sheets published by the UK Family Planning Information Service (May 1988).

METHOD	EFFECTIVENESS
THE COMBINED PILL (triphasic and biphasic pills/Everyday Pill)	99% (if taken properly)
MINI-PILL	98% (if taken properly)
INJECTABLE CONTRACEPTIVES (Depo-Provera/Noristerat)	Over 99%
IUD	96–99%
DIAPHRAGM or CAP (plus spermicide)	85–97% (with careful use)
SPONGE	75–91% (with careful use)
SHEATH	85–98% (with careful use)
'SAFE PERIOD' (body-temperature method)	85–93% (with careful use)
FEMALE STERILIZATION	Occasional failure: 1 in 300
MALE STERILIZATION	Occasional failure: 1 in 1,000

Effectiveness rates for reversible methods refer to the number of women out of 100 using the method for a year who do not get pregnant.

Post-coital effectiveness rates refer to the number of women out of 100 who do not become pregnant after using post-coital methods.

ing between periods. One of the main advantages is that, once fitted, there is no further involvement by the woman, except to check now and then that it is in the correct place by feeling the threads. An internal check-up by your doctor every year or so is essential.

BARRIER METHODS

Men and women started using barriers of various kinds to prevent pregnancy thousands of years ago.

Currently available are the diaphragm, cervical cap, vault cap and vimule cap. They are all made of soft rubber and fit over the neck of the womb (the cervix).

They are used with spermicide cream or jelly, and inserted before sex to form a barrier to sperm.

The newest barrier is the contraceptive sponge. Even though it is less reliable than the diaphragm, and therefore only suitable for women for whom pregnancy would not be disastrous, it overcomes some of the main objections to diaphragms and caps.

A major complaint by women is that barrier methods are too messy, interfere with spontaneous love-making and look unattractive. The sponge, which like the cap must be left in place for at least six hours after lovemaking, is impregnated with spermicide and after one use thrown away.

The male sheath is making a comeback. It is a reliable barrier method which rarely has any side effects. Today's sheaths are finer than ever before and often ribbed for increased sensation.

'SAFE-PERIOD' METHODS

These are usually used by couples who have objections to other methods for religious or other reasons. They are becoming increasingly popular with women who

Sheaths, the only contraceptive product available for men, can be bought readily from any chemist.

do not want to use medical or mechanical methods to avoid pregnancy. And as women become more aware of changes throughout their reproductive cycle, they are drawn to methods that are finely tuned to their own needs.

'Safe-period' methods aim to pinpoint when a woman is most fertile and then to avoid intercourse at this time. She will have to note signs of ovulation by taking her temperature every day (body-temperature method) or examining her cervical mucus (Billings method).

Careful record-keeping is essential, as is high motivation by both partners, with the acceptance that there will be times when they cannot have intercourse. These methods do need to be learned and are not suitable for women with irregular periods or for a while after childbirth.

'Safe-period' methods do not give the reliability that most couples demand. The effectiveness is increased when the temperature method is combined with the Billings method and other signs of ovulation.

Most people have heard about the 'morning-after' Pill, but fewer know about the post-coital IUD.

The post-coital Pill is in fact a special dose of contraceptive Pill containing oestrogen and progestogen, taken within 72 hours of intercourse. The fitting of a coil within five days after intercourse is the alternative.

Morning-after methods have become generally available and endorsed for safety in recent years. They are, it should be stressed, only for use in an emergency – when contraception has not been used or has failed.

The post-coital Pill method involves taking a special dose of hormones under a doctor's supervision. However, it will only work for the one occasion. Sometimes side-effects such as, nausea, and occasionally vomiting, are experienced. Once fitted, the post-coital coil will ensure continuous protection.

STERILIZATION

Female sterilization and male vasectomy are intended as permanent methods of birth control. They involve relatively simple operations that close the Fallopian tubes in a woman, and the tubes through which sperm travels in a man.

A vasectomy is usually done under local anaesthetic and takes a few minutes. Female sterilization takes longer and can be done under general or local anaesthetic.

There are several ways female sterilization can be carried out, the most common being by laparoscopy when the Fallopian tubes are blocked with rings or clips. Neither the male nor female operation affects the production of hormones responsible for sexual drive, so sexual feelings should not be changed.

Sterilization was once a last resort chosen by couples who had had many children. Today, it is increasingly chosen by couples who have decided that they have completed their family. In many countries one in five women in the fertile age range have been sterilized or their partners have had a vasectomy.

However, in a time of increasing marriage breakdown, there are also more requests for reversal. But reversal operations are frequently not effective.

THE 'SAFE PERIOD' METHODS

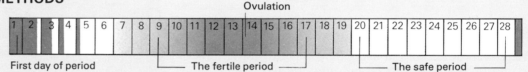

Ovulation

| 1 | 2 | 3 | 4 | 5 | 6 | 7 | 8 | 9 | 10 | 11 | 12 | 13 | 14 | 15 | 16 | 17 | 18 | 19 | 20 | 21 | 22 | 23 | 24 | 25 | 26 | 27 | 28 |

First day of period   —— The fertile period ——   —— The safe period ——

The principle of safe period methods of contraception is to learn to predict and recognize the time of the month when you are most fertile, and avoid intercourse at that time. Sex is restricted to 'safe' days, when you are less likely to conceive.

A woman is most likely to get pregnant at and around the time of ovulation – when the egg is released from the ovary into the Fallopian tube. This usually occurs about two weeks before the start of the next period, but there are various ways that a woman can pin-point the precise moment more accurately.

Since sperm can live for up to five days inside a woman, and an egg can live for about two days, a woman must not have sex for at least five days before ovulation and for several days afterwards.

Calculating the time of ovulation (when sex should be avoided) can be done in several ways:
☐ The body-temperature method
☐ The Billings (mucus) method
☐ The calendar method
☐ Combinations of these methods

The body-temperature method The woman takes her temperature every morning on waking up, and keeps a special chart. Immediately before ovulation, body temperature drops slightly – after the egg is released, it rises to a higher level than in the previous week.

The Billings (mucus) method This method works on the principle that ovulation can be detected by changes in cervical mucus. The woman is taught to examine her mucus and to recognize changes – such as increased amount and 'wetness'.

The calendar method The woman is shown how to calculate when she is most likely to ovulate by keeping a long-term record of her menstrual cycle. On its own this method is *very* unreliable and is not recommended.

Combined methods Combining methods and learning to recognize other 'symptoms' of ovulation increases reliability. With all these methods, skilled guidance is essential. See your doctor or family planning clinic for advice.

These techniques are most successful for women who have regular periods. Anything which makes periods irregular – from the recent birth of a baby to a change of routine – makes the time of ovulation difficult to predict. Pain-killing drugs can alter body temperature and consequently make the 'temperature method' unreliable.

SEXUAL DISEASES

Sexually transmitted diseases are on the increase throughout the world, and young people form a high proportion of those affected. But if diagnosed early some of these infections can be cured

Any disease that can be passed on from one person to another by sexual contact is called a sexually transmitted disease, or STD. In the past the term VD (short for venereal disease) was much more commonly used, and usually referred to gonorrhoea and syphilis, the more serious of the diseases, apart from the killer disease AIDS, which is discussed fully later in the book.

For many people, VD was not merely a term describing an infectious disease transmitted sexually – it was regarded as something that was only caught by people who indulged in immoral behaviour. This attitude has changed a great deal in recent years, so that today STDs, and departments of genito-urinary medicine where they are treated, are usually thought of with less embarrassment than in the past.

WHO SUFFERS?

Anyone can catch an STD by oral and anal sex as well as vaginal intercourse; in most cases the treatment is not painful or difficult, but as with most diseases, the earlier it is diagnosed, the easier it is to cure.

Generally, the most severe consequences of neglected STD fall upon women and their babies. Women are far less likely to have the recognizable symptoms that make early diagnosis easy. That is why the follow-up of contacts by an STD clinic is so important.

Not surprisingly, some 60 per cent of those infected worldwide are under 24. The effect on young women can be particularly devastating if the untreated disease leads to infertility. So, if you think you could have caught an infection, even though you have no symptoms, go for a check-up anyway – nobody is going to criticize you for being safe rather than sorry.

SYPHILIS

Syphilis, one of the most serious of all STDs, is becoming less common in Great Britain and the western world generally, while increasing in the developing world. There are about 20 to 50 million cases in the world every year. There were just over 3,000 cases reported in Great Britain in 1983, 6 per cent fewer than in the previous year – with ten times more men than women contracting the disease.

WHAT IS SYPHILIS?

Syphilis is caused by a corkscrew-shaped organism which is present in the blood and body fluids of an infected person. It can only live in the warm environment that the body provides, and it dies within a few hours outside it. The likelihood of your contracting syphilis if you have sex with an infected person is thought to be about one in two – particularly when it is in the early stages.

When the disease is passed on (by contact with a sore or ulcer), a hundred or more of the minute organisms, called triponemes, pass through the skin. After only half an hour they have passed to the lymph nodes in the groin and next they pass into the blood stream and are distributed to the whole body. It takes about three weeks before the body's defence mechanism begins to work against them.

THE FIRST SYMPTOMS

The first visible symptom of syphilis is a raised pimple on the vagina or penis (although it can sometimes occur on the mouth or anus from oral or anal contact).

Next, hard tissue forms around the pimple. The pimple becomes a painless ulcer or sore from which fluid oozes, and finally heals leaving a scar, usually taking about three weeks to do so.

Most people seek treatment when the sore appears, and the doctor will take a sample of the fluid from the sore to examine under a microscope and will also look to see if the lymph nodes of the groin are swollen.

The doctor will also take blood tests to see if antibodies to the organisms have been manufactured by the blood.

EFFECTS ON THE UNBORN CHILD

Transmission of syphilis to an unborn baby occurs by way of the placenta. A blood test done, for example, in the first ten weeks of pregnancy, can diagnose the disease in the mother before it is passed on to the baby – which does not happen until after the twentieth week. She can be cured with penicillin and produce a perfectly healthy baby.

TREATMENT

The chances of curing early syphilis by penicillin or other antibiotics are excellent, and even the advanced disease can be arrested. Daily injections of penicillin (together with Probenecid which maintains high levels of the antibiotic in the bloodstream) are given for about ten days, or a single dose can be injected into a muscle. Alternative antibiotics are given to those allergic to penicillin.

GONORRHOEA

Gonorrhoea is much more common than syphilis – about 50,000 new cases are diagnosed in Great Britain each year. It is the third most common STD, after non-specific genital infections and thrush, but much more common than herpes.

More than half of gonorrhoea cases are among under 24-year-olds, with three to five times as many cases among young men as among young women. Today there are probably between 200 and 500 million new cases every year in the world.

WHAT IS GONORRHOEA?

The gonorrhoea organism is small and bean-shaped, and is passed on by sexual intercourse – oral and anal as well as vaginal. It can therefore be passed from the urethra of a man, to the cervix, urethra, throat or rectum of his partner. It can be passed to a male as well as female partner. A woman can pass it on to the urethra of her male partner during penetration.

Since the organism (gonococcus) dies very quickly outside the human body, it is virtually impossible to pass it on without sexual intercourse. So you need not worry about catching it from a lavatory seat or towel. But if you do have sexual intercourse with someone who has gonorrhoea, you have more than an even chance of catching it.

THE SYMPTOMS

The symptoms are different in men and women. While only one man in ten is symptomless, more than half the women who develop the disease have no symptoms at all.

The first signs for a man occur between three and five days after contact. They start with a tingling of the man's urethra, followed by a thick, creamy-yellow discharge, which drips from the penis. At the same time there is a burning pain on passing urine.

Although at first he feels well in himself, if the infection is not treated and spreads, he may well begin to suffer from fever and headaches within ten to fourteen days. Infection can then travel to the prostate gland, the bladder, the testes or the epididymis. Scarring of the epididymis – the two long narrow tubes where sperm normally mature before they are ejaculated – can cause permanent sterility if both are affected.

Symptoms of gonorrhoea in a woman may include vaginal discharge or a burning feeling when passing urine. One painful complication occurs when the glands which supply secretions to keep the vagina moist – known as Bartholin's glands – become swollen and tender.

If the infection is not treated, it may spread

upwards, often during menstruation, and affect the Fallopian tubes. This may happen in as many as one in ten women who contract gonorrhoea, and is accompanied by fever, headaches, and severe pelvic pain. The inflammation of the tubes, known as salpingitis, can be serious enough to need emergency hospital admission, and the resultant scarring and blocking of the tubes can lead to permanent sterility.

TREATMENT

A positive diagnosis, found by microscopic examination of penile discharge, or of a smear taken from a woman's urethra, vagina or cervix, is followed by treatment with penicillin. If oral sex has taken place, a swab is taken from the throat, and if anal intercourse has occurred, one is taken from the rectum.

Treatment today usually consists of one large dose of penicillin in tablet form, together with Probenecid which maintains high levels of the antibiotic in the blood stream. While treatment is taking place, it is very important to avoid alcohol and sexual contact, usually for a matter of weeks.

A week following treatment, more swabs are taken and checked for gonococcus. If none is present the man is considered cured, but a woman needs to be checked again, after her next period. Certain types of penicillin-resistant gonorrhoea, found most frequently in South East Asia, need to be treated by another antibiotic called Spectinomycin.

PREVENTION

For both syphilis and gonorrhoea, the condom may provide a degree of protection, and it is accepted that the diaphragm or cap can protect the cervix from infection. Passing urine after sex may also help a woman to avoid gonorrhoea, although none of these measures guarantees protection.

CHANCROID

The sexually transmitted disease known as chancroid is most common in tropical climates, but with the increase in travel between tropical countries and the rest of the world, the ailment is likely to become more widespread.

Chancroid is caused by a small organism which is transmitted by sexual intercourse. Symptoms develop after three to seven days, with painful pimples on the man's penis or the woman's labia. When the pimples break to form ulcers, these too are painful (unlike syphilis ulcers) and they bleed easily. The lymph nodes of the groin become swollen and tender.

Diagnosis is made by taking a sample from the ulcer, and identifying the organism responsible under a microscope. It is cured by taking sulphonamides. These are not an antibiotic and therefore do not suppress syphilis if the two STDs occur together. When the chancroid is cured, further check-ups will be made for syphilis.

One of the most important elements in the treatment of STDs is the tracing of contacts, particularly as many women have no symptoms.

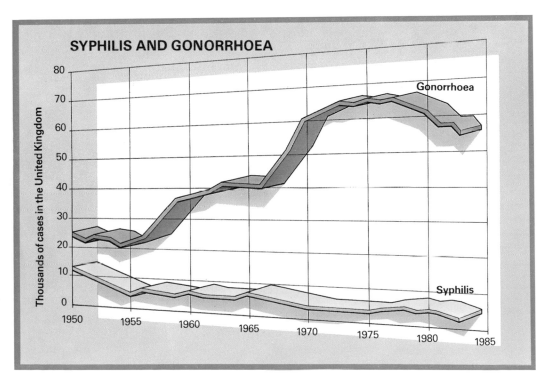

AIDS

The world faces a major epidemic of a disease with a hidden dimension, for the AIDS virus can be carried for years without symptoms becoming evident. Despite worldwide concerted efforts, no solution is predicted for the short term, although changes in sexual behaviour can mitigate the situation

Much of the hysteria about AIDS that is gripping the world, particularly the West, is generated by society's attitudes towards some of those groups most likely to be affected – homosexuals, bisexuals and intravenous drug users.

This has resulted in an outbreak of hysteria as devastating in its way as the disease itself, which has earned the tags of AFRAIDS and AIPS (AIDS Induced Panic Syndrome). Children have been barred from classrooms, dentists have refused to treat gay patients and cameramen have boycotted interview sessions featuring victims.

The disease itself has confounded doctors and scientists alike since it was officially recognized in July 1981 in San Francisco, and a cure is not expected in the near future, despite extensive research.

WHY AIDS KILLS

The acronym AIDS stands for Acquired Immune Deficiency Syndrome which spells out about as much and as little as we know about the disease. It is *acquired* and not inherited; it strikes at the *immune* system, the body's natural defence against hostile invading organisms; it produces a deficiency in its ability to fight infection; and it is a *syndrome* – a collection of symptoms which seem to occur together and very probably have the same cause.

AIDS-RELATED DISEASES

Victims die not from AIDS itself, but from one of a host of diseases to which the human body deprived of

As with most living organisms, the AIDS virus must kill in order to procreate and survive. Unfortunately, its natural prey the T4 cell – is part of the immune system. And while the virus is as fragile as a soap bubble outside the human body, once it reaches the blood stream it becomes, to date, impossible to destroy.

its immune system can fall prey.

Chief among these are Kaposi's sarcoma (a rare and disfiguring skin cancer) and a type of pneumonia (*Pneumocystis carinii pneumonia*) hardly ever seen except in cases of AIDS. Together or separately, these two diseases have caused about three-quarters of the deaths of AIDS victims in both Britain and the United States.

UNKNOWN ORIGIN

Equally puzzling is the origin of AIDS. Many researchers believe the virus was perhaps passed from animals to humans in day-to-day contact.

Monkeys in Africa, pigs in Haiti, even sheep in Iceland have all been singled out as possible one-time hosts of the virus, but no-one really knows how and why it claimed humans as its victims.

There is mounting evidence that AIDS is in fact an old disease from Africa, where the cancer Kaposi's sarcoma is thought to have been known long before the current outbreak.

AIDS IN THE USA

Wherever it came from, the disease has spread extremely rapidly over long distances in a very short space of time. The problem is that whereas most diseases increase arithmetically (2, 4, 6, 8 and so on) AIDS increases exponentially (2, 4, 8, 16, 32), and this is what has led to the cliff-face rise in the numbers affected. In America, five cases of *Pneumocystis carinii pneumonia* in Los Angeles and 26 cases of Kaposi's sarcoma in New York and California heralded the arrival of the disease in the summer of 1981.

THREAT TO HETEROSEXUALS

By the end of May 1988, nearly 64,000 cases of AIDS had been officially notified in the USA and nearly 36,000 deaths from the disease had been recorded. It is believed that the rapid increase in the number of cases in previous years was due to the fact that some homosexuals were considerably more promiscuous than heterosexual men or women. However, as the latest figures for gonorrhoea show that incidences within the gay community are declining – whereas heterosexual cases are still increasing – it can be assumed that homosexual promiscuity has declined. This, together with increasing awareness of safe sexual practices, has made doctors hopeful that the increase in gay AIDS cases will decline.

AIDS IN THE UK

Hot on the heels of the American outbreak of the disease came its British appearance, and although the numbers involved are far smaller, the rate of increase in the numbers of AIDS sufferers in the United Kingdom has been equally dramatic.

The first case of AIDS in the United Kingdom was reported in December 1981, with the first death, that of a 37-year-old man, on 4th July 1982. By June 1988 the number of AIDS cases reported in the UK stood at 1,598 and the number of AIDS-related deaths at 897.

AIDS WORLDWIDE

By 31st January 1988 the number of AIDS cases notified to the World Health Organization (WHO) had exceeded 77,000, although WHO estimates put the true number of AIDS sufferers worldwide at between 100,000 and 150,000.

Russia has finally acknowledged that it does have the beginnings of an AIDS problem, but the governments of other countries, particularly those dependent on their tourist trade, are keeping quiet about the actual incidence of the disease. Undoubtedly, AIDS is no respecter of borders – cases are being identified in developing nations as in the West, in small towns and in the country, as well as in larger cities.

Sexual transmission
Usually entering the bloodstream via the vulnerable linings of the rectum or urethra – although transmission may be by other means – the AIDS virus hunts down T4 lymphocytes (white blood cells).

Fatal attraction
Receptors on the T4 cell, designed to pick up hostile invaders, lock on to special chemical markers on the virus's surface. Now the T4 cell will begin to release antibodies, but to no avail.

THE SAFER SEX CODE
1. Only solo sex is guaranteed safe.
2. Avoid any contact with your partner's semen, bodily fluids or blood.
3. Have sex where you do not orgasm inside your partner's body, or if you feel you must do so, use a condom.

Supplied by the Terence Higgins Trust.

Insertion
As the antibodies begin their attack, the virus discards its outer coat. Now the core of the virus insinuates itself into the cell. Since the core contains RNA and not DNA, the cell is unaware of the danger.

Assimilation
Once safely in place, the virus continues to fool its unsuspecting host by using an enzyme to change its RNA into DNA. This genetic material is treated by T4 cells as if it were its very own.

NOT A HOMOSEXUAL DISEASE

Although AIDS has been dubbed by some as the gay plague and has even been described as being the result of the wrath of God brought to bear on homosexuals, it is by no means exclusive to the gay population, nor even the male population.

In Europe and the US, male homosexuals have made up the majority of victims to date, but other high risk groups include intravenous drug users, haemophiliacs using blood products, bisexuals and prostitutes. In the US and UK a number of sufferers are heterosexual men and women, proof of the fact that anyone who has sex is now at risk.

Outside of the western world, the concentration of AIDS in the gay population has been far less of a feature of the disease. In Central Africa, for example, where as many as one in 10 people are affected in some areas, AIDS is spreading rapidly through heterosexual contact and women are just as likely as men to fall victim to the disease, particularly prostitutes. This may be because of poor standards of hygiene in hospitals and clinics. But it may also be the result of the widespread practice of anal intercourse as a form of contraception in some African countries.

VIRUS ISOLATED

When people were first stricken by AIDS, doctors were mystified and the actual cause of this deadly disease was only isolated in 1985. The culprit is a virus which attacks the very cells which protect us from infection. This rod-shaped bug has been labelled the HTLV III virus (or human T cell lymphotropic virus, Type 3) by American scientists, and LAV (lymphaedenopathy associated virus) by French scientists. They have now compromised and the virus is known as LAV-HTLV III. Since the isolation of the original virus, another, more virulent, strain of the disease has been identified and others may exist.

How the AIDS virus spreads from one person to another is still not completely understood. Scientists have isolated it in most body fluids of AIDS victims – in blood, semen and saliva. But because the virus can be isolated in a laboratory test tube does not mean that it can be passed on through contact with all these fluids. AIDS is predominantly a blood-borne disease, although semen is also a likely carrier.

What is clear is that those in normal daily contact with AIDS victims are not necessarily in danger.

ANAL TRANSMISSION

The most common method of transmission is still through anal intercourse. The reason why anal intercourse allows the virus to cross over from one host to another is because the membranes of the rectum are much more delicate than those of the vagina, and hence far more likely to tear and bleed.

Unlike the vagina, the walls of the rectum allow fluids to pass through into the blood stream, so viruses from contaminated sperm could enter another person's body in this way.

There are two other ways in which the virus might be spread by blood to blood contact: by exchanging and using infected needles, a common practice among intravenous drug users, and by transfusing contaminated blood or blood products.

OTHERS AT RISK

Haemophiliacs have found themselves in a high risk group because of their treatment with the blood clotting agent, Factor VIII.

However, these two routes of transmission – blood transfusions and contaminated Factor VIII – should have been blocked by the introduction of tests for all blood donors and of heat-treating all blood to kill off any AIDS viruses present. These measures have been mandatory in the UK since September 1985.

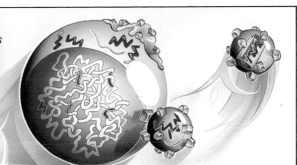

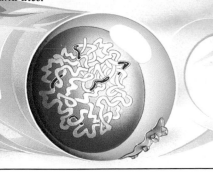

Cell death
The Aids DNA may lie hidden for up to five years within the T4 chromosomes. How and why it becomes activated remains a mystery – but when it does, the cell begins to make copies of the virus and dies.

DNA – *found only within the the cell nucleus, it stores the genetic code and can (uniquely) replicate itself*
RNA – *found throughout the cell, it can act as a messenger for DNA in synthesizing the protein chains that are part of the human body.*

MANY SYMPTOMS

When they do develop, the symptoms of AIDS are those of an array of diseases which the immune deficient victim has fallen prey to, making it difficult to tell whether someone actually has the disease. These include swollen glands in the neck, armpit or groin, weight loss, high fever and night sweats, diarrhoea and persistent coughs or shortness of breath.

There may also be skin changes with pink or purple flattish blotches or bumps occurring on or under the skin, inside the mouth, nose, eyelids or rectum or blemishes in the mouth.

Where any of these symptoms occur alone, or even in twos and threes, it is extremely unlikely that AIDS will be found to be the cause, and because the fear of AIDS can be almost as debilitating as the disease itself, it is important to seek medical advice.

COMPLETE CURE NOT YET IN SIGHT

As yet, the prospects for the prevention and cure of AIDS look none too hopeful.

No known cure has yet been found for the disease and the best that can be done, medically, for victims is to help alleviate the symptoms. Nor is there any effective vaccine at present, and according to scientists there is no chance of there being one before the 1990s.

The virus probably has several different forms, each capable of mutating (changing), which makes the development of a vaccine difficult. Many of the drugs currently being tested as possible cures for AIDS are aimed at stopping the virus reproducing after it has entered the body, but progress is slow. According to a report in the New England Journal of Medicine, doctors have isolated the virus in brain and spinal fluid from AIDS sufferers. The implications are that the virus 'hides' in the brain – and this could make eradication difficult, though probably not impossible.

Despite the anxiety among health care workers, and

those involved in caring for AIDS victims, their chances of contracting the disease themselves seem remote.

Apart from one case in the UK of a nurse who contracted the disease by accidentally innoculating herself with a small amount of blood from an AIDS patient, there have been no known cases of disease among doctors and nurses.

It is, however, known that an infected mother can pass on AIDS to her unborn child, possibly through the placenta or else during the actual birth when blood is lost by the mother.

VIRUS NOT NECESSARILY FATAL

As yet there is no test which shows categorically whether a person has AIDS. Anyone who has come into contact with the virus will make antibodies to it, and will show up as 'antibody positive'.

But although the presence of antibodies gives no protection against the disease, only 5–10 per cent of those who are found to have LAV-HTLV III antibodies in the blood will go on to develop a fatal case of AIDS.

Some will develop milder, less life-threatening infections, and a sizeable number may develop no obvious symptoms at all.

AIDS CARRIERS

Exactly what makes one person develop the disease while others remain unaffected is not known exactly, but carriers – those who have antibodies without symptoms – will still be capable of passing the virus to others, who in turn will stand much the same chance of developing AIDS.

The other worrying problem about AIDS is that symptoms may take anything from two, possibly as long as seven years to emerge, which means that sufferers may unwittingly be infecting a large number of other people before realizing that they have the disease.

INDEX

PICTURE CREDITS